worship4today

Part Three: Consolidating and Expanding Horizons

worship 4 today

A course for worship leaders and musicians

Part Three: Consolidating and Expanding Horizons

Helen Bent and Liz Tipple

CHURCH HOUSE PUBLISHING

Transforming Worship

Church House Publishing
Church House
Great Smith Street
London SW1P 3AZ

ISBN 978 0 7151 2262 4

Published 2014 by Church House Publishing
Copyright © Helen Bent and Liz Tipple

The opinions expressed in this book are those of the authors and do not necessarily reflect the official policy of the General Synod or The Archbishops' Council of the Church of England.

Printed and bound by CPI Group (UK) Ltd, Croydon, CR0 4YY.

CONTENTS

PART THREE: CONSOLIDATING AND EXPANDING HORIZONS

ASSESSMENT AND CONTINUING MINISTERIAL EDUCATION

APPENDICES

The course at a glance

The following is an overview of the *Worship4Today* course, including preparation stages, a session-by-session guide and follow up.

Stage	Date	Details
Pre-course planning		
Planning	Sep prior to start	• Plan course dates for the following academic year. • Choose key course leaders.
Invitation	Jan-Feb	• Send out a covering letter and initial course information to every parish, including dates for 'taster' sessions
Exploration	Apr-May	• Arrange 'taster' evenings for potential candidates. • Explain the aims of the course, how it works and invite individuals to consider taking part. Avoid Easter holidays.
Application	May-Jun	• Seek parish permission and support. • Complete and return application form.
Interview	Jun-Jul	• Interview each potential candidate to underline the commitment required and ensure that their expectations match the course content.
Preparation	Aug-Sep	• Course syllabus and information is sent to candidates. • A pre-course social is helpful, so that candidates have an opportunity to get to know one another a little.
Part one: Laying a firm foundation		
Session 1	Sep	**Title:** The theology of worship – What? Why? How? **Aim:** To explore worship and its basic ingredients. **Practical:** Establishing boundaries of confidentiality.
Session 2	Oct	**Title:** Who is the God we worship? **Aim:** To explore the nature of God, who He is and what He has done, and the worship cycle – our response, God's response. **Practical:** Worshipping together in small groups.
Session 3	Nov	**Title:** Worship in the Old Testament **Aim:** To give an overview of Old Testament worship, particularly in the Tabernacle and the Temple, and those who led worship there. **Practical:** A small group exercise using chosen material.
Session 4	Dec	**Title:** Leadership skills **Aim:** To discover qualities of leadership through studying the Levites and the leadership of Jesus. **Practical:** A small group exercise with a Christmas theme.

The course at a glance

Part two: Developing key skills		
Session 5	Jan	**Title:** The role of music in worship **Aim:** To explore a powerful medium and tool with reference to our emotions and aesthetic appreciation. **Practical:** To experience the English choral tradition and contemporary worship styles; and explore appropriate rehearsal techniques.
Session 6	Feb	**Title:** Worship in the Psalms **Aim:** To understand Israel's songbook, discovering the different types of psalms and appreciating their poetry. **Practical:** Writing psalms and exploring different settings.
Session 7	Mar	**Title:** Patterns of worship in the Anglican Church **Aim:** To understand basic service structures and how to choose appropriate material to nurture, disciple and sustain. **Practical:** Putting together part of a service.
Session 8	Apr	**Title:** Building a worship team **Aim:** To explore the pastoral and practical issues involved in developing a worship team, choir or music group. **Practical:** A music theory session at varying levels; a voice coaching workshop (both one hour).
Part three: Consolidating and expanding horizons		
Session 9	May (full Saturday)	**Title:** Practical worship day **Aim:** To give time for intensive input in a series of one hour workshops. **Suggested topics:** Leading up front; posture and movement in worship; AV technology; leading corporate prayer; signing in worship. Conclude with a short act of worship using material from all workshops.
Session 10	May	**Title:** Worship in the New Testament **Aim:** To look at Jesus as a worshipper and explore worship in the Early Church and in Revelation. **Practical:** Exploring improvisation skills and 'singing a new song to the Lord.'
Session 11	Jun	**Title:** The challenge of all-age worship **Aim:** To discover inclusive ways of engaging the whole congregation in meaningful worship. **Practical:** Exploring material appropriate for children and young people in small groups.

Project	Jun	Personal projects should be handed in at the June session.
Session 12	Jul	**Title:** Worship in a mission context **Aim:** To recognise how we model worship for others, particularly seekers and non-believers. **Practical:** Setting new vision and moving on. **End of course worship:** Holy Communion.
Portfolio	Jul	Personal portfolios should be handed in at the July session.
At the end of the course		
Review	Jun-Jul	Meet with each candidate and their incumbent to review their progress during the course and to discern the appropriate way forward.
Evaluation	Jul-Aug	Personal projects and portfolios are assessed and written feedback is given. An overall assessment of the candidate is made, including a recommendation for authorisation.
Authorisation	Sep	Candidates are authorised by the bishop together with other lay ministers, such as readers, pastoral workers and parish evangelists, at an appropriate service.
Optional extra session		
Arranged to suit	Spring term is best	**Title:** Drum workshop **Aim:** To enable a creative use of drums and percussion in worship, particularly with children and young people.

All these listed details are given for a course starting in September. If you are intending to start your course at a different date you will need to adjust all the dates, some practical tasks and homework tasks accordingly.

worship4today

session

Practical worship day

TEACHERS' NOTES

⑨ Practical worship day

SESSION PROGRAMME

5 mins	**Welcome and introduction to the session** Explain the different format with one hour practical workshops Finish with an act of worship using material from all the workshops
60 mins	**Worship leading 'up front'** Enabling worship to happen without getting in the way Choosing our words with care
15 mins	**Coffee break**
60 mins	**Posture and movement in worship** Looking at gesture, posture, movement, dance and use of flags
60 mins	**Using visual technology in worship** Introducing some basic guidelines and principles of good practice and debunking some fears of using technology
45 mins	**Lunch break**
60 mins	**Leading corporate prayer** Leading corporate intercessions effectively Exploring prayer stations and other creative ways to pray together
15 mins	**Tea break**
60 mins	**Signing in worship** (or an alternative) Introducing action with meaning to enhance our worship
20 mins	**Closing worship**

Allow five minutes comfort break between each workshop.

LIST OF MATERIALS NEEDED

- Food and drink, including a proper cooked lunch if there are facilities to provide it
- Flipchart and pens
- Laptop, data projector and screen
- CD player or mp3 facility
- Members' Handouts
- Sketch: 'How not to lead worship!' This sketch is based on one written by David Burfield, which first appeared in the Methodist Church Worship Leaders' Training Pack (Revised edition, Trustees for Methodist Church Purposes, 2000). The sketch has been modified

and updated and is used here with permission. The sketch needs to be prepared beforehand by an able actor/actress who can stand up and deliver it at the appropriate moment. This should be one of the course leaders or mentors, so that all course participants can observe

- A set of flags for the posture and movement workshop
- If possible, several extra laptops with PowerPoint and/or a worship programme installed for experimentation in the technology workshop
- Materials for prayer stations already set up beforehand (see Teachers' Notes for details).
- Sufficient copies of *A Guide to Leading Intercessions in Church* (see Appendix 1: this A4 document will reduce to make an A5 booklet)
- Sufficient prayer cards with verses of Scripture on one side and the Gaelic Blessing on the other (see Appendix 2: print back-to-back and cut into eight small cards)
- A plan for the closing worship with all necessary materials prepared beforehand, including any song words, liturgy or visuals on PowerPoint or using a worship software programme.

The full worship day is a good opportunity to bring in some specialist workshop leaders to broaden and enrich the input and provide a little respite for the usual course tutors on what can prove to be a long and tiring day. We have usually run the day with several visitors working alongside the overall course leaders, mixing and matching to play to their gifts and strengths.

We have always started with the worship leading 'up front' workshop, because this is the most formally taught session of the day. It also acts as a good introduction for what is to follow. Obviously it is possible to include alternative workshops within this day but, with the exception of the signing workshop, we actually think all the others are essentials for twenty-first century worship. Other workshops can always be added in as part of Continuing Ministerial Education for authorised worship leaders in the future.

We do encourage everyone to run *Sessions 9* and *10* in the same weekend, or at least close together. These two sessions are pivotal in building deeper relationships of trust between course participants, which will then continue long after the course has finished. However, if the *Worship4Today* material is being used within a parish setting, the workshops could be separated and run on different evenings to give more time to explore each area in more depth.

ROOM SET-UP

Ideally, there need to be several different spaces available for this session, so you may need to consider whether the usual venue is the best place for the full worship day.

Ensure there are sufficient chairs and tables where everyone can see the screen for the PowerPoint for the teaching sessions.

For the worship leading 'up front' workshop, participants will need hymn/song books and service booklets for the exercises on *Handout 1*, page 62. We recommend you specify material for each exercise to save time.

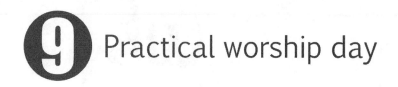

The posture and movement workshop and the signing workshop work best in a large open space to give everyone good visibility and room to move about freely, perhaps arranged with chairs in a large circle around the edge for the times when people need to sit down during these workshops. This space can also be used for the closing worship.

The technology workshop requires sufficient space to see a main screen as well as extra power sockets to operate additional laptops.

Prayer stations should be set up in advance. It is helpful to have them in a separate room to prevent participants 'jumping the gun', but if there is no extra space available they can be arranged discreetly in corners of the rooms already in use.

Serving a meal at lunchtime may require a small amount of rearrangement of tables, chairs and belongings, so allow time for this. Our mentors have usually cooked the lunch for us, but it could just as easily be done by others brought in for the occasion. Obviously, a menu should be planned in advance and any dietary requirements taken into consideration. We see from the Gospels that Jesus understood the value of getting alongside people over a meal, so please do not scrimp on this. Eating together and chatting informally forms an integral part of this full day.

ACKNOWLEDGEMENTS

We want to extend our special thanks to all those who have led workshops on the practical worship day in Sheffield since the course began. We are grateful for their wisdom and expertise and their generosity in helping to put these materials for *Session 9* together.

Our thanks go to Pam Jones and Lynn Broadhead for their help with flags and dance; Ann Walton together with Mike North, Phil Barringer, Sue King, Nicola Short and David Bent for their expertise on the use of technology in worship; Lynn Broadhead and Sue Burnage for their input on prayer and creating prayer stations; and Sue Wordsworth and Judy Leverton for their expertise in sign language in worship.

SESSION AIMS

- To give time for intensive input on specific topics
- To make these workshops as practical and 'hands-on' as possible
- To communicate principles and guidelines for good practice
- To have fun and enjoy one another's company

5 mins

WELCOME AND INTRODUCTION TO THE SESSION

Welcome participants and settle them quickly. Usually there is a real sense of anticipation in the air, as we prepare to spend a whole day immersed in worship.

Explain the different format with a series of one hour practical workshops throughout the day, culminating in an act of worship using material from all the workshops. Introduce any visitors coming to lead workshops, but keep it brief so that we maximise the time.

Quickly run through the aims from slide 2.

Pray

WORKSHOP 1 | WORSHIP LEADING 'UP FRONT'

10 mins | Sketch

We have always started straight into this workshop with a thought-provoking sketch around the theme of 'how not to do it' (see *Additional Handout*). This will need to be prepared beforehand by a budding actor/actress (preferably not one of the course participants).

You might like to blank the PowerPoint screen so it is not a visual distraction.

After the sketch, take some brief feedback on flipchart to identify areas of weakness. Then draw this part to a close by adding anything that has been missed. Possible observations might be:

- Inappropriate dress
- Lack of proper preparation
- Carelessness
- Undermining the confidence and security of the congregation
- A lack of respect for others including potential visitors
- Insulting, embarrassing or patronising the congregation
- Choosing own favourites
- Choosing inappropriate hymns
- Discouragement
- Interruption from mobile phones
- Lack of respect for church leadership
- Inappropriate waffle
- The tendency to use 'just' frequently and inappropriately

20 mins

Enabling worship to happen

Slide 4

Handout 1: Worship leading 'up front'

We want to facilitate an encounter with God in which we speak to God and He speaks to us without us getting in the way!

Let us consider how to avoid some of the sketch's mistakes and weaknesses by looking at some principles and practicalities.

Worship leaders or lead worshippers?

Slide 5

- **We are worshippers just as much as the congregation** – Although we may have been set apart to lead, it may be more helpful to see ourselves as 'lead worshippers' amongst a group of worshippers. The role is different, because we are giving the congregation some guidance and direction. However,
- **Together we are being led by the Holy Spirit** – The Holy Spirit is the one who ultimately leads us to worship 'in spirit and truth' (John 4:23-4). This is not an excuse for poor planning or insufficient preparation. The Holy Spirit can inspire the planning as well as inspiring the actual worship on the day.
- **We should be clear about our role in any particular service** – If we are in overall charge of a service, we cannot get completely lost in wonder, love and praise. We have a responsibility to stay connected to the congregation and to facilitate their worship.

Appearance

Slide 6

Appearance and dress will depend on the church, the context and the style of service, and local practices will vary.

- **What do I look like?** We mentioned this at the end of the last session. How we look says a lot about who we are. Sunday best can give a sense of honour and respect but can also sometimes appear distant and aloof, whereas more casual can indicate an approachable, relaxed informality. However, if we are too scruffy, it can suggest a lack of care and respect for God and others, and undermine the congregation's confidence in us. So,
- **What do I wear?** This is a serious issue if we are not wearing robes. Bright colours and loud patterns can be distracting as can torn or low slung jeans, short skirts or revealing low cut tops. We do need to consider whether our dress is appropriate and honouring to God.
- **Do I have any distracting habits or quirks?** This is a tough one, but we need to remember that our little habits and quirks are usually more noticeable to everyone else. They can also get worse when we are nervous. Glum faces and hands in pockets do not encourage others to fully engage with worship, and repeatedly pushing on our glasses or moving papers from one hand to the other can be distracting. Try getting someone to video you leading worship. This is scary but effective, especially if you play it on fast forward!

- Do I draw attention to myself or do I draw people to God? Our primary purpose is to help others to meet with God in the worship, and therefore we must remind ourselves regularly that worship leading is not about us! Our role is closer to that of conductor rather than soloist. We want to enable and encourage the worship of others drawing out their best for God without getting in the way.

Visibility

Slide 7

The use of space, especially at the front of the church, says important things about tradition, churchmanship and the style of worship. It also says something subconsciously about our priorities, so we need to consider carefully what is most dominant: the holy table; the pulpit; the service leader; or the singers and musicians? For example, if the musicians are arrayed across the front of the chancel, obscuring any view of the communion table, what does this say about what we value most? However, we are also talking physical practicalities here.

- **Who stands where?** Is it appropriate or the best place? And most important, what does it look like to the congregation? One of our team vicars is only five feet tall. She can hardly be seen at all if she uses the lectern, so this is neither the best nor most appropriate place for her to lead a service. Much better to lead from a place where she is easily visible. The musicians and singers need to see each other and they need to be able to communicate with the service leader. They also need to be visible to the congregation, if they are going to give a clear vocal lead.
- **Liturgical presidency** - We discussed this in *Session 7*. The liturgical president has the 'holding' brief over the whole service, preventing it becoming a series of unrelated parts. Therefore, he or she needs to be visible to everyone throughout if at all possible.
- **Complement and submit** - Everyone at the front is visible to the congregation, so we should be clear about our role and which parts we are leading to ensure we do not find ourselves in competition or conflict with other leaders. Our aim should always be to serve, to submit and to complement.

Atmosphere

Slide 8

Atmosphere makes a huge impression on people, and will vary from service to service. The atmosphere created by darkness and candles is in part what makes a Carol service or Christingle service so appealing. A sense of stillness and peace, together with candles, may attract some to a Taizé service whereas the bustle and activity of Messy Church may appeal to others. Atmosphere is difficult to put into words but we easily recognise when it is uncomfortable or strained. Therefore, whatever the context, we need to consciously cultivate an atmosphere which is …

- **Welcoming and inclusive** - Hopefully our congregation will usually include regulars, fringe people and visitors, mature Christians, new Christians, enquirers and unbelievers. It will also include those who are joyful and upbeat alongside those who are distressed and grieving. Some will have had a row with their partner or children on the way. Our task as worship leaders is to draw everyone in to make them all feel welcome, respected and included.
- **Inspire confidence and security** - It is vital to put a congregation at ease to help them to relax and participate as much as they are able. Entertainment can be a dirty word in worship circles but if people do not enjoy the worship experience and find it engaging and uplifting, what will encourage them to come back?
- **Recognise God's presence with us** - Whether this is done formally through the liturgy or informally through a few well chosen words, it is important to get that clear God-focus right away. This is the very reason why we are meeting together.

Attitude

Slide 9

- **Love and serve the congregation** - In the sketch, the lack of respect for others was writ large, and at times our service leader was plain rude. We may think we will never fall into these kinds of mistakes and it is certainly unlikely at that exaggerated level, but we can sometimes inadvertently embarrass or patronize. We have

9

perhaps been in a service where the leader does not think the congregation has entered in with sufficient enthusiasm. The liturgy or song is repeated, so that 'they can do better'. In our experience, a congregation does not respond well to being treated like a naughty class!

- **Discern what is happening** - Throughout a service, we have to keep alert to what is happening overall. Is the congregation fully involved or are some distracted and losing interest? Are there particularly noisy children disturbing the flow? There is a real art to gently guiding a congregation without discouraging them or undermining their integrity. A quiet pause can be a helpful way to settle the children and re-focus everyone on God.

- **Know when to stop!** We worked on the careful timing of a service in the practical task in *Session 4*. This is a good moment to re-emphasise the necessity to think through the length and timing of a service carefully. There is a point towards the end of every service when we are in danger of losing the congregation. Watch out for restlessness and people beginning to look at their watches. We should always aim to stop short of this point, so that we leave people with the sense that they wanted more.

- **Accept feedback** - None of us likes criticism, even the most constructive, but sometimes we do need to hear constructive ways to improve our leadership skills. Review each service afterwards and ask for some honest observation from others. This way we will avoid some of the pitfalls and bad habits.

Encourage relationship

Slide 10

As we said right at the beginning of the course, worship is at the heart of what it means to be a Christian and what it is to be Church. In our worship we want to encourage relationship ...

- **With God**, who is worthy of our praise and who desires to communicate with His people.
- **With each other** - Worship is a corporate activity. There is solidarity between worshippers and a sharing of one another's joys and sorrows.
- **With the wider Christian Church** - 'Common' worship reminds us of our connection with others who are worshipping elsewhere.
- **With the wider world** - We remember the wider world, its needs, and our responsibilities, particularly in our intercessions.

Relationship requires good communication, so we move on to consider what to say, what not to say, and how to say it, through a series of short practical exercises. Participants will need hymn/song books and service booklets for these exercises.

Choose words with care

10 mins

Exercise 1 – Beginning a service (see *Handout*, page 62)

Slide 11

Encourage participants to do these short exercises in pairs.

Participants are asked to prepare the beginning of the service giving the congregation some idea of what to expect. They should include a welcome, announce the first hymn and then lead into the first piece of liturgy. To save time, it will be helpful to specify the hymn and opening liturgy. As this workshop usually falls near Pentecost, we used: Hymn – 'O Breath of Life' and the general Greeting – 'Grace, mercy and peace'. Ask for a volunteer to demonstrate their version.

Allow five minutes for the planning, two minutes for the demonstration, and then three minutes to summarise, using the following points:

Understanding and sensitivity

Slide 12

- **Use appropriate language for the congregation** and try to avoid too much Christian jargon or church terminology.
- **Use explanation,** but don't give too much away. Encourage a healthy curiosity and expectancy.
- **Don't be apologetic or make excuses** - People do not want to know we felt unwell and did not have time to prepare properly. It may appeal for a sympathy vote but it is unprofessional, unnecessary and undermines the congregation's confidence.

- **Be prepared for the unexpected** - A pastoral crisis may affect all or part of the congregation and may suddenly render what we have prepared inappropriate: e.g. on the Sunday morning of Princess Diana's death many of us did not know until we arrived at church. Shock and disbelief affected everyone. On these occasions we may need to radically change things at the last minute. However, these are exceptional circumstances and last minute changes should not become a regular habit.

Communicating specific information

Slide 13

- **Hymn number/page number** - Not only do we need to make the numbers clear here, we may also need to indicate which book. It is helpful to give the numbers a second time.
- **Verses/parts** - Indicate clearly if certain verses are to be omitted or repeated. If the liturgy appears on a screen, people may need to know which is their part. Make it clear if congregational responses are in bold type or a different colour.
- **Background information** - It may be helpful to give the theme for the day or remind the congregation that we are part way through a sermon series.
- **Events** - This is particularly important for newcomers, who need to know when the offering will happen and if there are refreshments after the service. People with children need to know where the crèche is and when the children will go to their activities as well as the location of the toilets.

10 mins

Exercise 2 – Introducing the prayers (see *Handout*, page 62)

Slide 14

Participants are asked to introduce the Prayers of Intercession to the congregation, giving clear instructions for the inclusion of the Taizé chant, 'O Lord hear my prayer'.

 Ask for a volunteer to demonstrate their version. Allow five minutes for the planning, two minutes for the demonstration, and then three minutes to summarise, using the following points:

Giving instructions

Slide 15

If they are going to participate to the full, the congregation needs a clear idea of ...

* What to do;
* When to do it;
* How to do it.

The emphasis here is on clarity, so instructions should be succinct and to the point. We need sufficient words to communicate clearly but too much explanation will become tedious and off-putting.

Noteworthy phrases

Slide 16

It can be helpful to work out a few choice phrases in advance:

* **Would you please stand?** Suggest rather than telling people directly what they can and can't do.
* **Let us ...** This includes and draws people in, but also reminds them that the service leader is also a worshipper.
* **We encourage everyone to ...** Permission giving is vital, but also give permission not to: e.g. not everyone can stand up. This may apply to the elderly but also to parents with small children. We want to encourage everyone to feel comfortable and able to participate in whatever way they can.

- **We say together ...** Sometimes this is necessary, but at other times it is obvious we are all to say the words together. Nevertheless, it can be a helpful phrase to ensure everyone begins together at the same time.
- **We continue with ...** We may need to think out a few choice phrases to aid the flow, so that each part of the service becomes an integral part of the bigger whole.
- **Avoid 'just'!** This is a classic pitfall of informality, and we can so easily put *just* into every other sentence, especially in extemporary prayers. We don't even mean it! We don't just (merely) pray. Our prayer life is more vital than that. This colloquial use of *just* can undermine and water down the content of our prayers.

10 mins

Exercise 3 – Leading a block of sung worship in a service
(see *Handout*, page 62)

Slide 17

Participants are asked to introduce a sequence of three songs. They should choose a suitable order and whether the songs will be in a book or on a screen. The songs should be linked together appropriately. Again to save time, specify the three songs. We used: 'Holy Spirit, we welcome you' by Chris Bowater, 'Spirit of the Living God' by Paul Armstrong and 'There's a wind a-blowing' by David Ruiz.

Ask for a volunteer to demonstrate their version. Allow five minutes for the planning, two minutes for the demonstration, and then three minutes to summarise, using the following points:

Every word is precious

Slide 18

Think about different styles of worship. Cathedral services or big formal occasions will often proceed unannounced. Here the instructions are provided by the rubrics and the liturgy provides the links and the continuity.

However, in the more evangelical churches, blocks of sung worship are popular. We need to recognise what is in vogue at present and how it is handled. Learn from observing others. This is why it is so important for participants to visit churches of different churchmanship and styles.

- **Plan what to say beforehand** and keep it brief! People do not want to hear a mini sermon in between each song.
- **Purpose of words** - Do we actually need any words at all? Would it be better to link the songs musically and allow them to flow straight from one to another? This can work well if there is a clear link within the subject matter of the lyrics. However, where the link is more tenuous, the congregation may benefit from a little more guidance, otherwise they may have no idea why we chose these particular songs or why they might be relevant.
- **Use scripture** - A well chosen verse of scripture can provide a simple and effective link. This is often how the shorter pieces of liturgy work, the majority of which are based on scripture.
- **Use silence** - We can leave a pause between songs and allow space for reflection and space for God to speak. We do not have to fill every gap.
- **Are we being repetitive?** Are we saying the same thing twice, once informally and then again formally in the words of the liturgy?
- **Are we patronizing or preaching?** This can be a real issue. Teachers can be particularly prone to it and it is more subtle than naughty class syndrome. We never want to talk down to people or appear superior. When it comes to worship, we are all in this together.

Speak slowly and clearly

Slide 19

- **Use your natural voice** - No affected monotone or amateur dramatics!
- **Allow people time to engage with the liturgy** - Pace the phrases carefully and use pauses, so that the words flow in an unhurried manner.
- **Practise with a microphone** - Remember, a microphone helps to make a voice louder but it does not necessarily make our speech clearer. If we use a lapel microphone, we need to adjust it to the best position to be heard even if we turn away.

- **Practise voice-overs** - These can be effective to keep the worship flowing but can be difficult to do well. We will need co-operation and alertness from the sound desk. If we speak over music, can the congregation and musicians hear what is said? The spoken voice is usually softer than the singing voice, so a microphone may need adjusting at the sound desk for the voice-over to work.

Finally check whether there are any questions.

15 mins

COFFEE BREAK

WORKSHOP 2

POSTURE AND MOVEMENT IN WORSHIP

Although the usual course leaders will be able to take everyone through the first part of this workshop on posture and gesture, it is essential to invite someone appropriate to lead the section on dance. We have always tried to offer some testimony and demonstration from a dancer together with some simple instructions for free dance and then an opportunity for everyone to join together in a communal dance. How this works out in practice will be dependent on who is available within the local area. Although a simple PowerPoint presentation is provided, course leaders may prefer to run this workshop without using it.

There is a well known English proverb: 'Actions speak louder than words.' This can apply in many walks of life and worship is no exception. We have probably all experienced the poignancy of lighting a candle at a Memorial service; maybe some have experienced foot or hand washing on Maundy Thursday. These are specific actions for specific occasions, but our regular worship can also be greatly enriched by action and movement, changes in posture and the use of symbolic gestures. Some of these will be explored creatively within this workshop and the prayer workshop later in the day.

There is a biblical precedent for movement and the use of meaningful posture and gesture during worship. The ancient Israelites were undoubtedly far more demonstrative than the average reserved British congregation! Biblical examples are given and where appropriate attention is drawn to the Hebrew and Greek. All the information is

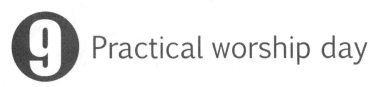

summarised in *Handout 2*, but we recommend that this is given out at the end of the workshop so that the main emphasis here is on experiential learning.

Right from the beginning, demonstrate from the front and encourage all participants to try out each posture, gesture or movement whilst at the same time allowing them permission not to do anything they find uncomfortable or inappropriate. (NB. Some may have physical difficulties which prevent kneeling or lying prostrate) We have tried to include gestures from across the traditions in order to encourage greater understanding of different churchmanship and to be as inclusive as possible. However, the list is not exhaustive and others may be able to offer additional suggestions.

20 mins

Posture and gesture

Slide 3

If the coffee has been served in a different place from the large open space, a good way to begin this workshop is by processing from one room to another perhaps led by a cross if available to give a clear lead.

A procession is defined as a number of people moving forward in orderly succession, especially at a ceremony. It might be a procession of choir and ministers at the beginning or end of a service, perhaps following behind the cross (crucifer) and lights (acolytes, i.e. candle bearers). It implies ritual, majesty, and dignity. Alternatively, a procession could involve the whole congregation either inside or outside the church building more akin to the return of the ark to Jerusalem during the reign of King David (2 Samuel 6:1ff) or the triumphal entry of Jesus into Jerusalem on Palm Sunday (Matthew 21:8ff). These are both acts of rejoicing and acts of witness, which attract the attention of others.

Standing - We usually stand at the beginning of a service to demonstrate our respect for God. It also indicates an expectancy, an alertness and a steadfastness. We are ready and we mean business! (See 2 Chronicles 7:6; Revelation 7:9)

When Ezra read from the Book of the Law, the people stood up. (Nehemiah 8:5) We might stand in a similar way for the reading of the Gospel. This might also be accompanied by a procession of the

book of the Gospels down into the nave, where the Good News is proclaimed in the midst of the people.

Genuflection is practised in Anglo-catholic parishes and involves a bending of the knee or bowing down as a sign of reverence or adoration in worship. This is usually directed toward the altar/holy table. We find references to worshipping and bowing down in Old and New Testaments:

But I, by your great mercy, will come into your house; in reverence will I bow down towards your holy temple. (Psalms 5:7)

Shachah (Heb) - to worship and bow down.

At the name of Jesus every knee will bow. (Philippians 2:10)

Kampto (Gk) - to bend or bow.

Sign of the cross - As early as the 2nd Century, the Christian writer Tertullian refers to making the sign of the cross on the forehead in daily comings and goings: 'In all the ordinary actions of everyday life, we trace the sign of the cross.' During Medieval times, it took on a more sacramental aspect, being seen as 'a lawful outward ceremony and honourable badge' *(Canon XXX, 1603)* and a reminder of the Trinity. (From *A New Dictionary of Liturgy and Worship,* ed. J. G. Davies, SCM Press Ltd, 1986)

The sign of the cross is made from forehead (in the name of the Father) to lower chest (in the name of the Son), shoulder to shoulder (in the name of the Holy Spirit). It is used by the clergy as a sign of blessing, but also by the people as a form of prayer and openness to God's grace. This gesture is associated with significant points in the liturgy: Greeting, Absolution, Gospel, before receiving the sacrament, Blessing, and before reading the Gospel, also small gestures on forehead, lips and heart. This might be accompanied silently by the following prayer often used by the preacher before the sermon:

May the words of my lips and the meditation of my/our heart(s) be acceptable in your sight, O Lord, our Rock and our Redeemer.
(Based on Psalm 19:14)

Holy kiss can be a sign of greeting and a token of love for one another at the beginning of a service or during the peace (1 Corinthians 16:20). However, it can also be a sign of deep respect and honour for God, which extends to holy objects such as the Bible, altar or icons of saints. This is an important part of Eastern Orthodox worship.

Proskuneo (Gk) – to come towards to kiss; a practice in ancient Greek and Roman cultures to kiss the feet of a statue or living person in adoration. (See also the woman who kissed the feet of Jesus in Luke 7:45)

Sharing peace as a sign of forgiveness, friendship and unity usually takes place before taking Holy Communion (Matthew 5:23-4; 1 Corinthians 11:17ff). This is usually done by shaking hands, 'offering the right hand of fellowship' (Galatians 2:9) or an embrace. Although some people find sharing the Peace difficult, it reminds us of the importance of touch. However, it can become increasingly protracted and its true meaning lost in idle chatter.

Mea culpa – My fault; my mistake (Latin) Occasionally we may notice the beating of the breast three times as an act of contrition sometimes observed by the priest before partaking of Holy Communion as a sign that they too need to confess their sins to almighty God.

The tax collector would not even look up to heaven, but beat his breast and said, 'God, have mercy on me, a sinner.' (Luke 18:13)

Slide 4

Clapping can be a sign of joy or appreciation, so try some applause.

Taqa (Heb) – to clatter, to slap the hands together, to clang an instrument; to clasp the hand of another in friendship.

Clap your hands all you nations; shout to God with cries of joy. (Psalm 47:1)

Praise GOD, everybody! Applaud GOD, all people! (Psalms 117:1, The Message)

Macha (Heb) – to rub or strike the hands together (in exultation); to clap. (Psalm 98:8 - rivers clap; Isaiah 55:12 - fields clap).

Clapping is also associated with preparation for battle (together with stamping of feet) as part of a war cry (Ezekiel 25:6). Think about the power and defiance in a slow hand clap of protest. We might want to consider this a useful tool in spiritual warfare.

Wave offerings involved lifting an item before the Lord. In the Old Testament, this was usually done by the priest.

T(e)nuwphah (Heb) – to brandish, offer, shake, wave (an offering).

Leviticus mentions 'heave' offerings; i.e. a breast of lamb was lifted vertically and offered to God (Leviticus 7:34). This is similar to the offering of our monetary collection or the elevation of the bread and wine during the communion prayer. 'Wave' offerings involved lifting a gift of grain and waving it horizontally from side to side (Leviticus 23:9-12)

In the New Testament, we find people waving palms and clothing during the triumphal entry of Jesus into Jerusalem on Palm Sunday. (John 12:13)

Today we might join in a Mexican wave at a sports event: a communal wave travels round an arena section by section as each group catches on, usually followed by a great roar from the crowd. Why not try it around the room followed by a shout of praise such as 'Alleluia' or 'Jesus is Lord'!

Lifting hands tends to be associated primarily with the charismatic churches, but we will certainly find priests of every churchmanship raising their hands during the communion prayer as part of the four-fold action of taking bread, giving thanks, breaking it and sharing it with the congregation.

At times, it may be in vogue to raise one hand whilst at other times both hands are raised. Scripture refers to both options:

Towdah (Heb) – to raise the right hand in agreement with God's word, in covenant; to extend the hand in thanksgiving and adoration.

He who sacrifices thank-offerings (with an extended hand implied) honours me, and he prepares the way so that I may show him the salvation of God. (Psalm 50:23)

God also extends his hand to us:

So do not fear, for I am with you; do not be dismayed, for I am your God. I will strengthen you and help you; I will uphold you with my righteous right hand. (Isaiah 41:10)

Yadah (Heb) – to worship with extended hands; to lift up hands in worship to the Lord.

I will praise (with extended hands implied) you, O LORD, with all my heart; I will tell of all your wonders. (Psalm 9:1)

When King Jehoshaphat sent his singers out at the head of his army, they were to praise and worship in this way with outstretched hands.

We can open our arms wide in a position of vulnerability or abandonment, a physical reminder of the cross and a symbol of sacrifice and surrender, giving our whole self to God. Alternatively, we can hold our hands cupped as a symbol of offering to God or a readiness to receive from God.

Laying on of hands can be used in a variety of ways.

As a sign of blessing: People were bringing little children to Jesus to have him touch them. (Mark 10:13)

We do this as part of the baptism service or as an alternative to receiving the bread and wine at communion.

For commissioning; e.g. the choice of deacons to wait at tables in Acts 6: They presented these men to the apostles, who prayed and laid their hands on them. (Acts 6:6)

We see a similar action at services of ordination and authorisation.

For the healing of the sick: Jesus laid his hands on many sick people and healed them. (See a man with leprosy and Peter's mother-in-law in Matthew 8 and Jairus' daughter in Mark 5:41)

Anointing with oil as a sign of God's grace and blessing frequently accompanies the laying on of hands. Oils are blessed and set apart on Maundy Thursday for anointing at baptism, at ordination or commissioning (oil of chrism), and for anointing the sick and dying.

This is in line with the instruction in James:

Is any one of you sick? He should call the elders of the church to pray over him and anoint him with oil in the name of the Lord.
(James 5:14; see also the disciples in Mark 6:13)

Kneeling is a posture of reverence and adoration.

Barak (Heb) – to kneel (down), to give reverence to God as an act of adoration.

Come, let us bow down in worship,
let us kneel before the Lord our maker; (Psalm 95:6)

With removal of pews and hassocks from churches, kneeling seems to have gone out of fashion, and yet it makes a difference to our prayer life.

Cranmer encouraged communicants to 'make humble confession to Almighty God, meekly kneeling upon your knees.' (BCP Communion)

He also referred to '*devoutly kneeling*' in prayer in the rubrics to Morning and Evening Prayer in the Book of Common Prayer.

The adoption of this kind of submissive and humble posture reinforces our words of confession or our pleas for help during intercessory prayer. (See the Canaanite woman in Matthew 15:25)

Prostration implies lying face down in awe or in an attitude of complete submission and abandonment to God in prayer.

Shachah (Heb) – to fall down flat, to prostrate in homage to royalty or God.

Come, let us bow down in worship. (Psalm 95:6)

Pipto (Gk) – to fall down (literally or figuratively).

At his revelation of Jesus, John fell at his feet as though dead. (Revelation 1:17)

King David pleaded with God for the life of his son by lying face down on the ground (2 Samuel 12:16). Together with fasting, his posture underlines the desperation and sincerity of his prayers.

This is a rarity nowadays, although some ordinands will prostrate themselves publicly during the prayers prior to their ordination, and prostration is occasionally to be found within charismatic worship.

N.B. We can find no references in scripture to 'sitting' in worship, although with the removal of pews and kneelers this is now frequently our default posture.

10 mins

Use of flags in worship

Slide 5

Although this is often associated with the children and young people within our congregations, the use of flags in worship is an expressive art and a skill in its own right. Again we find good biblical evidence. Indeed, the Lord Himself is described as our banner by Moses:

Jehovah-nissi (Heb) – The Lord is my banner. (Exodus 17:15)

Flags were used

- To denote families (Numbers 2:2)
- As a rallying point in times of war

In that day the Root of Jesse will stand as a banner for the peoples; the nations will rally to him, and his place of rest will be glorious. (Isaiah 11:10)

- Symbols of rejoicing and praise. (Psalm 20:5)

Dagal (Heb) – to raise a flag; to be conspicuous with banners.

We will rejoice in your salvation, and in the name of our God we will set up our banners! (Psalms 20:5)

Compare these references with Jesus' triumphal entry into Jerusalem, when the crowds used cloaks and palms to wave and carpet the road. (Matthew 21:8ff)

A **good flag** will be made of a lightweight, crease-resistant fabric, which is the same on both sides. It will be attached securely to a dowel (stronger than a bamboo cane) with a 15-20cm (6-8in) handgrip; any longer and the handle will get in the way. The size of a flag is a matter of personal preference, although too big becomes unwieldy and children obviously need proportionally smaller ones. Instructions for making flags are on the handout.

Encourage everyone to take up a flag and have a go. Participants will need more space than they anticipate in order to avoid others! Choose appropriate recorded worship music to facilitate movement. Experiment with wide flowing sweeps, both high and low. Circles to the

23

right need to be countered with circles to the left to avoid the flag becoming tangled. Then take some quick feedback.

Summarise

The use of flags is a relatively new expression of worship, developing in Britain over the past thirty years. It has been pioneered and given credibility, particularly amongst men, by

Andy Au, pastor of City Gate Church, Brighton and director of *Movement in Worship,* which he founded in the early 1980s. Andy is an expert with flags and has played a pioneering role in the use of flags in worship. Andy is keen to encourage men in dance using staves (big sticks!). At the time of writing, he is currently working with Psalm-drummers, experimenting with pulse and rhythm to develop what he describes as 'dynamic mass sculpture'. To find out more, details are given on *Handout 2.*

Hopefully by now, all the experimentation with posture and gesture and the flag waving will have helped participants to relax before tackling dance.

25 mins

Dance

Slide 6

Before we go any further, we must state that it is impossible to encapsulate dance in text. Dance has to be 'experienced', so concentrate on the practical here rather than giving the biblical background and rationale. *Handout 2* will fill in the gaps.

We can all dance - Programmes like *The X-Factor* have made dance and singing into spectator sports, but these are activities for participation. Just the same as singing (where everyone has a voice), everyone has arms and legs and therefore has the potential to dance. In many other cultures, where singing and dancing are an integral part of community life and its ceremonies, this whole idea of 'I can't sing/dance' simply does not exist. Some may have a particular gift, but all nevertheless take part. And before anyone asks. 'What about those with physical disabilities?' Graham Kendrick gives a wonderful description of a guy in a wheelchair dancing before the Lord in his book *Worship* (Kingsway Publications Ltd, 1984, page 99).

Dance was a regular part of Israel's celebration and their rites of passage, and it was therefore quite natural that dance should flow over into the worship arena. Remember how Miriam led the women with tambourines and dancing to celebrate Israel's great deliverance from Pharoah. The Bible encourages us all to dance!

Let them praise his name with dancing. (Psalm 149:3)

Chiyl/chuwl (Heb) for dance used here also means to twist or whirl in a circular manner.

Testimony and demonstration - If at all possible, include some testimony and demonstration of a sacred/liturgical dance at this point from a competent dancer or group of dancers. Then ask them to lead participants through the following practical points:

Movements - It is helpful to point out that a wide range of movements can be used making full use of the body and personal space as well as full use of the stage or room space.

Simple movements can be made at every level and in every direction: from the floor, bowing, bending, standing, arm extensions, stretching, turning, etc. Such movements can be slow or fast, smooth and flowing or angular and jerky.

Movement can be used to illustrate words and interpret a song or text. Dances can be done individually or co-ordinated in groups. They can be planned or spontaneous.

There is a need to dress appropriately and be aware of any hazards such as slippery floors, steps or burning candles.

Encourage participants to practise at home first. Lock the door, close the curtains, put on a favourite worship CD and have a go! It is surprising how quickly we can move from practising to actually worshipping.

A simple communal dance - Now give everyone the opportunity to try a simple dance together. Encourage everyone to have a go, but make it very clear that people can participate at their level (e.g. there may be some who are able to join in by moving their arms whilst sitting, but would struggle with anything else).

We used an Israeli circle dance set to traditional Israeli music with simple traditional steps, but other dances could be equally effective. We can use the resources we have around us in terms of people who

have experienced different forms of dance, particularly those from other countries: e.g. dance has been used as a form of protest in South Africa; many cultures celebrate harvest through dance. This is about trying something different and seeing if it works for you in your context.

A dance or series of movements needs simple, clear explanation if folk are going to fully take part. And be enthusiastic!

Encourage everyone to reflect back on the experience and take some quick feedback.

5 mins

Summarise

Slide 7

Many Hebrew and Greek words for exuberant praise and rejoicing imply the need for movement to express such joy adequately. As ever, the English translation fails to do justice to everything encapsulated within one Hebrew or Greek word.

Chagag (Heb) means to celebrate a festival or to march in a sacred procession, but it also means to dance or to move in a circle until giddy!

We are probably all familiar with the phrase from Psalm 118:

This is the day the LORD has made;
let us rejoice and be glad in it. (Psalms 118:24)

Giyl/guwl (Heb), the word for 'rejoice and be glad' used here, also means to spin round under the influence of any violent emotion.

This is the same word used by Habakkuk in his exhortation to continue to praise and worship even when everything is going wrong:

Though the fig-tree does not bud and there are no grapes on the vines, though the olive crop fails and the fields produce no food, though there are no sheep in the pen and no cattle in the stalls, yet I will rejoice (jump for joy) in the LORD, I will be joyful (spin round) in God my Saviour. The Sovereign LORD is my strength; he makes my feet like the feet of a deer, he enables me to go on the heights. (Habakkuk 3:17-19)

In *Sessions 3* and *4*, we came across the return of the ark of the covenant to Jerusalem.

David, wearing a linen ephod, danced before the LORD with all his might, while he and the entire house of Israel brought up the ark of the Lord with shouts and the sound of trumpets. As the ark of the Lord was entering the City of David, Michal daughter of Saul watched from a window. And when she saw King David leaping and dancing before the Lord, she despised him in her heart. (2 Samuel 6: 14-16)

The Hebrew word used here - *'Pazaz'* - meaning to spring or leap, is similar to our own word 'pizzazz', meaning energy, style and sparkle. David gave himself wholly to worship, dancing with all his might not caring what anyone else thought. Michal, on the other hand, was singularly unimpressed, and perhaps ashamed and embarrassed by the king's behaviour. She sneers at the king:

How the king of Israel has distinguished himself today, disrobing in the sight of the slave girls of his servants as any vulgar fellow would. (2 Samuel 6:20)

A question of attitude

We may feel dance is definitely not for us, but leave everyone with a final challenge. God sees more than the dance. God sees our hearts. Will we be like David, who was prepared to dance before the Lord with all his might, irrespective of who was looking? Or will we be like his wife, Michal, who despised the way the king behaved in front of all the people?

Handout 2: Posture and movement in worship

Finally, draw everyone's attention to *Handout 2*, which summarises all that we have experienced within this workshop.

WORKSHOP 3 | USING VISUAL TECHNOLOGY IN WORSHIP

Slide 2

Some of us are natural geeks but others of us can too easily become techno-phobic. The purpose of this workshop is to introduce some basic guidelines and principles of good practice and debunk some fears of

using technology. Hopefully it will give us some useful insights into the whole process of putting together and running a worship programme on a Sunday morning. In any cohort of participants we may well have one or two technical wizards, so this may be an ideal opportunity for them to play to their strengths and share their talents and experience with others in the group.

Although this workshop can be facilitated by one leader up front, it is much more interesting and informative if it can be as 'hands on' as possible. It will be helpful to have one laptop set up with data projector and screen, but have one or two other laptops available with PowerPoint and/or a worship software programme and people who know how to use them. Allow a good half of the time for demonstration on the screen and then time for experimentation in small groups with a little bit of feedback and summary at the end. We have provided very full notes, but to save time on the day it might be pertinent to focus on the PowerPoint presentation and use the Teachers' Notes as helpful background for the workshop leaders.

Handout 3: Visual technology in worship

Link with current culture

30 mins

Whether we like it or not, we live in a world of Information Technology (IT). Visual images and sound bites stimulate our senses all day long. Our children are growing up with computers and access to all sorts through Google, iPlayer and iTunes, using icons and symbols on their mobiles or iPods. Technology is part of their everyday world at home and at school. Consequently, expectations are high. If we are going to use technology in worship, we need to do it well: firstly, because God deserves our best; secondly, because we want to keep the congregation on board; and thirdly, because visitors may find it 'naff' if it is not good.

Worship first

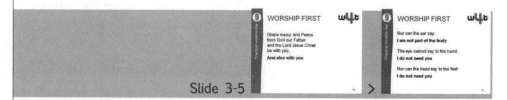

Slide 3-5

We are talking here about technology in the context of worship, so let's begin with some worship.

Read through slides 3-5 together.

The liturgy has been laid out exactly as it is in the book. Therefore, it looks familiar to regulars who naturally respond to sections in bold type without any prompting.

Visuals can be used to enhance worship by

Slide 6

- **Illustrating points** with a few headings and bullet points, but not too much information on any one slide. 'Keep it simple' is still the watch word.
- **Stimulating imagination** with additional images or photographs but be aware that this can also limit imagination by guiding it in a specific direction.
- **Giving information succinctly** - This is especially useful for giving notices in an interesting way without taking time during the service. Why not have notices scrolling round at the beginning and end of services?
- **Facilitating the introduction of new songs** - This is a great way to save typing and save trees!
- **Facilitating the use of varied liturgy** - So many parishes limited their use of *Common Worship* by producing a set of service booklets, but with projection we can use the full library of resources easily. The *Visual Liturgy* software package is already available to help.
- **Using material produced by others** - Every creative activity takes time, so sometimes we may need to use ready-made presentations. Make a note of good websites and be prepared to share amongst the *Worship4Today* network. Please be aware of copyright laws and fully acknowledge other people's work.

However, with all this we must remember that ...

Slide 7

Worship comes first - Technology, images and gimmicks are there to *serve* and *enable* worship:

- Not to dominate;
- Not to distract;
- Not to be clever.

3Rs - Regularly Reflect and Review - As with every style and every aid to worship, we need to reflect honestly on what we are doing and make appropriate adjustments and modifications as we go along. We must continue to ask ourselves:

- What works well and enhances worship?
- What distracts?

With these two questions in mind, we want to run through some basic tools and top tips for doing visuals well.

Good practice for screen design

The best way to get the hang of PowerPoint and screen design is to take time to play; mess around; push every button; have fun and see what it can do! The following list is not exhaustive and any experts within the group may want to add their own hot tips as we go.

The slides follow the order on the handout but we recommend that participants focus primarily on the screen.

Font

Slide 8

Choose one or two font styles that are clear and easy to read and stick to them.

- Arial is clear
- Times New Roman is easy to read
- **Comic sans MS is useful with children**
- Other fonts, particularly fancy ones, should be used with caution.

Slide 9

And be aware that

- **Size matters!** Font size varies according to style. In Arial, text must be at least 24pt; most people agree 32pt is best; some would say 40pt is better; above 48pt cramps the page layout. Using bold and shadow or outline can also help to emphasise text.

Text

Slide 10-20   >

- **Avoid writing over the top of 'loud' images**, which make the text difficult to read; perhaps put text over grass or sky.
- **Start text at the same place** on each screen whenever possible so the eye knows where to look. Left justification is easiest to follow.
- **Break up lines in sensible places** with no more than eight lines of song lyrics per slide
- **Lower case is easier to read than CAPITALS**
- **Keep to key words and don't overload with text** - This can be a big turn off for many people, so keep focused on the message you want to convey. Use bullet points and then expand on each point from personal notes. Try to keep each title or bullet point on one line.

If there is a lot of text to display for Bible readings and songs, run it over several slides.

Colour

Slide 21

Backgrounds should be kept subtle and not too bright:

- **Use a good contrast**
  - Black or blue text on pale background
  - White or yellow on dark background
- **Consider those with sight problems**, particularly the colour blind and those suffering from dyslexia. Expert opinion varies, but generally issues on screen will be the same as on paper. Yellow on blue is recommended by some as the easiest for most people to read.

- Use colour to separate types of information
  - Leader in white
  - Congregation in yellow

  This will be more obvious than a simple contrast between ordinary text and bold text, which can be almost indistinguishable in certain fonts.
- Use colour to emphasise a point – but carefully.

Templates and logos ...

Slide 22-25

- **Are useful to keep consistency**; e.g. *W4T* logo and format used throughout this course. These set and maintain a house style, which is easily recognisable, using a consistent border, logo and slide title format throughout.
- **Maintain a mood or theme** during a particular season or sermon series. All templates and logos should be self-explanatory. If using a border with people on it, make sure people look into the content of the slide rather than out from it even if it means reversing a picture. This effect draws the congregation in as well. Sections of pictures can be cropped to make borders.
- **Should be in sympathy with the local context** - In a medieval church, a stone coloured background and photographs of the church may help the use of visuals remain in keeping with the building. We might use a design from the stained glass in the church as a matching border.

Slide 26

Signals

These are images or colours that indicate where we are or what is happening in a service. They should be clear, consistent and self explanatory, but not over used. These could be in the form of a simple progress bar, highlighting where we are in terms of Gathering, Word, Prayer, Sacrament, Conclusion, or we could show a simple icon of a bible or the appropriate hymnbook in the corner.

Animation and transitions

Just because we can have things flying in or dissolving out does not mean that they will necessarily enhance a presentation. *Fade* seems uninteresting but it may actually be least intrusive.

Slide 27

Transitions ...

- Should go unnoticed unless making a particular point
- Should be the same all the way through. If transitions change after every slide, the presentation looks amateurish.
- Watch out for any unintentional auto slide advance.

The features should never obscure the message. And don't design slides that make us wait for information. Slowly crawling in from the bottom may have seemed good on the desktop, but when we are standing waiting for the animation to catch up it can be embarrassing. Animation should be customized to add to the storyline not detract from it.

Summary of distractions

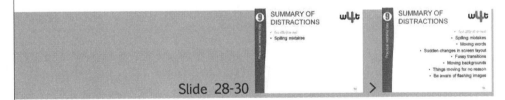

Slide 28-30

- **Text difficult to read** – font, size, colour blends.
- **Spelling mistakes** can be really irritating for some. Try to eliminate any mistakes as soon as they are spotted to avoid the same mistake appearing week on week.
- **Moving words** must appear in an appropriate way and at an appropriate speed and then remain long enough to be read and absorbed.
- **Sudden changes in screen layout** can subconsciously unsettle the congregation.
- **Fussy transitions** draw the eye away from the main message.
- **Moving backgrounds** can be very effective when used sparingly, but they can be a real distraction with song lyrics or liturgy, because the eye is automatically drawn to the thing that moves.

- Things moving for no reason can be unsettling, and too many things moving together can be chaotic with points being lost in sensory overload. Finally,
- Be aware of flashing images and photosensitivity, which can cause big problems for some.

Some tips to maintain consistency

Slide 31

- Copy or overwrite previous presentations, so that the congregation get used to the same format.
- Use hymnbooks on disk or same internet sources, so that song lyrics are always presented in the same style. Some will have a capital letter for the start of every new line, whether it needs it or not.
- Cut and paste wherever possible to avoid spelling mistakes and other typos.
- Evolve a house style - This takes time, so do not be rushed. Better to let it happen gradually over the first six months or so. And in general don't be tempted to change things just for the sake of it.

Using images

Slide 32-36

Visual images can enhance aesthetically, but they are also an aid to memory and learning.

- Use visually powerful images that reinforce text and again try to match the image style from slide to slide.
- Clip art rarely works well - Using clip art is now considered a deadly sin! It is much better to use proper pictures and photographs with a good mix of traditional and contemporary images for spiritual inspiration.
- Don't overwhelm the text - We don't want too much crammed on to any one slide. It is much better to use more slides with less information on each.

- Try to get a good balance on the screen with generally no more than two images per screen carefully positioned with the text. Think about each slide as something we wish to publish or print. Make sure there are equal borders down each side/top and bottom, round pictures, etc.
- Leave enough border to allow for the 'cropping' effect of projection - When the presentation is projected onto a screen, it is unlikely to line up exactly. Some screens have rounded corners too. Allowing big borders on all four sides will avoid losing important parts of the presentation.

Finding images

Slide 37

This is where the internet comes into its own!

- Use 'Google Images' search engine and other internet resources extensively but responsibly. Choose pictures with care; some will be too small to project with good definition and clarity; some may need to be cropped or resized to fit into the presentation. Some internet pictures may be copyrighted.
- Take digital camera images (with sufficient pixels) - Again, quality of image matters but our own pictures enable us to connect with our locality and congregation in a direct way.
- Scan from printed images, but these must be clear.

Adding sound and video

Slide 38

This requires a little more technical expertise, but is not that complicated! The sound file should be WMA (Windows Media Audio) or WAV (Waveform Audio) file format or mp3 depending on age of software. The video file also has limited formats. WMV (Windows Media Video) is a safe option.

- Ideally embed video and audio files into the presentation - They should be saved as part of the presentation, so the PowerPoint file will be large. This means that if their location on the computer is changed, then they will still play. They should also load quicker if they are embedded. Whatever the situation, the audio/video file needs to be located on the computer it is running from.
- Amplification will be needed if running from a laptop - Laptop speakers are not big enough or loud enough for even a small group.

Summary

Slide 39

- **Worship is our aim – technology is the servant** - This is a machine, so we should be in control, not the other way around!
- **Keep it simple** - Remember too much information or 'noise' on the screen is not good communication.
- **Be consistent** - This makes life easier for everyone: the person putting together the presentation, the person operating the presentation and the people looking at it.
- **All rules can be broken** but only if there is a good reason.

Books and manuals can be overwhelming as well as confusing, so it may be easier to 'learn by doing' alongside someone who is already familiar with PowerPoint.

Church presentation software

Slide 40

Both free (such as *ZionWorx*) and commercial programmes (such as *EasyWorship* and *SongPro*) are available, so do plenty of research first before you settle on one particular programme. Some are more straightforward to use than others but the simpler programmes may not have such good functions available for integrating and playing media clips. If you are planning to pay for software, then check the licence cover, especially if it is a team ministry with multiple users. Some basic licences prohibit the use of a second screen and projector and will require extra payment for an upgrade. It can get expensive quickly. Visit

other churches to see different programmes working in situ as well as reading up on websites and listening to the sales pitch.

To allow time for 'hands on' experimentation, we suggest that the following points are drawn out and emphasised. These will be reinforced and expanded by further details given in *Handout 3*.

The crucial factor is **Dual monitor configuration,** which provides an operator screen and a presentation screen. This allows the operator full control for creating or editing a presentation during a service without affecting the main screen. Some software now includes an additional stage screen option for leaders and musicians. This in turn allows greater flexibility without losing the rest of the band! Much of what we have already said about putting together a presentation continues to apply here. Suffice it to say that any programme needs to include ...

- **Extensive formatting options** for fonts, sizes, colours, backgrounds, images and animation.
- **Integrated Bible and song databases** with good and varied search facilities. This can avoid hours of typing and enables a verse of scripture or a different song to be displayed in seconds. Some programmes will automatically collect CCLI data for the annual return, saving painstaking recording of songs.
- **Easy to import PowerPoint files** for sermon, prayers or notices.

Full web and audio integration and a live camera feed can all be useful additions but these are not essentials. Any memory facilities, which can store worship resources and service data may save time later.

Practical tips for service leader or preacher

Slide 41

Whoever is putting the service presentation together, always

- **Try to create the presentation on the computer that will run it on the day** - Variations between versions of software, updates and screen resolutions can make something that worked fine at home not work at all somewhere else.
- **Operate the PowerPoint presentation yourself if possible,** using a hand-held slide advancer ('Wireless Presenter'). Alternatively, give the AV operator a full script of the presentation highlighting slide changes to denote clicks and auto entries.

- **Don't keep looking over your shoulder to see what is on the screen** This can be irritating and looks unprofessional. We are talking to the congregation not addressing the screen! If possible, use a separate monitor at the front; if this is not possible, practise with the operator, and then trust them to do their job.

Practical tips for the operator

Slide 42

- **Practise setting up** - Different laptops and data projectors sometimes have difficulty talking to each other, so always try everything out beforehand.
- **Correct order may matter**, otherwise we may find that the data projector refuses to talk to the laptop. Connect all mains cables and leads between projector and laptop first. Turn on each component in the right order, usually laptop first, then the data projector automatically recognises the type of laptop.
- **Don't forget the extra sound cable if playing a film clip** - This is one that catches us out time and again!
- **Practise keeping pace** - It is vital to have the correct words on the screen at the moment we need them. The operator must learn to anticipate and change to the next slide at just the right moment, so that liturgy flows seamlessly and song words appear unimpeded from verse to verse. This is an intuitive skill which takes time to master.
- **Practise with different service leaders and musicians** so that you are familiar with their individual styles. A few joint rehearsals for service leaders, musicians and the technical team will pay great dividends.
- **Practise editing and adding whilst something else is happening** - This is a vital skill to master, allowing for an immediate change in order or the addition of an extra scripture or song.
- **Practise in bright sunlight**, especially during the winter when the angle of the sun is low. Try to test colour combinations in situ and at the time of day they will be shown. Most combinations will work at night but might not show up well on Sunday morning with sun streaming through the windows and at that point there may not be enough time to change every slide.
- **Learn from feedback** - Practice will make progress. Every mistake provides an opportunity to grow and improve.

25 mins

Examples and exercises

Now it is time for some experimentation in small groups of three to four people per laptop. Divide people according to experience and skill, ideally with some PowerPoint experience in each group. Some short exercises are given on pages 75-77 of *Handout 3*. There won't be time for them all, so suggest that everyone tries exercises one and two and then concentrates on either exercise three or four. Exercises five and six can be explored at home. You will need to provide a hymn/song text and a piece of responsive liturgy.

5 mins

Feedback and final comments

Draw everyone back together and take some quick feedback before summarising with the following points.

What happens if ...

With all things technical, what happens if the technology fails or the projector bulb blows? What happens if there is a power cut? Do we have a plan B at the ready? Most of us come unstuck at least once, thinking it won't happen to us! Will we be completely panicked, or do we have a set of old songbooks or service sheets tucked away in a cupboard for such a time as this?

And finally ...

Technology is not always the answer and there can be some serious disadvantages, which should not be overlooked:

- If we are moved or challenged by particular words, we cannot linger and meditate on them further. We have already moved on to the next frame.
- For the uninitiated, there is often no way of knowing what is coming next or when the service will come to an end.
- Sometimes visual technology will compete unhelpfully with other visuals and sometimes other visual aids will actually work better. However, visuals of any kind will only work well if everyone can see them. If a significant number cannot see the screen, we may need to think again, and are we prepared to produce large print hard copies of every service for the visually impaired?
- Most church buildings were not built with 21st century visual technology in mind, so sight lines can be limited by distance or obscured by pillars. Some churches will use two screens, others will add television monitors on pillars for the far corners, but there may be a loss of focus if people are looking in different directions. If the screen is too high, those near the front may get cricked necks.

We must face the hard questions we asked at the beginning:

- Will data projection enhance worship or will it be a distraction?
- And, if we use data projection for everything, will it begin to lose its effectiveness?

Don't forget ... the projector can be turned off!

A little technical knowledge and understanding can be a great asset, so we would encourage all participants to spend some time learning the basics about their church sound system too. It is so easy to miss the crucial on/off button and wonder why the whole system is not working properly. An additional workshop including PA might be arranged as a follow-up for those who want to develop their technical expertise further.

Some helpful books for further exploration:

Tim Stratford, *Liturgy and technology*, Grove no. W154, 1999.
Ian Tarrant, *How to worship with data projection,* Grove no. W192, 2007.
These booklets are backed up by Grove's online resources at www.grovebooks.co.uk

45 mins

LUNCH BREAK

WORKSHOP 4

LEADING CORPORATE PRAYER

Slide 2

Although this session may begin with some teaching and discussion, we also want it to include movement and interaction. The use of prayer stations may be new to some, and can open up a whole new dimension to intercessory prayer.

5 mins

Brainstorm

Slide 3

Think about the different types of prayer we use both privately and corporately. Share BRIEFLY with one another in pairs.

Feedback on flipchart.

Handout 4: Leading corporate prayer

10 mins

Patterns of prayer

Slide 4

If we think about the structure of a Sunday service, we will notice that there are patterns to our prayers. One such pattern is given the acronym A-C-T-S, representing adoration, confession, thanksgiving and supplication (or intercession). Traditionally, these four describe essential components of our conversation and relationship with God. They also provide a simple and memorable framework for the different types of prayer used within a service:

Adoration - We recognise God's presence with us at the beginning of a service. We come to praise and worship God for who He is, Father, Son and Holy Spirit, and for what He has done as our Creator, Redeemer and Sustainer. Adoration fulfils the commandment to love God with all our heart, mind, soul and strength and implies a lingering in God's presence without rushing away. Opening prayers may incorporate facts about God alongside an invitation to worship:

Faithful one, whose word is life:
come with saving power
to free our praise,
inspire our prayer
and shape our lives
for the kingdom of your Son,
Jesus Christ our Lord.
Amen

(New Patterns for Worship, The Archbishops' Council 2002, A36 in Gathering and Greeting)

Confession - We examine our thoughts and behaviour and clear away all the things that get in the way of our relationship with God. We acknowledge our mistakes and failings, selfishness and guilt. We express

our sorrow and take responsibility for them before hearing God's assurance of forgiveness. Sometimes we include a resolve to amend our ways:

In your mercy
forgive what we have been,
help us to amend what we shall be;
that we may do justly,
love mercy,
and walk humbly with you, our God.

(Confession from *Common Worship: Services and Prayers for the Church of England,* The Archbishops' Council 2000, p.39 & 169)

Thanksgiving - From early childhood we are taught to say 'thank you' when someone gives us something or does something for us. It is a natural response to God's forgiveness and grace. We have many things to be thankful for, and yet this area of prayer can frequently be overlooked.

Gratitude is a vital aspect of prayer for the 21st century church, working in a consumer culture in which we take so much for granted. Everything we have is a gift from a generous God, who genuinely deserves our thanks. Anglican liturgy has a history of thanksgiving seen in the General Thanksgiving from the *Book of Common Prayer.*

Almighty God, Father of all mercies,
We thine unworthy servants
Do give thee most humble and hearty thanks
For all thy goodness and loving kindness to us ...

('A General Thanksgiving' from *The Book of Common Prayer*)

Supplication or intercession (when offered on behalf of others) - We ask God for something we need or for something needed by others. It is perhaps the most basic and instinctive of prayers, practised in some form at some time by the majority of the population. A wise saying suggests that there are no atheists in a sinking ship and each person prays to his God for deliverance (Cf. Jonah 1:6). This type of prayer will include prayers for the world, for the Church, for the local community, and for the sick and bereaved.

New Patterns for Worship (The Archbishops' Council, 2002) includes some helpful directives for leading each of these four types of prayer, based on stories from four churches.

These four different types of prayer are all included within the liturgy. These liturgies are not merely words to be said, but words to be prayed

as they are spoken *('lex orandi')*. Another old Latin saying also picks up the theme: '*Qui bene cantat bis orat*': 'He who sings *well*, prays twice.' (the 'well' is often omitted in translation). Although this phrase has frequently been attributed to St Augustine, scholars cannot find anything similar within his writings. The phrase has also been associated with St Gregory, St Basil, Thomas Aquinas or Luther. Original author aside, the phrase reminds us that many of our hymns and worship songs are in themselves prayers. Our singing too can be another form of prayer.

The Lord's Prayer

Slide 5

When one of the disciples asked Jesus to teach them how to pray, Jesus gave them the example of what we now know as the 'Lord's Prayer'. The original context is one of private prayer:

But when you pray, go into your room, close the door and pray to your Father, who is unseen. Then your Father, who sees what is done in secret, will reward you. (Matthew 6:6)

However, the prayer links closely to the A-C-T-S pattern. The Lord's Prayer itself contains the essential components of adoration: *Our Father in heaven, hallowed be your name;* confession: *forgive us our sins;* thanksgiving and praise: *for the kingdom, the power and the glory are yours;* and supplication: *give us today our daily bread.*

This prayer is now included as a corporate prayer in almost every act of worship. The Lord's Prayer is considered one of the four key Christian texts to be taught as part of the preparation for baptism or confirmation. It continues to be taught as the primary Christian text in school.

10 mins

Intercessory prayer

Slide 6

We now want to home in on leading intercessory prayer as this is a part of worship often led by lay people. Lay leadership of the intercessions

not only brings a variety of approaches and insights, it also underlines the importance of the whole people of God sharing together in these corporate prayers:

Again, I tell you that if two of you on earth agree about anything you ask for, it will be done for you by my Father in heaven. For where two or three come together in my name, there am I with them.
(Matthew 18:19-20)

When we agree together in prayer, we are deliberately putting our trust in God - together. We are crying out to Him to change those situations that we cannot change. This corporate prayer is powerful.

Why should we intercede?

Slide 7

John Pritchard, in his *Intercessions Handbook* (SPCK, 1997, p.6-9), suggests there are three main reasons why we intercede:

- **A deep instinct** - To reiterate what we have already said, there is a deep human instinct to pray when in trouble, and to reach out to a heavenly Father who knows how to give good gifts to his children (see Matthew 7:9). 'The danger is that God is treated as a celestial cash-point' who can be manipulated round to our way of thinking. However, 'at the heart of this instinct is the instinct to love.' If we truly love people, we will want the best for them and we will care sufficiently to engage in the 'serious task of holding them daily before God.'
- **A biblical invitation** - 'It is the consistent expectation of the Bible that we will bring our needs and the needs of others to God.' This is exemplified throughout scripture, through direct conversations between God and individual people: e.g. Abraham's bold discussion with God to spare Sodom and Gomorrah (Genesis 18:16ff) or Elijah's persistent prayer for rain to relieve famine (see 1 Kings 18). Jesus also encourages us to be bold and ask for what we need, and to persist if at first we do not receive an answer (Luke 11:1-13). This is the way Jesus himself asked the Father for what he needed. And when we do not know how to pray, Pritchard reminds us: 'One of the most exciting discoveries we make in intercession is that the Holy Spirit will be guiding and sorting out our prayers anyway.' (see Romans 8:26)

- A long tradition - 'Intercession has always been at the centre of our public liturgies ... The Church has always seen it as a holy duty to bear the world to God in regular prayer.' We clearly have a responsibility to pray, and we see this responsibility taken seriously every time we meet to worship.

For whom should we pray?

Slide 8

Traditionally we pray for the Church, the world, the community, the sick, and the dying. However, we don't have to pray for everything and everybody every time we pray. Specific topics may lend themselves to a particular service, or current news items may already dominate people's thinking.

Intercessions can take many forms: following one of the set patterns suggested within *Common Worship*; using the form of a litany with a bidding and response; using petitions followed by a silence; using the prayers of others from published collections; writing prayers especially for the occasion. We can pray in any form but clear patterns and obvious topics will give clarity and flow, and help others to follow and engage.

Intercessory prayer is not ...

Slide 9

Before we move on to a few practicalities, let us quickly clarify what intercessory prayer is not. It is not ...

- **Individual prayer writ large** - We will each pray differently alone in private, dependent on our personality, age, experience of God, and personal preference. What is helpful to me personally may or may not be helpful to others. Intercessory prayer in church is first and foremost the corporate prayer of the whole people of God and therefore must be accessible to the whole people of God.

- **A litany of the news** - Our prayers should be more than a wish list of needs. True intercession is about loving concern, sincere care and the solidarity of standing alongside others in need.
- **Telling God what He already knows** - We have no need to tell God that George is having a hip operation in Ward 10 of the local hospital. Nor is the prayer time the place to give this information to the congregation. Much better to choose our words with care and encourage everyone to pray for George's speedy recovery rather than locate him!
- **An opportunity to preach a second sermon** - We may be bursting to add extra pearls of wisdom to the sermon but during the prayers is not the appropriate place. We may be disappointed that we are not given a platform to preach but now is not the time to let our personal issues surface.
- **An opportunity to criticise others** or to say things that we would not dare to say to their face. Nor is the prayer time the place to tell God what we think of the latest 'hot' issues or to tell the congregation what we think God thinks!
- **Too long!** The length of intercessions will vary from church to church but clearly the role of those leading prayers is not to cover everything or the service will last all day. Think through the overall span of the service, the position of the prayers within that, and what might be an appropriate length. We want people to engage and pray without getting restless.

We may laugh at some of these pitfalls, but they are all too easy for all of us to fall into sometimes.

A few helpful pointers

Slide 10

We have provided a detailed booklet: *A Guide to Leading Intercessions in Church* in Appendix 1 to this session. This will cover many of the basic, practical dos and don'ts, so do encourage everyone to read it carefully and use it when preparing intercessions for a service. However, we want to flag up a few general points here:

- **Prepare thoroughly** - We must set aside adequate time to prepare, but not too early in the week or we may need to re-write to include the latest news. We need to consider the theme of the service and who will be present as well as current news, international, national and local. Thorough preparation does not limit our ability to amend

prayers at the last minute, building links with the sermon or including a last minute crisis. Using paper with wide margins enables extra notes to be added easily.

- **Exercise pastoral sensitivity** - We will all be aware of people who are sick, dying, or simply having 'a hard time'. Some people will have told us all about their problems, but they do not expect the whole congregation to hear about them during the intercessions. We must respect confidentiality and resist the temptation to 'share' personal details risking embarrassment to an individual or family.

- **Can we all say 'Amen'?** We must be careful how we pray for difficult situations. We cannot 'push people into praying something they do not believe can happen' (from *How to ... Lead the Prayers* by A. de Lange & L. Simpson, Grove W169, 2002). Can everyone join in our prayer with integrity?

- **Use silence**, which can be very powerful. Silence creates a bridge between corporate prayer, where we share common petitions, and private prayer, where we reflect together on what has been said and add our own individual prayers. However, make sure that the congregation knows what to expect. Reassure them by telling them approximately how long the silences will last.

- **Clear delivery** - Those leading intercessions need to be in position and ready. They also need to be audible and to speak slowly and clearly; now is not the moment to bow the head or drop the voice, especially when kneeling. The congregation will not be able to join in if they cannot hear what is being prayed. Biddings and responses should be clearly introduced with *short* paragraphs and creative pauses in between, so that the bidding and response is not forgotten. The end of the prayer time can be made obvious by joining together in a short communal paragraph or the Lord's Prayer.

- **A model for others** - Good quality intercessions provide a model for prayer for both the regular gathered congregation and for newcomers, who may not know how to pray.

- **Creative participation** - We can get the congregation actively involved by using projected images relating to prayer topics, or encouraging them to write down and offer their own prayers, or using a simple object such as a pebble or candle. Keep ideas simple and make sure that the congregation is given clear instructions.

This nicely leads into spending some time using prayer stations.

20 mins

Prayer stations

Slide 11

After the theory, this is the time for active engagement. Participants are offered the opportunity to explore several different prayer stations and to engage in creative ways of praying together. Encourage everyone to take their time and to be open to God's promptings. They may visit all the stations or they may find themselves lingering at one. We have around twenty minutes and leaders should draw everyone back at the end of that time.

For leaders

A simple definition - 'A prayer station is a small place with something to look at or do, which will stimulate meditation and prayer.' (From *Labyrinths and Prayer Stations* by Ian Tarrant and Sally Dakin, Grove W180, 2004)

The objective of the prayer station is not merely an exhibit to admire, but an invitation to participate in some way. The prayer stations will need to be set up beforehand with a good mix of activities: passive, active, written, creative. We want to encourage participants to both 'be' and 'do'. This is a good opportunity to mix effectively ancient traditions with contemporary material. The revered artwork of old masters or icons and traditional prayers such as the 'Jesus Prayer' or 'Celtic breastplate' prayers can find a place alongside contemporary media using current newspapers, a short film loop on a laptop or a live-feed camera from the street outside the venue.

The possibilities for prayer stations are endless, and may follow the A-C-T-S pattern, relate to the season, or the current hot topics. We have usually used four stations to give sufficient space and variety without becoming unmanageable in the time frame. Include some 'safe' activities, such as lighting a candle, holding a pebble, or writing the name of someone in need on a post-it. We recommend a strong scriptural input for each station together with clear instructions, so that everyone knows exactly what to do. We also recommend that there is suitable music playing in the background. This helps people to move about without having to be silent, and if anyone is crying, it is less obvious.

Over the years, we have used:

- Planting hope (Uplifting and encouraging with something to take away)
- Newspaper prayer (Topical, readily accessible to all and easy to create)
- Confession using sand (Very powerful and well worth the effort)
- Meditation on stones and water (Simple and meaningful but non-threatening)

Instructions for these can all be readily found on the creative prayer website (www.creativeprayer.com). Details of this and other useful websites are given on the handout. Other tips and pointers for creating prayer stations are also included on the handout.

This kind of prayer activity might be used occasionally as an alternative form of intercession but, within the context of a regular service, we must carefully consider the length of time that the activity will require.

10 mins

Two other creative ways of praying

Slide 12

Remaining in an attitude of prayer, we want to introduce two further ideas before taking some feedback.

• Holding prayers

We all have times when a situation is so traumatic or hopeless that we have no idea how to pray. At these times all we can do is 'hold' the people and situations before God and trust the Holy Spirit to lead us.

In the same way, the Spirit helps us in our weakness. We do not know what we ought to pray for, but the Spirit himself intercedes for us with groans that words cannot express. (Romans 8:26)

We have found praying with a simple song can be most helpful on such occasions. We have used 'A Celtic Rune' by Liam Lawton with simple words and movements. We are able to identify with the sufferings of Christ, whilst lifting situations to the God, who, like us, holds these needs in His heart. The words are very simple, so there is no need to have copies. Music is available from CJM Music Ltd. It can be sung unaccompanied or accompanied, in unison or in harmony. Suggest that participants stand, although the movements are possible in a sitting position.

These simple gestures are readily accessible for all ages:

Lord, hear our prayer (Hold the right hand out in front palm upwards and watching the palm, move it out to the side)
Lord, hear our prayer (Hold the left hand out in front palm upwards and watching the palm, move it out to the side to form a crucifixion pose)
Lord, in your mercy (Bring hands together cupped and lift them up to God)

Lord, hear our prayer *(Clasp hands together and draw them back to the heart)*

The singing can be interspersed with simple petitions followed either by silence or, if the song is accompanied, by an instrumental verse.

Maggi Dawn's 'I will wait for your peace to come to me' (Kingsway's Thankyou Music, 1993) is another good option.

* Blessing one another

Although we tend to associate blessing primarily with the priest at the end of a service, the early Celtic Christians had a practice of liberally blessing everything! At its simplest, this was a type of greeting: 'Blessed be' or a bit like our sharing of the Peace, using words like 'Blessings of God be with you'. However, prayers of blessing could focus on the morning or the evening or extend to marriage, homes, hospitality, friendship, and so on. These were simple requests for God's favour to rest upon whomever or whatever was blessed.

Give each person a card of blessing *(see Appendix 2)*. On one side, it has an encouraging verse of scripture and on the other it has a traditional Gaelic Blessing. Then in pairs, ask each person to *slowly* pray the scripture and the blessing over their partner. To avoid any embarrassment, encourage everyone to start together, then change over and again start everyone together.

5 mins

Feedback

Leave sufficient time at the end for participants to share some of their experiences.

What have they found helpful or moving? Why?
What has proved difficult? Why?

15 mins

TEA BREAK

WORKSHOP 5	SIGNING IN WORSHIP (or an alternative)

Slide 2

It is essential to buy in specialist expertise for this workshop. The Diocesan Chaplain to the Deaf should be able to suggest a suitable person who is well versed in signing for worship and has the appropriate teaching gifts. We were fortunate to discover a gifted signer amongst the original working party during the setting up of *Worship4Today*, who could teach with clarity, enthusiasm and humour. Every year this workshop has proved a real eye-opener and highlight for participants, which is why we have stuck firmly to it.

However, other options could also be explored in the final workshop and this may be an ideal opportunity to draw on particular gifts discovered amongst the current group of participants. Other possibilities might include: an introduction to drama and mime, including the use of dramatic readings; storytelling in worship; the use of puppets; an introduction to creative arts; and the use of other visuals in worship. Alternatively, you could make each of the other four workshops a little longer leaving more time for further experimentation.

We probably all have experience of using action songs with the children during worship. Action songs can work well with younger children, but these days can be found increasingly lacking amongst our sophisticated older children. Our teens and adult congregation alike may find them thoroughly embarrassing if they are expected to join in. However, introducing actions that actually mean something through sign language makes all the difference and can enhance worship on several different levels.

Sign language can prove liberating for the participant as the movement interprets words through a different kind of physical expression. Words, and therefore worship, are given a completely new depth. This can be moving and uplifting to both participant and observer, quite apart from communicating with any deaf people in the congregation. Each signer/workshop facilitator will have their own approach, but the outline below may suggest a helpful structure for the workshop. We are assuming that the workshop leader will provide their own handouts and so we only include some basic information within the course materials for this workshop.

5 mins

Testimony

Sign language is a wonderful skill and fascinating means of communication. If we are exposed to it for long enough, we are likely to get hooked! Encourage the signer to begin with their own personal story of why they chose to learn to sign and how it has affected their life generally and their life of worship in particular.

5 mins

Deaf culture and common sense

Slide 3

For many of the deaf community, signing is their first language. Signing in worship enables them to access God and meet with Him in a deeper way. The deaf will usually *sit* for worship, in a position where they can see the words on a screen but where their main focus is the signer. Starting from a recognised pool of signs, they may all use slightly different signs to interpret their own emotions and response towards God in their own way. Like the rest of us, the deaf can literally go through the motions or their whole being can express their love for Jesus. The deaf may also move in time to the music of songs if they are able to feel the vibrations through the floor.

Be aware that deaf people will worship and pray with their eyes open, so that they do not lose a second sense. It is not always helpful to recommend that a congregation close their eyes.

Slide 4

It is helpful to wear black or plain coloured clothes. Bold or busy patterns may distract and make signs more difficult to see. The deaf look at us as a whole when we are communicating; it is not just about the signs, so ...

Do

- Speak normally, don't exaggerate;
- Use short sentences;
- Use facial expressions;
- Use body language;
- Stand still.

Don't

- Hide your mouth;
- Turn away from the deaf person;
- Shout at a deaf person;
- Stand in front of a window or light source.

Signing is not just about using our hands. As we all know, we can say one thing and our body language can say quite another. We want our words, our sign language and our body language to work together in harmony to communicate as fully as possible.

Slide 5

Signing is a pictorial language which images the story. It is rarely one sign to one word. Small words may be missed out completely and whole phrases may be easier to interpret than individual words. If we think in pictures, we may also need to change the word order: e.g. a person crosses over a bridge. The bridge has to come first otherwise the person has nothing to cross! The person comes second and then the action of crossing. Gradually an action picture is built up.

Slide 6

Movement, direction and speed can be linked to facial expression and body language. We may look upwards when we speak of God and downwards when we speak of the devil and sin. When we speak of Jesus as a baby the direction of our gaze will be different from when we speak of Jesus, the risen Lord, who has now ascended back to heaven.

The size and speed of signs can also communicate depth of emotion: e.g. *'excited'* might be interpreted by a small, slow movement, but *'really excited'* might be interpreted by a larger, quicker movement.

These signs enhance the worship of the whole congregation. Our understanding is expanded by *seeing* the words interpreted visually.

A few basics

15 mins

Slide 7

It works well to start the actual signing with a few basics, so we have learnt:

- The alphabet;
- Spelling our names;
- Words for family and friends: mother, father, brother, sister, friend, etc;
- A few useful phrases: hello, goodbye, thank you, etc.

Then we move on to ...

A few worship words

Christian worship words are not necessarily part of the everyday language of the deaf community and certain words may need some re-interpretation. We have learnt:

- Some names of God - Father, Son, Holy Spirit;
- The name of Jesus;
- Some general worship words: praise, worship, shout, sing, pray;
- Some commonly used worship words: holy, glory, forever.

Signing to worship songs

30 mins

We then go on to sing with sign language. Traditional hymns can be difficult, because deep theological words can be hard to interpret. It is much easier to go for everyday language using meaningful words that people will readily understand.

Sometimes the difficulties in interpreting particular lines in a song will highlight lines which everyone finds difficult to comprehend: e.g. the final line of 'Strength will rise' by Brenton Brown and Ken Riley talks about rising on wings like eagles. This might need preparation and explanation in order to understand what it is actually saying.

Over the years we have used a variety of contemporary worship songs, but the following ones work particularly well. There will only be time to learn two or three songs, so try to choose a good mix of different styles and content.

Come, now is the time to worship by Brian Doerksen

This song is not too fast. It is simple and repetitive with words that are easily understood and personalised.

Father, we love you by Donna Adkins

This song is another good starting point because it repeats so much and enables us to put a lot of feeling into it.

My Jesus, my Saviour by Darlene Zschech

This is a song that most people know well and it lends itself beautifully to signing. It encapsulates intimacy, reassurance, and exuberant praise, and signing adds a profound dimension of self-offering to the words:

Let every breath, all that I am,
never cease to worship You.

Light of the world by Tim Hughes

This is a great song for story telling with its reference to the birth, crucifixion and ascension of Jesus.

We bow down and confess by Viola Grafstrom

There is a great sense of awe as this song is signed. Through signing, the words are given a new depth of meaning.

Longing for light (Christ, be our light) by Bernadette Farrell

This is a longer song but simple to sign, and enables us to engage with a world in need.

More love, more power by Jude del Hierro

Signing here can bring a tangible physical expression and prayerful depth to the words, as we ask for more of God in our lives.

And I will worship You
and I will seek Your face
with all of my heart
with all of my mind
with all of my strength
for You are my Lord.

Signing here can draw us closer to God by using the whole of our being, perhaps akin to David dancing before the Lord with all his might, only without the dance!

Taizé chants

These can work well, because they are simple and repetitive. 'In the Lord I'll be ever thankful' and 'O Lord, hear my prayer' are favourites of the deaf community in Sheffield.

The Lord's Prayer

Learning how to sign the Lord's Prayer is a really useful tool, and again works well.

Feedback

Leave sufficient time at the end for participants to share some of their experiences.

5 mins

What have they found helpful or moving? Why?
What has proved difficult? Why?

Some helpful books for further exploration:

Richard Chubb, *Lifting Holy Hands: A dictionary of signs used in Church services*, Advisory Board of Ministry Paper No. 7, June 1994.
Bob Shrine, *The Church and the Deaf Community*, Grove no. P126, 2011
Dictionary of British Sign Language, Faber and Faber, 1993.
Andrew Owen, *Signs of God*.
Cath Smith, *Signs Make Sense,* Human horizons series, 1990.
Cath Smith, *Sign In Sight,* Souvenir Press, 1992.
Forest Books are suppliers of learning resources to all aspects of deafness including excellent resources for learning sign language (www.forestbooks.com).

Some other helpful websites:

www.signsofgod.org.uk - This site encourages people to develop and improve their use of BSL in Christian settings. It also publicises events and training.

www.deafchurch.co.uk - Look in the index for information on deaf-Anglicans-together.

www.gosign.org.uk - *Go! Sign – Christ in the deaf community:* using BSL, this site raises awareness of deaf issues in the wider Christian community.

20 mins

CLOSING WORSHIP

Finish this session with a short act of worship using material drawn from each workshop. If at all possible, put song words and liturgy on PowerPoint. Encourage freedom of expression throughout, so that participants are able to explore some of their new found learning further if they wish.

Ensure that there are flags available and space for movement.

An outline of what has been used in previous courses can be found in the *Teachers' Notes Appendix 3.* Service materials will need to be prepared beforehand.

At the end of the day, encourage participants to continue to reflect on their experiences and what they have learnt through them. Finally, give a brief reminder of the preparation for the next session: *Worship in the New Testament.*

worship4today
PREPARATION FOR
NEXT TIME

Worship in the New Testament ⑩

Slide 8

worship 4 today

session

9

Practical worship day

WORSHIP LEADING 'UP FRONT'

Enabling worship to happen ...

... without getting in the way!

Worship leaders or lead worshippers?

- We are worshippers just as much as the congregation
- Together we are being led by the Holy Spirit
- We should be clear about our role in any particular service

Appearance

- What do I look like?
- What do I wear?
- Do I have any distracting habits or quirks?
- Do I draw attention to myself or do I draw people to God?

Visibility

- Who stands where? Appropriateness?
- Liturgical presidency
- Complement and submit

Atmosphere

- Welcoming and inclusive
- Inspire confidence and security
- Recognise God's presence with us

Attitude

- Love and serve the congregation
- Discern what is happening
- Know when to stop!
- Accept feedback

Encourage relationship

- With God
- With each other
- With the wider Christian Church
- With the wider world

Choose words with care

What to say, what not to say and how to say it!

Understanding and sensitivity

- Use appropriate language for the congregation
- Use explanation
- Don't be apologetic or make excuses
- Be prepared for the unexpected

Communicating specific information

- Hymn number/page number – which book?
- Verses/parts
- Background information
- Events (offering, children's activities, refreshments, etc)

Giving instructions

- What to do
- When to do it
- How to do it

Noteworthy phrases

- Would you please stand? (Suggest, don't tell)
- Let us ... (Include)
- We encourage everyone to ... (But give permission not to)
- We say together ... (Necessary or obvious?)
- We continue with ... (Aid the flow)
- Avoid *just* ...!   (An informal pitfall)

Every word is precious

- Plan what to say beforehand
- Purpose of words – do we need any?
- Use scripture
- Use silence
- Are we being repetitive?
- Are we patronizing or preaching?

Speak slowly and clearly

- Use your natural voice
- Allow people time to engage with the liturgy
- Practise with a microphone
- Practise voice-overs

Exercise 1: Beginning a service

Prepare the beginning of the service giving the congregation some idea of what to expect. Include a welcome, announce the first hymn and then lead into the first piece of liturgy.

Exercise 2: Introducing the prayers

Introduce the Prayers of Intercession to the congregation, giving clear instructions for the inclusion of the Taizé chant, 'O Lord hear my prayer'.

Exercise 3: Leading a block of sung worship in a service

- Introduce the three specified songs.
- Choose a suitable order.
- Choose whether the songs are in a book or on a screen.
- How will you link them together?
- If songs are in a book, how will you ensure everyone knows all the numbers?

POSTURE AND MOVEMENT IN WORSHIP

WORKSHOP 2

(All Hebrew and Greek definitions come from the *Hebrew and Chaldee Dictionary* and *Greek Dictionary* respectively, *Strong's Exhaustive Concordance of the Bible,* pub. Hendrickson)

Procession

A number of people moving forward in orderly succession especially at a ceremony. Implies ritual, majesty, dignity. Might include ministers, singers and people/congregation.
Returning the ark to Jerusalem (2 Samuel 6:1ff); Jesus' triumphal entry into Jerusalem (Matthew 21:8ff).

Standing

Demonstrates respect for God and for those who minister, expectancy, alertness and steadfastness (we are ready and we mean business!).
Standing to worship (2 Chronicles 7:6, Revelation 7:9)
Standing for the reading of the Gospel (cf. Nehemiah 8:5)

Genuflection

To bend the knee or bow down as a sign of reverence or adoration in worship. Usually directed toward the altar/holy table.
Shachah (Heb) – to worship and bow down (Psalm 5:7)
Kampto (Gk) – to bend or bow (Philippians 2:10)

Sign of the cross

Tertullian wrote in the 2nd century: 'In all the ordinary actions of everyday life, we trace the sign of the cross.' It is 'a lawful outward ceremony and honourable badge' *(Canon XXX, 1603)* and a reminder of the Trinity. (From *A New Dictionary of Liturgy and Worship,* ed. J. G. Davies, SCM Press Ltd, 1986).
Used at significant points during the liturgy: Greeting, Absolution, Gospel, before receiving the sacrament, Blessing; before reading the Gospel, also small gestures on forehead, lips and heart. (See Psalm 19:14)

Holy kiss

A sign of greeting (1 Corinthians 16:20).
A sign of deep respect and honour.
Proskuneo (Gk) – to come towards to kiss; a practice in ancient Greek and Roman cultures to kiss the feet of a statue or living person in adoration (see the woman who kissed the feet of Jesus in Luke 7:45). Still part of Eastern Orthodox worship. Some people will kiss the Bible, altar or icons.

Sharing peace

As a sign of forgiveness, friendship and unity before taking Holy Communion (Matthew 5:23-4; 1 Corinthians 11:17ff; Galatians 2:9)

Mea culpa	My fault, my mistake (Latin). The beating of the breast three times as an act of contrition. (Nahum 2:7; Luke 18:13)
Clapping	A sign of joy. *Taqa* (Heb) – to clatter, to slap the hands together, to clang an instrument; to clasp the hand of another in friendship (Psalm 47:1). *Macha* (Heb) – to rub or strike the hands together (in exultation); to clap. (Psalms 63:3-4; 117:1; also Psalm 98:8 - rivers clap; Isaiah 55:12 - fields clap). Also a preparation for battle, together with stamping of feet (Ezekiel 25:6)
Wave offering	Lifting an item before the Lord. *T(e)nuwphah* (Heb) – to brandish, offer, shake, wave (an offering) Old Testament - Usually by the priest. 'Heave' offering: i.e. breast of lamb lifted vertically and offered to God (Leviticus 7:34ff). Cf. The elevation of the elements during HC or our monetary collection. Wave offering: sheaf lifted and waved horizontally side to side (Leviticus 23:9-12). New Testament – people waving palms and clothing (John 12:13).
Lifting hands	Scripture speaks of holding up holy hands in prayer Cf. priest at Eucharist
Lifting one hand	*Towdah* (Heb) – to raise the right hand in agreement with God's word, in covenant. God extends His hand to us and we to Him. (Psalm 50:23; Isaiah 41:10)
Lifting both hands	*Yadah* (Heb) – to worship with extended hands; to lift up hands in worship to the Lord. (Psalm 9:1:2 Chronicles 20:21)
Arms wide	A symbol of vulnerability or abandonment; a reminder of the cross, surrender, sacrifice, giving whole self to God.
Hands cupped	Ready to offer something to God, or ready to receive from God.
Laying on of hands	In blessing (Mark 10:16; Luke 18:15); for commissioning (Acts 6:6); for the healing of the sick (Matthew 8; Mark 5:41).
Anointing	With oil as a sign of God's grace and blessing. Oils are blessed and set apart on Maundy Thursday for anointing at baptism, at ordination or commissioning, and for anointing the sick and dying. (See the disciples in Mark 6:13 and instructions in James 5:14)

Kneeling		A posture of reverence and adoration. (Psalm 95:6) *Barak* (Heb) – to kneel (down), to give reverence to God as an act of adoration. Confession and submission: 'meekly kneeling upon your knees' *(BCP Communion)*. 'Devoutly kneeling' for prayer. *(BCP Morning and Evening Prayer)* Intercessory prayer and pleas for help. (Matthew 15:25)
Prostration		Lying face down in awe or supplication. *Shachah* (Heb) – to fall down flat, to prostrate in homage to royalty or God (Psalm 95:6). *Pipto* (Gk) – to fall down, literally or figuratively. (Revelation 1:17); complete submission and abandonment to God; pleading with God in prayer (Cf. David pleading with God for his son in 2 Samuel 12:16).

Flags in worship

Jehovah-nissi (Heb) – The Lord is my banner. (Exodus 17:15)

Dagal (Heb) – to raise a flag; to be conspicuous with banners. (Psalm 20:5)

Flags were used

- To denote families (Numbers 2:2)
- As a rallying point in times of war (Isaiah 11:10)
- As symbols of rejoicing and praise (Psalm 20:5)

How to make flags

Fabric

- Choose a lightweight, crease-resistant fabric which is the same on both sides. Organza is sheer and a bit sparkly; chiffon is soft and sheer with a matt finish; a lightweight, silky polyester can work well too. Taffeta makes a snapping noise, which can create a useful sound effect for warfare praise. Material with a metallic shimmer reflects the light and can also create a stunning visual effect.
- The size of the flag partly depends on the width of material, which usually comes in 90cm (36in), 112cm (44in) or 150cm (60in) widths. This may well be a matter of trial and error. Everyone seems to make flags of a size that suits them in terms of what they can handle.

- Sew a straight hem on three sides of each flag. On the fourth side, sew a channel for a pole. Sew the top end of the channel closed so that the pole will not poke through the end. Make sure the channel seam is sturdy and secure.

Flag Poles

- Dowel rods are best and come in different thicknesses as well as lengths. 9mm or 3/8in works well.
- Bamboo canes are a cheaper option, but are less durable and prove too flimsy for larger flags.
- Allow between 15-20cm (6-8in) for a hand grip. Much longer and the handle will become unwieldy.
- Sandpaper the cut edges to avoid rough areas damaging the fabric or hands.

Small flags are good for smaller children, made as above but scaled down.

Keeping flags on their poles

- The channel for the pole should fit tightly.
- Staple the flag to the pole top and bottom to hold it fast.
- Hold on to the bottom of the flag whilst waving for extra security and control.

For more information ...

... check out Andy Au, Pastor of City Gate Church, Brighton and founder and director of *Movement in Worship* since the early 1980s:

- Pioneering role in the use of flags in worship
- Encouraging men in dance using staves (plural of staff, i.e. big sticks!)
- Working with Psalm-drummers (a network of Christian drummers and percussionists) experimenting with pulse and rhythm
- Developing 'Dynamic Mass Sculpture'

Website: www.citygatebrighton.org.uk with direct link to *Movement in Worship.*

Dance in worship

We can all dance

- Same as singing (where everyone has a voice)
- Everyone has arms and legs
- Therefore everyone can dance

In many cultures, singing and dancing are an integral part of ...

- Community life
- Ceremonies and rites of passage
- This whole idea of 'I can't sing/dance' does not exist
- Some may have a particular gift
- All take part

Dance was a regular part of Israel's culture and celebration

- Flows naturally into worship
- The Bible is full of references to dance:
  - Miriam and the women (Exodus 15:20)
  - Jepthah's daughter (Judges 11:34)
  - After victory in battle (1 Samuel 21:11)
  - King David (2 Samuel 6:14ff and 1 Chronicles 15:29ff)
  - The return of the prodigal (Luke 15:25)

Dance can be ...

- Individual or corporate
- Traditional or contemporary
- Planned (with set steps) or spontaneous (freestyle)
- Sacred or secular
- An interpretation of a song or text or free expression
- Observed or participative

Movements

- Use of full personal space
- Use of full stage or room space
- Movements at every level and in every direction:
  - From the floor, bowing, bending, standing, arm extensions, stretching, turning
- Slow or fast movements
- Smooth and flowing or angular and jerky movements
- Repeated movements
- Movements to illustrate words

Top tips

Do

- Focus on God and not on who's looking
- Listen to the Holy Spirit
- Take off shoes
- Enjoy!

Don't

- Wear inappropriate clothing
- Wear tight clothing that makes movement difficult
- Ignore potential hazards: slippery floors, steps or burning candles

Practise at home first

- Lock the door
- Close the curtains
- Put on a favourite worship CD
- Have a go!
- Practice can soon become worship

A question of attitude

God sees more than the dance. God sees our hearts.

Will we be like David, who was prepared to dance before the Lord with all his might, irrespective of who was looking?

Or will we be like his wife, Michal, who despised the way the king behaved in front of all the people?

Biblical words for dance in worship

Many Hebrew and Greek words for exuberant praise and rejoicing imply the need for movement to express such joy adequately. The English translation does not usually do them justice.

Orcheomai (Gk) – To dance (implying regular motion)
Matthew 11:17

Machowl (Heb) – A (round) dance; dancing
Psalm 30:11

Choros (Gk) – A ring; dancing; i.e. a round dance
Luke 15:25

Mechowlah (Heb) – A dance or company of dancers
Exodus 15:20; 1 Samuel 18:6

Chagag (Heb) – To move in a circle; to march in a sacred procession; to observe a festival; to dance, to celebrate, to be giddy, to reel to and fro
Psalm 42:4

Chiyl/chuwl (Heb) – To twist or whirl in a circular manner; to dance
Psalm 149:3

Giyl/guwl (Heb) – To spin round under the influence of any violent emotion, usually to be glad and joyful, to rejoice.
1 Chronicles 16:31; Psalm 118:24; Habakkuk 3:18

Dalag (Heb) – To spring or leap
Song of Solomon 2:8 or Isaiah 35:6

Pazaz (Heb) – To spring or leap
2 Samuel 6:16

Pacach (Heb) – To hop, skip over, dance
1 Kings 18:26

Raqad (Heb) – To stamp, to spring about, to jump for joy, to leap or skip
1 Chronicles 15:29; Ecclesiastes 3:4

Agalliao (Gk) – To jump for joy; to be (exceeding) glad
Matthew 5:12; Revelation 19:7

Skirtao (Gk) – To jump for joy (including the movement of a baby in the womb)
Luke 1:41; Luke 6:23

VISUAL TECHNOLOGY IN WORSHIP

Link with current culture

- Information technology (IT)

- Visual image

- Sound bites

- Icons and symbols

Expectations are high, so we need to do it well!

Visuals can be used to enhance worship by ...

- Illustrating points

- Stimulating imagination

- Giving information succinctly

- Facilitating the introduction of new songs

- Facilitating the use of varied liturgy

- Using material produced by others

However ...

Worship always comes first

Technology, images and gimmicks are there to **serve** worship.

3Rs - Regularly Reflect and Review

- What works well and enhances worship?

- What distracts?

Good practice for screen design

Font

- Keep to one or two font styles
  - Arial is clear
  - Times New Roman is easy to read
  - Comic sans MS is useful with children
  - Other fonts should be used with caution
- Size matters: font size varies according to style
  - In Arial, at least 24; 32 best? Above 48 cramps the page

Text

- Avoid writing over the top of 'loud' images
- Start text at the same place on each screen if possible
- Left justification is easiest to follow
- Break up lines in sensible places
- No more than eight lines of song lyrics per slide
- Lower case is easier to read than CAPITALS
- Keep to key words and don't overload with text
- Try to keep each title or bullet point on one line

Colour

- Use a good contrast
  - Black or blue text on pale background
  - White or yellow on dark background
- Consider those with sight problems
- Use colour to separate types of information
  - Leader in white
  - Congregation in yellow
- Use colour to emphasise a point – but carefully

Templates and logos

- Are useful to keep consistency; e.g. *W4T* logo and format
- Set and maintain a house style
- Maintain a mood or theme
- Should be self-explanatory
- Should be in sympathy with the local context

Signals

These are images or colours that indicate where we are or what is happening in a service. They should:

- Be clear and consistent
- Be self-explanatory
- Not be overused

Animation and transitions

- Should go unnoticed unless making a particular point
- Should be the same all the way through
- Watch out for any unintentional auto slide advance

Summary of distractions

- Text difficult to read – font, size, colour blends
- Spelling mistakes
- Moving words/entry/speeds
- Sudden changes in screen layout
- Fussy transitions
- Moving backgrounds
- Things moving for no reason
- Too many things moving together
- Anything that flashes

Some tips to maintain consistency

- Copy/overwrite previous presentations
- Use hymnbooks on disk or same internet sources
- Cut and paste wherever possible
- Evolve a house style
- Don't change things just for the sake of it

Using images

- Use visually powerful images that reinforce text
- Try to match image styles
- Clip art rarely works well – use with caution
- Don't overwhelm the text
- Try to get a good balance on the screen
- Generally no more than two images per screen
- Leave enough border to allow for the 'cropping' effect of projection

Finding images

- Use 'Google Images' search engine
- Use internet extensively but responsibly
- Be aware of possible copyright on pictures
- Take digital camera images (with sufficient pixels)
- Scan from printed images, but these must be clear

Adding sound and video

- The sound file should be WMA (Windows Media Audio) or WAV (Waveform Audio) or mp3 depending on age of software
- The video file also has limited formats – WMV (Windows Media Video) is a safe option
- Ideally embed video and audio files into the presentation
- The audio/video file needs to be located on the computer it is running from
- Amplification will be needed if running from a laptop

Summary

- Worship is our aim – technology is the servant
- Keep it simple
- Be consistent
- All rules can be broken – but only if there is a good reason

Church presentation software

What are the essentials?

- Dual monitor configuration
  - An operator screen and a presentation screen
  - Some software includes an additional stage screen option for leaders and musicians
- Full control for creating or editing a presentation during a service without affecting the main screen
- Extensive formatting options
  - Different font styles and sizes
  - Different colours
  - Graphic or motion background images
  - Simple drag-and-drop system
- Smooth and appropriate transitions from slide to slide
  - Appear
  - Dissolve in
  - Fade

- Integrated Bible databases with good search facilities
  - Search by chapter and verse
  - Search by key word(s)
  - Several different translations
- Integrated song database
  - Easy access without lots of typing
  - Search by title, chorus or first line
  - Facility to add new songs
  - Able to display any song lyrics in seconds
  - Compliant with CCLI licensing laws
  - Linked to CCLI SongSelect
  - Automatically records CCLI data for annual return
- Easy to import PowerPoint files for ...
  - Sermon
  - Prayers
  - Notices

Useful but not necessarily essential

- Full web and audio integration for the addition of
  - Audio files
  - Pre-queued or custom made DVD clips
  - YouTube clips
- Moving images from a live camera feed
- Memory facilities to save
  - Service lists
  - Associated style information

Practical tips for service leader or preacher

- Try to make the presentation on the computer that will run it on the day
- Operate the presentation yourself if possible
- Alternatively give the operator a full script of the presentation highlighting slide changes
- Don't keep looking over your shoulder to see what is on the screen. If possible use a separate monitor at front

Practical tips for the operator

- Practise setting up
- Correct order may matter
  - Connect all mains cables and leads between projector and laptop
  - Turn on each component in the right order, usually laptop first. Then the data projector automatically recognises the type of laptop

- Don't forget the extra sound cable if playing a film clip
- Practise keeping pace
  - Correct words on screen when needed
- Practise with different service leaders and musicians
- Practise editing and adding whilst something else is happening
- Practise in bright sunlight!
- Learn from feedback – remember every mistake is an opportunity to grow and improve

What happens if ...

- The technology fails or the projector bulb blows?
- There is a power cut?
- Do you have a Plan B at the ready?

And finally

There are times when data projection is not the solution.

- It would compete unhelpfully with other visuals
- Other visual aids will work better
- A significant number could not see the screen
- Operating data projection would be a distraction

Don't forget ... the projector can be turned off!

Useful exercises

Take time to play!

Push every button and see what AV can do.

Exercise 1 – Experiment with different fonts and different sizes

Start with the basic PowerPoint slide, using the given text boxes for title and bullets. Try out Arial, Times Roman, Tahoma, Verdana, Trebuchet, Comic Sans MS.

Try a range of sizes from 24-48 in each font.

Experiment with bold and shadow to compare different styles for clarity.

Exercise 2 – Experiment with different backgrounds and colours for text

Using the slide(s) you have already created, experiment with possible options for background colours.

Try out some plain background colours and a few pictures.

Try a range of colours for the text to contrast well with the various backgrounds.

Exercise 3 – Design song lyrics slides using a given text

- Type in or cut and paste the lyrics into PowerPoint.
- Choose an appropriate background colour or picture.
- Choose an appropriate font colour to contrast well.
- Size the font to suit line length with line breaks in sensible places.
- How much of the song will fit reasonably on each slide?

Exercise 4 – Design liturgy slides using a given text

- Type in or cut and paste the liturgy into PowerPoint.
- Choose an appropriate background colour or picture.
- Choose an appropriate font colour to contrast well.
- Clearly distinguish between leader and congregation.
- Size the font to suit line length with line breaks in sensible places.
- How much of the liturgy will fit reasonably on each slide?

Exercise 5 – Design a service/sermon series template for a series of services and sermons based on the life of King David.

- The same template will be used as the starting point for the service and sermon each week. The series will feature David as shepherd, warrior, fugitive, worshipper, friend, adulterer, and king.
- Include the title for the whole series: 'King David, a man after God's heart' (see Acts 13:22) as well as a subtitle for the current week.
- Choose an appropriate font colour and size.
- Choose an appropriate background colour.
- Insert a picture if appropriate.

Exercise 6 – Design some slides to accompany the intercessions
for an all-age harvest service

- Experiment with fonts, colour and size to draw out the key words.
- Experiment with backgrounds and pictures – this may be a good opportunity to search for suitable pictures and images on the internet.
- You may change, add or re-order words if you wish.
- You do not have to show all the words on the screen.

Harvest intercession

The word HARVEST has many other words within it. We will use some of these in our prayers.

Lord of the HARVEST, we bring to you our prayers for the world in which we live.

We think of the word HAVE. In this world of need we thank you Lord for all that we HAVE …

We think of the word STARVE. We pray for those who STARVE through lack of food …

We think of the word SHARE. We pray for a fairer SHARE of the world's resources …

We think of the word TEARS. We pray for all who will shed TEARS this day …

We think of the word REST. We pray for those who are weary and in need of REST …

LEADING CORPORATE PRAYER

Patterns of prayer

A simple acronym: A-C-T-S

- Adoration

- Confession

- Thanksgiving

- Supplication

The Lord's Prayer

- Jesus teaches his disciples to pray. (Matthew 6:6ff)

- A key Christian text. (See *CW Christian Initiation*, p.40-42)

- Used in almost every service.

- Still the key Christian text taught in schools.

Intercessory prayer

Corporate prayer

- The prayer of the whole people of God (Matthew 18:19-20)

Why should we intercede?

- A deep instinct

- A biblical invitation

- A long tradition

Traditionally we pray for

- The Church
- The world
- The community
- The sick
- The dying

Intercessory prayer is not ...

- Individual prayer writ large

- A litany of the news

- Telling God what He already knows

- An opportunity to preach a second sermon

- An opportunity to criticise others

- Too long!

A few helpful pointers

- Prepare thoroughly

- Exercise pastoral sensitivity

- Can we all say 'Amen'?

- Use silence

- Use creative participation

- Model prayer for others

Delivery

- Be in position and ready

- Keep body and head upright especially if kneeling

- Speak clearly and project the voice

- Use a microphone if available

- Clearly introduce biddings and responses

- Leave creative pauses

- Make the end of the prayer time obvious

We could draw the prayers to a close with the 'Lord's Prayer' or we could join together in a short paragraph such as:

Merciful Father, accept these prayers
for the sake of your Son, our Saviour Jesus Christ.
Amen

(from *Common Worship,* Holy Communion Service)

Prayer stations

A simple definition

'A prayer station is a small place, with something to look at or do, which will stimulate meditation and prayer.' (From *Labyrinths and Prayer Stations* by Ian Tarrant and Sally Dakin, Grove W180, 2004). The objective of the prayer station is not merely an exhibit to admire but an invitation to participate in some way.

Tips and pointers for creating prayer stations

- A good mix of activities: passive, active, written, creative.
- A good mix of 'being' and 'doing' in prayer.
- Include some 'safe' activities such as lighting a candle, holding a pebble or writing a name on a post-it.
- A strong scriptural input for each station.
- Clear instructions.
- Suitable music in the background.

Holding prayers

- When we don't know how or what to pray.
- Allowing the Spirit within to pray. (see Romans 8:26)

Blessings

- A simple request for God's favour to rest upon...

Useful websites

www.creativeprayer.com contains a wealth of good ideas.
www.engageworship.org useful material by Sam and Sara Hargreaves.
www.leeabbey.org.uk useful material by Revd Emma Ineson.

Organisations like *YWAM* and *Christian Aid* will frequently include resources and ideas for prayer stations for particular events or occasions like missions to particular places or the annual *Christian Aid* week in May.

Useful books

A list of useful books is included in the *Guide to Leading Intercessions* booklet which accompanies this session. Also check out Grove booklets: W179 *Confessing our sins*, W180 *Labyrinths and Prayer Stations*, W181 *Liquid Worship*, W206 *How to help others pray out loud in groups*.

SIGNING FOR WORSHIP

Deaf culture and common sense

In the deaf community

- Signing is their first language

- Signing gives access to God

- They will usually **sit** for worship

- Their main focus is the signer

- They may all use slightly different signs to interpret their own emotions and response towards God

- They may also move in time to the music of songs as they feel the vibrations

- They will worship and pray with their eyes open

The deaf look at us as a whole when we are communicating, so ...

Do

- Speak normally
- Use short sentences
- Use facial expressions
- Use body language
- Stand still

Don't

- Hide your mouth
- Turn away from the deaf person
- Shout at a deaf person
- Stand in front of a window or light source

Signing is not just about using our hands

- The words
- The signs
- Our body language

should all work together in harmony

81

Signing

- A pictorial language which images the story

- Rarely one sign to one word

- Small words may be missed out completely

- Phrases may be easier to interpret than individual words

- Word order may change

Movement, direction and speed

We look ...

- Up to God

- Down to the devil and sin

- At Jesus as a baby in our arms

- At Jesus, risen and ascended, up in the sky

The size and speed of a sign may indicate depth of emotion.

Our understanding is expanded by *seeing* words interpreted visually.

Some helpful books and websites for further exploration:

Richard Chubb, *Lifting Holy Hands: A dictionary of signs used in Church services*, Advisory Board of Ministry Paper No. 7, June 1994
Bob Shrine, *The Church and the Deaf Community*, Grove P126, 2011
Dictionary of British Sign Language, Faber and Faber, 1993
Andrew Owen, *Signs of God*
Cath Smith, *Signs Make Sense,* Human horizons series
Cath Smith, *Sign In Sight,* Souvenir Press, 1992
Forest Books are suppliers of learning resources to all aspects of deafness including excellent resources for learning sign language (www.forestbooks.com).

www.signsofgod.org.uk - This site encourages people to develop and improve their use of BSL in Christian settings. Also publicises events and training
www.deafchurch.co.uk - Look in the index for information on deaf-Anglicans-together.
www.gosign.org.uk - *Go! Sign – Christ in the deaf community:* using BSL, this site raises awareness of deaf issues in the wider Christian community.

SKETCH: HOW NOT TO LEAD WORSHIP!

This sketch is based on one written by David Burfield, which first appeared in the *Methodist Church Worship Leaders' Training Pack, Revised Edition* (Trustees for Methodist Church Purposes, 2000). The sketch has been modified and updated and is used here with permission. To be acted out whilst the group observes. You will need to arrange in advance for a mobile phone to ring at the appropriate moment.

A scruffily dressed service leader goes to the lectern, produces a bag and starts rummaging through. Looking somewhat hassled, books and crumpled papers are quickly arranged. The bag is carelessly discarded on the floor next to the lectern. S/he then looks up and peers threateningly at the gathered congregation, bashes the mic and shouts:

Is this working this week?

The service leader begins the service.

It's disappointing that so few are gathered for worship this morning, especially when I have made a special effort to be with you. The trouble with congregations today is that they stay away with the least excuse or they arrive late, like the lady just coming in now.

I have just been asked to give out a notice in addition to the 41 already on your printed notice sheet.

The service leader hunts among the books and papers and eventually withdraws a crumpled piece of paper from a pocket.

The 'Young Wives Group' (actually, they're quite middle-aged now) in conjunction with the 'Old Codgers Keep Fit Club' (they're hopeful!) and 'The Church Renegades' have raised the magnificent sum of eight pounds and seventeen pence at last Saturday's coffee morning. The vicar is relieved that this will be enough to cover the cost of heating the church hall and replacing the cups they dropped. A further coffee morning will be held on Saturday 19th November (providing they've bought new cups by then!) – the 19th is actually a Sunday, should it be the 18th?

And now I just have some Banns of Marriage to read. Are the young people in question here today? No? It is a pity that young couples these days just can't be bothered to turn up. I publish the banns of marriage between ... Now, where was I? Ah yes, your vicar has asked me to preach on the Lectionary readings for today, but there aren't any readings I care for and so we shall be thinking together about the love of God.

I have chosen to begin our service with a children's hymn. Oh, there aren't any children present! Never mind – we will just sing it any way. It's a particular favourite of my mother-in-law and we had it at our son's christening.

Reads first line.

All things bright and beautiful ... the words will appear on the screen, assuming the data projector operator can keep up this week. How many of you know this? I see there are a few of you who don't know the tune so I will just ask the organist to play it through for us first.

During the singing (one chorus will be sufficient), the leader begins to find the next page and has a drink of water. No eye contact is made with the congregation. The service leader continues:

At the beginning of the service we call to mind our sins, but first there will be a time of silence for you to be still before God.

A very short pause.

Times of silence are very helpful because they are something we miss out on in daily life. So often our minds are full of things. Like the latest episode of our favourite soap opera, or forgetting to download the latest emails, or worrying if we've remembered to turn the oven on ... or off, or if our cars are safe in the car park bearing in mind that cars were broken into last Sunday whilst the preacher was speaking.

So, let us confess our sins to God, who forgives us in Christ.
Almighty God, our heavenly Father, we have sinned against you
and against our neighbour in thought, and word, and deed.

A few lines into the confession a mobile phone goes off. The service leader looks around with an accusing look.

Exasperated:

Who did us the discourtesy of not turning off their mobile phone when we began the service?

When no one responds, the service leader realises the phone in question is in the discarded bag beside the lectern!

Dear me. It's just **my** phone ringing. How hilarious! Fancy me forgetting to turn off **my** phone.

May almighty God forgive us for all our unfortunate mistakes, through Jesus Christ our Lord. Amen.

Now, stand to sing the Gloria. Oh, the organist doesn't have the music. Never mind, we will say it if the organist can't be bothered to prepare properly.

Glory to God in the highest ...

worship4today

A GUIDE TO LEADING INTERCESSIONS IN CHURCH

INTRODUCTION

This booklet was originally prepared by the Sheffield Diocesan Worship and Liturgy Committee to help those who lead intercessions in their parishes. It is reproduced here with permission.

This is not a definitive guide to leading intercessory prayer, but contains helpful hints and ideas to help the Church pray effectively.

'True intercession ...
... is about solidarity,
not wish lists.
It grows out of our relationship
with our heavenly Father
and our love for one another.
We pray because we love,
not merely to acquire things.'

From
Worship changes lives,
Ed. Paul Bradshaw & Peter Moger, CHP, 2008, p.34

CORPORATE PRAYER IS POWERFUL

Again, truly I tell you, if two of you agree on earth about anything you ask, it will be done for you by my Father in heaven. For where two or three are gathered in my name, I am there among them.
(Matthew 18:19-20)

Good quality intercessions provide a model for prayer for the gathered congregation and newcomers.

WHAT IS INTERCESSORY PRAYER?

Intercessory Prayer is ...

- The corporate prayer of the whole church.

- A biblical invitation to bring our needs and the needs of others to God.

- A humble and earnest petition.

- Part of a long tradition, praying on behalf of congregation, community, and world.

- A way of loving people.

- Acknowledging our connection with and concern for the world.

Intercessory Prayer is not ...

- Individual prayer writ large.

- Confession.

- Meditation.

- Sermon.

- Critical or judgmental.

- Telling God what we think of the 'hot' issues or telling people what God thinks.

PREPARATION

Do ...

- Set aside time to prepare, but not too early in the week or you may need to re-write to include the latest news.

- Read through the bible readings for the service.

- Be aware of special themes for certain services: e.g. Mother's Day, Sea Sunday, Education Sunday, etc.

- Liaise with the preacher and service leader.

- Look at the newspapers and TV news for the current topics.

- Be aware of what is happening in your local community.

- Use printed prayers from books if they are appropriate.

- Check the news/internet/teletext before you leave to make sure you don't miss anything important.

- Be aware of who will be present: baptism family? Town council?

Don't ...

- Preach a second sermon.

- Use the prayers to criticise others.

- Try to pray for everything every time.

- Make the prayers longer than the sermon!

- Tell God what he already knows. ('O Lord, George is having a hip operation in Ward 10 of the General Hospital ...')

- Be out of date.

STRUCTURE THE INTERCESSIONS

Why?

To help to enable others in prayer.

To keep prayers short and succinct.

To give focus and direction.

Whom or what to pray for?

Divide the prayers up into topics to give clarity and flow.
Try not to use the same topics all the time.

Traditionally, we pray for:

- The Church
- The world
- The local community
- Those who suffer
- The communion of saints

However, we can pray in any form, but clear structures and patterns help people to follow and engage.

A consistent pattern should be used throughout the prayers:

We give thanks for ...   especially we pray for ...

Bless those who ... that they may ...

We hold before God ...

BIDDINGS AND RESPONSES

Biddings and responses can give prayers a sense of rhythm and flow. They help people to know how and when to end each prayer. They allow people structured space to pray their own prayers.

They should be short and memorable

Bidding	Lord, in your mercy	
Response	**hear our prayer.**	F2
Bidding	Lord, hear us.	
Response	**Lord, graciously hear us.**	F4
Bidding	Lord, meet us in the silence	
Response	**and hear our prayer.**	F9

Prayers should be consistently addressed ...

... to Father, Son or Holy Spirit

Prayers might begin 'Let us pray to the Father.'

Bidding	Father, Lord of creation,	
Response	**in your mercy, hear us.**	F47
Or	'Jesus said' ...	
Bidding	Saviour, we hear your call.	
Response	**Help us to follow.**	F43
Or	We pray to God to fill us with his Spirit ...	
Bidding	Lord, come to bless us.	
Response	**Fill us with your Spirit.**	F63

These and other examples can be found in *New Patterns For Worship* in the section on 'Prayer', p.171-218.

PASTORAL SENSITIVITY

You may know of people who are sick, dying, or simply having 'a hard time'. Some people will tell you all about their problems,

BUT

they do not expect the whole congregation to hear about them during the intercessions.

Do ...

- Be loving and caring.

- Treat others as you would like to be treated.

- Respect confidentiality.

Don't ...

- Be tempted to 'share' personal details.

- Use personal information without asking the person first.

- Embarrass an individual or family.

Can we all say Amen?

- Be careful when you pray for difficult situations.

- Can everyone join in your prayer with integrity?

- 'Do not push people into praying something they do not believe can happen.' (From *How to ... Lead the Prayers,* Grove no. W169)

DELIVERY

When?

- Know when the prayers come in the service.
- Know when you should go to your place to lead.

Where?

- Will the prayers be led from the lectern?
- Will the prayers be led from the body of congregation?
- Will you be using a microphone?

How long?

- Be sensitive to the overall length and flow of the service.

- If necessary, be prepared to miss a section out rather than making a long service even longer!

How?

- Allow the congregation time to sit or kneel and then time to settle before you start. Watch to see when they are ready.

- Clear speech is very important, so keep your body and your head upright especially if you are kneeling.

- Use the microphone. Speak slowly and clearly (mumbling becomes louder but less intelligible with a microphone).

- Choose words carefully. Avoid words like 'just'! Be specific and not apologetic.

- Make the end of the prayer time clear. It helps everyone feel comfortable and secure.

MORE THAN WORDS ALONE

All our senses - hearing, sight, touch, taste, smell – can be used. All things can be *'God's holy gifts for God's holy people.'* (Common Worship Holy Communion Service, p.180)

Images or symbols

- Can be helpful.
- God can connect with His people through ordinary life.

Hearing, seeing, doing

- Can transform our lives.

Examples

Candles	Seeds
Pebbles	Glass beads
Water	Acetate confession
Sand	Soil
Post-it notes	Patchwork
Pictures	Icons
Images on data projector	Globe
Food items	Balloons
Incense	Anointing oil
Nails (on Good Friday)	Flowers (on Easter Sunday)

USING SILENCE

Prayer is what starts when the words stop

Don't be afraid of silence. Creative pauses enable others to reflect on what has been said and leave room for people to add their own prayers.

You can guide people's thinking with open phrases, such as, 'We hold before God ...' or, 'Let us think about the week to come ...'

The congregation will be more relaxed and able to participate fully if they know what to expect. Reassure them by telling them approximately how long the silence will last.

When we don't know what we ought to pray for ...

The Spirit helps us in our weakness ... that very Spirit intercedes for us with groans that words cannot express. (Romans 8:26-7)

USING MUSIC

Music reaches places that words cannot touch

- **A simple sung response** might be used in between the intercessions, such as 'O Lord, hear my prayer'. There are many suitable Taizé, Iona or other simple chants to choose from.

- **A well known hymn** with intercessions between each verse.

- **A piece of music** might be played. It could be a hymn or spiritual song, a secular song or an instrumental piece. A gentle instrumental version of 'Be still, for the presence of the Lord' may help us to focus on simply being still! Or music might be accompanied by images or news items as in Simon and Garfunkel's rendering of 'Silent Night' with the reading of headlines superimposed.

USEFUL BOOKS

A. Ashwin, *The Book of a Thousand Prayers,* Zondervan, 1996

Archbishops' Council, *New Patterns for Worship,* CHP, 2002

Ed. P. Bradshaw & P. Moger, *Worship Changes Lives: How it works, why it matters,* CHP, 2008

Hear our Prayer – Gospel based for Sundays, Holy Days and Festival Years A, B, C, Canterbury Press, 2003

R. Chapman , *The Intercessor's Guide: How to Lead and Write Intercessory Prayers,* Canterbury Press, 2007

R. Chapman , *Leading Intercessions,* Canterbury Press, 1997

S. Dakin, *Praying with Stuff,* Grove no.S107, 2008

A. de Lange & L. Simpson, *How to ... Lead the Prayers,* Grove no.W169, 2002

J. Pritchard, *The Intercessions Handbook,* SPCK, 1997

J. Pritchard, *The Second Intercessions Handbook,* SPCK, 2004

I. Tarrant & S. Dakin, *Labyrinths and Prayer Stations,* Grove no.W180, 2004

S. Wallace, *Multi-sensory Prayer,* Scripture Union, 2000

AND FINALLY ...

Pray thankfully ... 1 Timothy 2:1

Pray briefly ... avoid long, drawn-out details

Pray clearly ... use words and ideas people will know

Pray specifically ... ask God to do definite things

Pray expectantly ... something is going to happen

Pray humbly ... you do not have all the answers (2 Chronicles 7:14)

Pray boldly ... that is our privilege (1 John 5:14)

From *How to ... Lead the Prayers* by A. de Lange & L. Simpson (Grove no.W169)

God says:
'I will never leave you;
I will never forsake you.'
So we say with confidence,
'The Lord is my helper;
I will not be afraid.'

Hebrews 13:5

Be strong and courageous.
Do not be terrified;
do not be discouraged,
for the Lord your God is with you
wherever you go.

Joshua 1:9

Do not be anxious about anything,
but in everything, by prayer and petition,
with thanksgiving, present your requests to
God. And the peace of God,
which passes all understanding,
will guard your hearts and minds
in Christ Jesus.

Philippians 4:6-7

Are not two sparrows sold for a penny?
Yet not one of them will fall to the ground
without the Father knowing.
Even the very hairs of your head are all
numbered. So don't be afraid;
you are worth more than many sparrows.

Matthew 10:29-31

Trust in the Lord and do good;
dwell in the land and enjoy safe pasture.
Delight yourself in the Lord
and He will give you
the desires of your heart.

Psalm 37:3-4

Bless the Lord, O my soul,
and forget not all His benefits. He forgives all
my sins and heals all my diseases; He
rescues my life from the pit and crowns me
with love and compassion. He satisfies my
desires with good things, so that my youth is
renewed like the eagle's.

Psalm 103:2-5

This is what the Lord says:
'Fear not, for I have redeemed you.
I have called you by name; you are mine.
When you pass through the waters
I will be with you;
when you pass through the rivers,
they will not sweep over you ...
Do not be afraid, for I am with you.'

Isaiah 43:1, 2 & 5

Jesus says:
'Ask and it will be given to you;
seek and you will find; knock and the door
will be opened to you.
For everyone who asks receives;
everyone who seeks finds;
and to those who knock,
the door will be opened.'

Luke 11:9-10

Traditional Gaelic Blessing

May the road rise up to meet you.
May the wind be always on your back.
May the sun shine warm upon your face;
the rains fall soft upon your fields,
and until we meet again,
may God hold you in the palm of his hand.
Amen.

Traditional Gaelic Blessing

May the road rise up to meet you.
May the wind be always on your back.
May the sun shine warm upon your face;
the rains fall soft upon your fields,
and until we meet again,
may God hold you in the palm of his hand.
Amen.

Traditional Gaelic Blessing

May the road rise up to meet you.
May the wind be always on your back.
May the sun shine warm upon your face;
the rains fall soft upon your fields,
and until we meet again,
may God hold you in the palm of his hand.
Amen.

Traditional Gaelic Blessing

May the road rise up to meet you.
May the wind be always on your back.
May the sun shine warm upon your face;
the rains fall soft upon your fields,
and until we meet again,
may God hold you in the palm of his hand.
Amen.

Traditional Gaelic Blessing

May the road rise up to meet you.
May the wind be always on your back.
May the sun shine warm upon your face;
the rains fall soft upon your fields,
and until we meet again,
may God hold you in the palm of his hand.
Amen.

Traditional Gaelic Blessing

May the road rise up to meet you.
May the wind be always on your back.
May the sun shine warm upon your face;
the rains fall soft upon your fields,
and until we meet again,
may God hold you in the palm of his hand.
Amen.

Traditional Gaelic Blessing

May the road rise up to meet you.
May the wind be always on your back.
May the sun shine warm upon your face;
the rains fall soft upon your fields,
and until we meet again,
may God hold you in the palm of his hand.
Amen.

Traditional Gaelic Blessing

May the road rise up to meet you.
May the wind be always on your back.
May the sun shine warm upon your face;
the rains fall soft upon your fields,
and until we meet again,
may God hold you in the palm of his hand.
Amen.

CLOSING WORSHIP OUTLINE

This will need to be carefully prepared in advance in liaison with all the workshop leaders. It is helpful to put all words on PowerPoint to allow maximum freedom for expression and spontaneity. It also gives an opportunity to demonstrate a good example of using PowerPoint for worship.

Simple introduction

- A verse of scripture plus a visual image
- Or short liturgical greeting

Hymn/song

- Of thanksgiving
- Or to fit the season (this day can often coincide with Rogation or Pentecost if the course follows the academic year)

Liturgy

- Responsive liturgy of thanks
- Or simple Kyrie confession

Song with signing

- Choose the most suitable one from the workshop

Reading

- From the Lectionary for the day

Reflection

- Very brief
- Linked to the reading
- Perhaps a poem or short meditation
- With a few images or pictures on the PowerPoint
- A suitable short video on the PowerPoint (maximum two minutes)

Prayers

- Using an idea from the workshop or a new idea
- Choose from pebbles, candles, glass beads, post-its, paper shapes, etc
- Must be something that can be done quickly

Song

- Looking forward to *Session 10*
- To send out

Blessing

worship4today

session

10

Worship in the New Testament

TEACHERS' NOTES

SESSION PROGRAMME

5 mins **Welcome and introduction to the session**
Give reminders about deadlines and hand-in dates
Explain about end of course reviews and assessments

80 mins **Worship in the New Testament**
Jesus the worshipper
- Jesus the Jew
- Worship in spirit and truth
- From Passover to communion

Worship in the Early Church
- Regular worship - anywhere
- Coming prepared - hymns, psalms and spiritual songs
- Conduct and encounter

Worship in Revelation
- Worship in heaven
- On earth as in heaven

20 mins **Tea break**

30 mins **Introduction to improvisation**
Here comes the bride, the Gospel, the collection!
- Filling in, extending and maintaining the flow

New songs - printed or improvised
- Using existing songs as a basis for improvisation

45 mins **Small groups**

20 mins **Worship all together**
Singing with the mind and with the Spirit

10 mins **Feedback all together**

LIST OF MATERIALS NEEDED

- Food and drink
- Flipchart and pens
- Laptop, data projector and screen
- Bibles
- Members' Handouts, including *Preparation Sheet* for session 11 (we recommend this is printed on different coloured paper to distinguish it)

For the improvisation workshop, you will need:

- If the main course leaders are not proficient musicians, it will be necessary to bring in musicians - singer, keyboard player and/or guitarist - to assist with the practical improvisation part of this session.
- Pack of music resources for each person for the practical work. It will be helpful to have the resources and *Handout 4* in order in the pack for ease. Although the music is primarily for study purposes, please be aware of copyright issues when reproducing music and check that you have the required cover to do so.

SUGGESTED RESOURCES FOR IMPROVISATION

Suggestions for improvisation	Our choices have changed from year to year, but we have used
Filling in time gaps (waiting for bride, Gospel procession, collection)	*Theme from Finlandia* by Sibelius
Extending hymns or songs	*Praise my soul* and *Here is love* *In Christ alone* by Stuart Townend *Holy, holy (lift up his name)* by Nathan Fellingham
Using an existing song as a base for changing the words	*Adoramus te O Christe* from Taizé *O come let us adore him* by J F Wade
Using a chord sequence from an existing song	*For Thou, O Lord, art high* by Pete Sanchez Jr *Let our praise to you be as incense* by Brent Chambers *All who are thirsty* by Brenton Brown and Glenn Robertson
Using chord patterns and melodic riffs	See *Additional Handout* for this session

We also provide writing paper, art paper, pencils and pastels for those participants who are not specifically musicians but who want to be spontaneously creative in other ways. Each group will need bibles.

ROOM SET-UP

Ensure there are sufficient chairs and tables where everyone can see the screen for the PowerPoint. You will also need separate rooms for small group work with sufficient chairs and, if possible, a keyboard.

⑩ Worship in the New Testament

SESSION AIMS

GUIDELINES

- To give an overview of New Testament worship
- To explore the worship of Jesus, the Early Church and heaven as it is portrayed in the book of Revelation
- To experiment with improvisation skills, both words and music
- To 'sing a new song to the Lord'

5 mins

WELCOME AND INTRODUCTION TO THE SESSION

Welcome participants and settle them quickly. Having spent a whole day together for *Session 9*, hopefully there will be a healthy buzz and sense of expectation.

Take some brief feedback from the full workshop day:

- What were the highlights?
- What were the challenges?

Deal with other administrative tasks swiftly, including:

- Give out *Preparation Sheet for Session 11.*
- *Personal projects:* Remind everyone that these should be handed in at the next session on **(give date)**, so it is now time to pull everything together and present it in its final form. If anyone is having difficulties at this stage, encourage them to discuss their projects with the course leaders.
- *Reviews:* Remind everyone that there will be an end of course review between *Session 11* and *12.* They will be invited to come with their incumbent and a member of their 'link group' or their 'buddy.' The review will take the form of a conversation based on a series of specific questions to enable the participants to reflect on their learning and the way in which their ministry is developing. It will be helpful to have a list of dates and time slots available.

NB. Letters should be sent to the participants and their incumbents, inviting them to take part in an end of course review. Further information, sample letters and suggested review questions are contained in the appendices to the *Assessment and CME* section.

As we come to explore worship in the New Testament, try to conduct the whole session in a worshipful atmosphere and allow the scriptures to make their own impact. This is very much an overview and an appetiser to encourage further personal study. We are well aware that we could easily spend a whole session on each section.

⑩ Worship in the New Testament

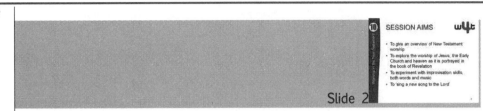

Slide 2

Quickly run through the session aims from slide 2.

Pray

30 mins

JESUS THE WORSHIPPER

Slide 3

Handout 1: Jesus the worshipper

Question: What have we observed about Jesus as a worshipper based on the passages of scripture set as preparation?

Share BRIEFLY with one another in pairs.

Share any significant thoughts.

As we consider Jesus as a worshipper, we will explore how he lived in the Jewish culture, following the Jewish religion and the Jewish way of life, and what new dimensions he added. We should also keep in mind the parallel thought of ourselves as worshippers within the culture, neighbourhood and traditions in which we live. Part of our calling as Christian worshippers is to be within our culture and neighbourhood whilst at the same time being 'different' and 'set apart'.

Jesus the Jew

Slide 4

Jesus:

- **Grew up in a Jewish culture (Luke 2:21-39)** - His parents presented him at the temple according to the custom for a first-born male baby. Here we receive the first inkling of Jesus being something

special. The devout Simeon was waiting to see the Christ before he died. Here we see Simeon's insight and his recognition of Jesus as the 'Christ' with his words:

Sovereign Lord, as you have promised, you now dismiss your servant in peace. For my eyes have seen your salvation ...
(Luke 2:29-30)

- **Attended the synagogue as a boy** - Mary and Joseph were devout and observed the usual regular practices of Jewish worship and tradition, so we can safely assume they were regular worshippers at the synagogue.

And the child grew and became strong; he was filled with wisdom, and the grace of God was upon him. (Luke 2:40)

- **Knew his Old Testament scripture** - Like all other Jewish boys, Jesus would have been instructed in the Torah from an early age.

- **Made pilgrimages to Jerusalem for major festivals** (Passover, Tabernacles, etc) - It was after the feast of Passover that Mary and Joseph lost Jesus, returning to Jerusalem to find him conversing so knowledgeably with the teachers *in his Father's house.*

Then he went down to Nazareth with them and was obedient to them. But his mother treasured all these things in her heart. And Jesus grew in wisdom and stature, and in favour with God and people. (Luke 2:51-52)

Again and again Mary recognised the special nature of her son as he grew up.

- **'Went to church' as an adult,** following all the regular Jewish customs. As he attended his local synagogue, Jesus was being part of his local worshipping community just like us.

Although he was doing everything like everyone else, from very early on Jesus was emerging as someone different, whom people respected, someone to whom others were drawn.

Jesus the Rabbi

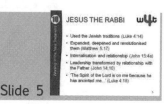

Slide 5

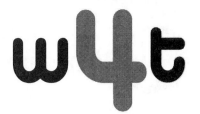

As an adult, Jesus became an itinerant preacher. He was regarded as a rabbi, a title given to a teacher or master of disciples, someone whom people respected enough to follow. Just like other Jewish rabbis, Jesus gathered disciples and taught them to pray, to teach and to preach.

At the Transfiguration, on the mountain with Peter, James and John, Peter says, 'Rabbi, it is good for us to be here.' (Mark 9:5) and at the Last Supper, when Jesus says one of his disciples will betray him, Judas replies: 'Surely not I, Rabbi?' (Matthew 26:25). Rabbi was a natural title for his disciples to use.

How was Jesus different from other rabbis?

Rather than teach the 'traditions of the Father' as handed down in the books of the Law, Jesus was sent to teach the 'will of *his* Father'. He spent time with his Father in prayer and had a relationship with Him. He did what he saw the Father doing (John 5:19) and unlike other teachers, Jesus taught as one with authority (Matthew 7:29).

After he had been baptised and was full of the Holy Spirit (Luke 3:21), it seems that God enabled Jesus to add a whole new dimension.

- Jesus used the Jewish traditions of which he was a part - He did not reject them as such, but

- He expanded, deepened and revolutionised them - Jesus says, 'Do not think that I have come to abolish the Law or the Prophets; I have not come to abolish them but to fulfil them.' (Matthew 5:17)

- Internalisation and relationship grow out of acknowledgement and obedience. The Jewish laws are no longer mere rules for people to get right but a way of life to take into themselves as part of an ongoing relationship rather than an ongoing tradition. This carries a promise from Jesus:

  'Remain in me, and I will remain in you.' (John 15:4a)

- Jesus' leadership was transformed by his relationship with the Father

  'Don't you believe that I am in the Father, and that the Father is in me? The words I say to you are not just my own. Rather, it is the Father, living in me, who is doing his work.' (John 14:10)

  How true is this for us?

Jesus was becoming more and more widely known:

'Jesus returned to Galilee in the power of the Spirit, and news about him spread through the whole countryside. He taught in their synagogues, and everyone praised him. He went to Nazareth, where he had been brought up, and on the Sabbath day he went into the synagogue, as was his custom.' (Luke 4:14-16)

In a sense, it looks as if Jesus took advantage of his position, but there is something much deeper going on. We read on from here as part of the preparation for this session. The synagogue was his 'home church.' By then, he was a 'visiting preacher' in the synagogues of Galilee. He was asked to 'read the lesson and teach' in Nazareth. The Old Testament scrolls were kept in a special place and handed to the reader by a special attendant. Jesus stood up to read (customary) and read from the book of Isaiah.

- **The Spirit of the Lord is on me, because he has anointed me to preach good news (Luke 4:18, quoting Isaiah 61:1ff)**

Then he sat down (again customary) to deliver his audacious piece of teaching:

The eyes of everyone in the synagogue were fastened on him, and he began by saying to them, 'Today this scripture is fulfilled in your hearing.' (Luke 4:20-21)

Jesus was revolutionary and challenging within the traditions of which he was a part.

Jesus at the Jewish festivals

We are going to use mainly John's gospel to illustrate some examples of how Jesus lived and ministered.

Slide 6

- Clearing the temple just before Passover (John 2:12) - Jesus was present with everyone else for the Passover Feast. The animals were there because Jews travelling long distances needed to buy them for sacrifice. When he saw the dishonest traders making money out of the worshippers, Jesus was 'consumed with zeal' for

His Father's house of prayer and worship, and turned the money lenders and traders out.

Now while he was in Jerusalem at the Passover Feast, many people saw the miraculous signs he was doing and believed in his name. (John 2:23)

- **Healing at the pool of Bethesda** (John 5) - Jesus was in Jerusalem for a Jewish feast, probably Passover again. He healed the man at the pool on the Sabbath at the normal Jewish gathering.

- **'I am the Bread of Life'** - John 6 is full of hugely profound teaching. We rightly get hooked up on it, but the context is the local synagogue as people prepare for the forthcoming Passover. There are already hints of what will come during the Last Supper:

He said this while teaching in the synagogue in Capernaum. (John 6:59)

- **The Feast of Tabernacles** (John 7) - This was the great Jewish feast of thanksgiving for the fruit harvest and for God's goodness. Also known as the Feast of Booths, Jewish families made temporary booths from tree branches and foliage as a reminder of the fragile dwellings of the Israelites as they wandered in the wilderness after the exodus from Egypt. (We talked about the significance of remembering past events in our worship when we looked at worship in the Old Testament.) The feast lasted several days. Jesus arrived half way through and capitalised on the occasion in order to teach in the temple courts every day. Festivals can provide an ideal outreach opportunity.

- **'The Father is IN me and I am IN the Father'** (John 10:22ff) - Jesus was speaking at the winter Feast of Dedication in the temple in Jerusalem. His teaching is profound and provocative.

There are numerous more examples of Jesus bringing his own incredibly profound and revolutionary dimension to regular acts of worship and customary Jewish festivals. Jesus was working within the traditions, moving amongst the people, led by the Holy Spirit.

Pause for a moment to consider:

- How did people react to Jesus?
- Any other thoughts so far?

Beyond the boundaries

Slide 7

The woman at the well

Ask someone to read John 4:4-24 and then draw out the following points:

Here Jesus shows us that although he was part of Jewish culture and tradition,

- **He was not limited or restricted by Jewish practices** – His teaching went far beyond the rituals, traditions and prejudices. In this one episode …

- **Jesus overturned everything that was normal, accepted practice** Firstly Jesus spoke to a woman (v.7). Jewish religious teachers did not do this. Then he accepted a drink from this woman, and a Samaritan woman at that.

  The Samaritan woman said to him, 'You are a Jew and I am a Samaritan woman. How can you ask me for a drink?' (For Jews do not associate with Samaritans.) (John 4:9)

  Jewish law stated that a Jew would become ceremonially unclean by drinking from a vessel handled by a Samaritan, so Jesus had already overturned several norms. He then went on to show himself to have special powers by telling the woman her own life story. (John 4:17-18)

  'Sir,' the woman said, 'I can see that you are a prophet. Our fathers worshipped on this mountain, but you Jews claim that the place where we must worship is in Jerusalem.' (John 4:19-20)

  Instigated by the woman, the conversation moves on to the new topic of worship. At this point …

- **Jesus explored a whole new concept of worship** – He dismissed the old arguments between Jews and Samaritans about the right place to worship and took the conversation in a completely unexpected direction.

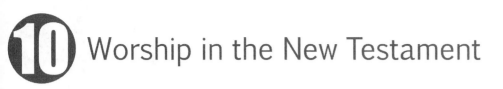

In spirit and truth

Slide 8

- **The place of worship is irrelevant**

  Jesus declared, 'Believe me, woman, a time is coming when you will worship the Father neither on this mountain nor in Jerusalem.' (John 4:21)

  Jesus puts the emphasis back on relationship with the God who can be known:

  'You Samaritans worship what you do not know; we worship what we do know, for salvation is from the Jews.' (John 4:22)

- **God is Spirit and his worshippers must worship _in_ spirit and _in_ truth (v.24)** - Here we see again that interesting mix of transcendence and immanence in the God who is Spirit and totally other, yet who wants to draw close to us in personal encounter.

- **_Proskuneo_ (Gk) – To worship; to come towards to kiss** (as a dog might lick his master's hand) **in a token of reverence** - Among Orientals, especially the Persians, to fall upon the ground and touch the ground with the forehead as an expression of profound reverence. True worship involves both awe and intimacy.

- **_Pneuma_ (Gk) - breath; wind; figuratively, spirit (human or divine)** - The Spirit of God connects with our human spirit to enable our worship in a unique way, reflecting the kind of relationship which Jesus had with his heavenly Father. Worship in spirit and truth takes us to a new level.

- **_Aletheia_ (Gk) – truth (in things about God); not hidden; not concealed; free from falsehood, pretence or deceit.**

  (Definitions taken from Thayer's Greek-English Lexicon of the New Testament Greek by Joseph H. Thayer, published by Hendrickson)

Our worship should be full of genuine adoration and intimacy as well as profound respect. In true worship, God is no longer hidden but revealed in increasing glory. We reflect that image back without falsehood or pretence in our worship as we come to know God better.

- **Worship is accessible to everyone**

  The woman said, 'I know that Messiah (called Christ) is coming. When he comes, he will explain everything to us.' Then Jesus declared, 'I who speak to you am he.' (v.25-26)

  This is allegedly the only place prior to his trial that Jesus specifically revealed himself as the Messiah, and he chose to do so to the lowest of the low, an immoral, outcast, Samaritan woman. We are all able to offer worship to God no matter who we are or where we are.

The ultimate revolution

Slide 9

The Last Supper

Jesus' final meal with his disciples was held on the evening of preparation for Jewish Passover, which was a time of remembering God's mercy towards the Jews and their deliverance from the final plague in Egypt. A perfect lamb had been selected for sacrifice and the blood splashed around the door frames, so that the angel of death would 'pass over' and the Israelites would be protected.

- **Jesus began with familiar Jewish traditions** - Jesus, who was born into Jewish culture, fulfilled these traditions within himself interpreting them in a new way.

- **Jesus took them 'into' himself** - According to Luke, they ate the Passover meal first and then Jesus told the disciples that he was the 'Passover Lamb', sealing a new covenant:

  In the same way, after the supper he took the cup, saying, 'This cup is the new covenant in my blood, which is poured out for you.' (Luke 22:20)

- Jesus is 'heir' of the Old Testament covenants - Echoing John the Baptist's statement right at the beginning of Jesus' ministry: 'Behold, the Lamb of God, who takes away the sin of the world!' (John 1:29), in not so many words Jesus declares himself the heir and fulfillment of the Old Testament promises.

  Through the symbolism of bread and wine, Jesus gave the disciples, and us, a means of living 'in Christ', moving ...

- From external tradition to internal transformation - The sacrament of Holy Communion is an outward sign of that inner reality. As we eat the bread and drink the wine, we receive God's grace afresh; we are renewed and strengthened within through the power of the Holy Spirit.

- Jesus establishes a new pattern ... of taking, giving thanks, breaking and giving

  And he took bread, gave thanks and broke it, and gave it to them, saying, 'This is my body given for you; do this in remembrance of me.' (Luke 22:19)

  This now forms the basis of our Holy Communion liturgy, which we continue to celebrate regularly in remembrance of Jesus' sacrifice once for all on the cross. The four-fold action of taking, giving thanks, breaking and giving was drawn out by Dom Gregory Dix in his influential book *The Shape of Liturgy*.

As one ...

Slide 10

As we share around the Lord's table, we commune with one another.

- Communion - We share intimately and feel in close touch with our Lord and Saviour, as well as with one another. The word itself comes from the Latin *communio* meaning sharing in common, but it also picks up the old French *com un* meaning 'as one'.

- *Koinonia* is the Greek word for this close fellowship and intimate participation. The word is used throughout the New Testament to describe relationship within the Early Church as well as the act of breaking bread together. Believers come together in faith and love.

- Eucharist comes from another Greek word *eucharisteo* meaning thankfulness, gratitude or the giving of thanks. Closely related to the Greek words *charis* (grace) and *charismata* (gift), the emphasis here is on our thankfulness to God for His gifts of grace.

All these different names reflect different aspects of Holy Communion and its significance for us today.

Slide 11

It may be helpful to pause here for two minutes' quiet meditation. Use the picture on the screen possibly together with some wordless music.

WORSHIP IN THE EARLY CHURCH

Slide 12

Handout 2: Worship in the Early Church

Regular gatherings

We have already heard how many encounters with Jesus happened within the context of regular worship. Indeed, the writer of Hebrews warns us:

Let us not give up meeting together, as some are in the habit of doing, but let us encourage one another ... (Hebrews 10:25)

We can all slide into bad habits, but just after the Ascension everyone was really keen!

Slide 13

25 mins

- **Upper Room** (Acts 1 and 2) - The first regular gatherings were held in the Upper Room, which was already a significant place of worship and prayer for the disciples. This was the room where they had eaten the Last Supper and received Jesus' last instructions before his arrest. It was the room where they had hidden behind locked doors for fear of the Jews after the crucifixion. This was where the risen Christ had appeared to them and spoken words of peace. And this was the room where they worshipped and waited day by day for the coming of the Holy Spirit on the day of Pentecost. The supposed site is now a major tourist attraction. Imagine the exuberant disciples spilling out from the Upper Room into the narrow Jerusalem streets, where passersby were surprised by what they saw and heard:

'We hear them declaring the wonders of God in our own tongues!' (Acts 2:11)

Slide 14

- **The temple**

They stayed continually at the temple, praising God. (Luke 24:53)

The disciples were still good Jews, worshipping regularly in the temple and the temple courts. It was on one of these regular trips to the temple at the time of prayer, that Peter and John met the lame man. Healed in the name of Jesus Christ of Nazareth ...

He went with them into the temple courts, walking and jumping, and praising God. (Acts 3:8)

Both the Upper Room and the temple site are significant today. They continue as places of pilgrimage and prayer for Jews and Christians as well as tourists from many different nations.

Slide 15

- **The local synagogue**

  As his custom was, Paul went into the synagogue, and on three Sabbath days he reasoned with them from the scriptures. (Acts 17:2)

  Throughout Acts, we find Paul using regular synagogue worship as a platform to proclaim the good news.

Slide 16

- **In homes** - The 'House Church' movement was not invented in the 20th century, but in a desire to get back to authentic New Testament worship they modelled their style of meetings on the worship of the Early Church:

  Every day they continued to meet together in the temple courts ...

  But they also:

  ... broke bread in their homes and ate together with glad and sincere hearts, praising God and enjoying the favour of all the people. (Acts 2:46-47)

  Post-Pentecost, the believers were devoted to prayer and worship, enjoying the *koinonia* that we mentioned earlier.

  Lydia was already a worshipper of God but she learnt more through Paul's teaching and opened up her house to him (Acts 16:14-15). It is likely that believers met regularly at her house.

  Priscilla and Aquila, a married couple, were also early converts, whom Paul met in Corinth (Acts 18:2ff). After travelling with Paul to Ephesus, they appear to have established a church there in their house (see Paul's greeting in Romans 16:3-5).

  If we read the end of Paul's letters, we find various greetings to various people and the churches which met in their houses.

Worship anywhere, anytime

Jesus had already made it clear to the woman at the well that worship would no longer be centred on the temple in Jerusalem, or for that matter any other specific building or geographical location. The Early Church worshipped anywhere, anytime.

Slide 17

- **Mount of Olives** (Luke 24:50-53; Acts 1:1-12) - This had been a significant place of prayer and worship for Jesus. This is where Jesus had given his final instruction to his disciples to wait for the coming of the Holy Spirit. He had blessed them and then the Ascension had taken place here whilst the disciples worshipped.

Slide 18

- **By the river**

  On the Sabbath we went outside the city gate to the river, where we expected to find a place of prayer. We sat down and began to speak to the women who had gathered there. (Acts 16:13)

  Paul went to pray down by the river. As a result, Lydia was converted along with her household, and a new church was born. Prayer and worship outside can be a powerful witness to others.

  However, sometimes we can worship in the most unlikely places.

Slide 19

- **In prison** - Paul and Silas had been arrested for causing an uproar in the city of Philippi. They were put in chains in the deepest cell, where their response to their captivity and ill-treatment was worship:

  About midnight Paul and Silas were praying and singing hymns to God, and the other prisoners were listening to them. (Acts 16:25)

  They worshipped so loudly that all the other prisoners were listening. Then there came a mighty earthquake. Surprisingly, none of the prisoners tried to escape and again many people came to faith. When the going gets tough, do we still respond with worship?

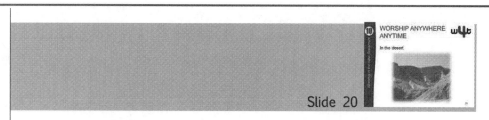

Slide 20

- **In the desert** - Philip, on the other hand, found himself on the desert road, sitting beside an Ethiopian official as he read from the book of Isaiah. Philip was able to explain the scriptures as they went along, and what was the result?

  As they travelled along the road, they came to some water and the eunuch said, 'Look, here is water. Why shouldn't I be baptised?' And he gave orders to stop the chariot. Then both Philip and the eunuch went down into the water and Philip baptised him. (Acts 8:36-38)

  This impromptu baptism service in the middle of the desert sent the Ethiopian eunuch on his way rejoicing.

Coming prepared

Slide 21

The early Christians were encouraged to come prepared to worship:

Speak to one another with psalms, hymns and spiritual songs. Sing and make music in your heart to the Lord, always giving thanks to God the Father for everything, in the name of our Lord Jesus Christ. (Ephesians 5:19-20)

- **Bring psalms, hymns and spiritual songs** - We talked a little about this in *Session 5*, when we were thinking about the role of music in worship. We need all three genres included in our worship, because they all enable and enhance our worship in different ways. More than that, we are instructed to come with these songs already in our hearts and minds.

- **Sing and make music in your hearts to the Lord** (v.20) - Singing brings pleasure to God and does us good. This might include new spontaneous songs as well as familiar ones. It might also include singing in tongues, which Paul describes as a gift of the Holy Spirit (see Acts 2:4 and 1 Corinthians 12:28).

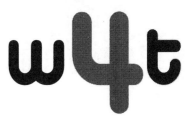

- Give thanks for everything (v.20; also Philippians 4:4-7) - All our worship should be conducted in an attitude of thanksgiving. Thanksgiving encourages a deeper appreciation of God's goodness and is a great antidote to self absorption.

Question: Whether we are leading, part of the worship team or a member of the congregation, what difference might it make if we all came to worship better prepared?

Share BRIEFLY with one another in pairs.

Share any significant thoughts.

Proper conduct of worship

Slide 22

Worship in the Early Church was not without its issues. We find some of them addressed in Paul's letters as he writes to specific churches in specific places. Although our culture is very different, we can still draw out some important principles.

- The Lord's Supper (1 Corinthians 11:17-34) - Paul was disappointed to hear of divisions in the church at Corinth:

When you come together, it is not the Lord's Supper you eat, for as you eat, each of you goes ahead without waiting for anybody else. One remains hungry, another gets drunk. Don't you have homes to eat and drink in? Or do you despise the church of God and humiliate those who have nothing? (1 Corinthians 11:20-22)

The Corinthians were reprimanded for their lack of care and consideration for those who had little. They seemed to have a general lack of respect for the togetherness and fellowship, which Jesus had originally encouraged between his disciples. It also appears that the bread and wine had lost some of its symbolism, prompting Paul to remind the church that this was a proclamation of Christ's death to be continued in his memory 'until he comes again' (v.26). Paul follows this up with a stern warning. If we take communion 'in an unworthy manner' (v.27), we may bring judgement in the form of weakness and sickness on ourselves (v.29-30).

- **Orderly worship** (1 Corinthians 12-14) - When we read instructions about women with their heads covered and women not teaching, we need to remember that this is a letter written to a particular cultural context. Essentially, Paul wants to encourage fitting conduct and propriety, where everything is done in a way that builds up the body of believers (1 Corinthians 12). This principle readily applies to us today and is echoed in the Canons of the Church of England when they state that our worship should glorify God and edify or build up the people.

  We should remember that Paul's famous passage about love is actually in the context of our behaviour in worship. If we do not express love for God and love for one another in our worship, then we are nothing.

  According to 1 Corinthians 14, worship should contain elements for our 'strengthening, encouragement and comfort' (v.3), 'but everything should be done in a fitting and orderly way' (v.40). We are reminded again of the need for balance between structure and planning on the one hand and spontaneity and freedom on the other. Even spontaneity needs to be practised and developed. We will be exploring this more later when we look at improvisation skills in our practical session.

- **Sound doctrine** (Acts 6:1ff; 2 Timothy 3:16-17) - We have been reminded many times that worship is the context in which we are informed and formed as believers. For this reason the apostles placed a high priority on prayer and the ministry of the word (see Acts 6:4). Paul reminds Timothy that:

  All Scripture is God-breathed and is useful for teaching, rebuking, correcting and training in righteousness, so that the people of God may be thoroughly equipped for every good work.
  (2 Timothy 3:16-17)

  We do well to heed Paul's advice and choose liturgy, songs and prayers that are biblical, theologically balanced and doctrinally sound.

Encountering God

Slide 23

Finally, for the Early Church, worship was a place of expectation and encounter.

- **A place of conversion** - On the day of Pentecost, traditionally remembered as the birthday of the Church, the international crowd heard the believers praising God in their own languages (Acts 2:11). This spontaneous outburst of Pentecostal praise led there and then to the conversion of three thousand people, but as the believers continued to meet together daily for teaching, prayer and praise, 'the Lord added to their number daily those who were being saved' (Acts 2:47).

When Christians come together to worship, others come to faith.

- **A place of transformation** - Paul discovered that worship in spirit and truth made him more like Jesus:

Now the Lord is the Spirit, and where the Spirit of the Lord is, there is freedom. And we, who with unveiled faces all reflect the Lord's glory, are being transformed into his likeness with ever-increasing glory, which comes from the Lord, who is the Spirit.
(2 Corinthians 3:17-18)

The more time *we spend* with God in worship, the more like Him *we become*. In 2007, the Liturgical Commission presented a report to General Synod called *Transforming Worship* (GS 1651, The Archbishops' Council, 2007). They later published a small booklet for parish use: *Worship changes lives: How it works, why it matters* (edited by Paul Bradshaw and Peter Moger, The Archbishops' Council, 2008). These both underline the premise that we become the people God wants us to be through worship. They also remind us that worship and mission are inextricably linked. The Early Church believed passionately that worship changed lives. It was part of their daily experience. If we take this potential for transformation seriously, the Anglican Church could be radically changed in the future on a daily basis.

- **Offering ourselves and our money** - Sharing their goods in common was another hallmark of the Early Church:

From time to time those who owned lands or houses sold them, brought the money from the sales and put it at the apostles' feet, and it was distributed to anyone as he had need. (Acts 4:34-35)

Barnabas got it right, offering a generous gift for God's work:

Barnabas (which means Son of Encouragement), sold a field he owned and brought the money and put it at the apostles' feet. (Acts 4:37)

Ananias and Sapphira on the other hand got it wrong:

They also sold a piece of property. With his wife's full knowledge Ananias kept back part of the money for himself, but brought the rest and put it at the apostles' feet. (Acts 5:1-2)

They tried to pass this off as the whole amount and their dishonesty cost them their lives. Paul later encourages the Corinthian church to decide what each person should give and then offer it with a cheerful and generous attitude (see 2 Corinthians 8 and 9). Honesty and integrity are essentials of worship.

Everything that we are and everything that we have is a gift from God, so we offer our money gratefully (see Offertory Prayer: 'Yours, Lord, is the greatness.'). This also links back to the verse in Romans 12 that we read in our very first session:

Therefore, I urge you, in view of God's mercy, to offer your bodies as living sacrifices, holy and pleasing to God – this is your spiritual act of worship. (Romans 12:1)

Worship was a way of life to the Early Church, and it can be a way of life for us too.

- **Commissioning** – Finally, worship was the context for setting particular individuals apart for specific tasks and ministries. Matthias, the replacement for Judas amongst the apostles, was chosen within the context of prayer and worship (Acts 1:21-26). Later, in the church at Antioch ...

While they were worshipping the Lord and fasting, the Holy Spirit said, 'Set apart for me Barnabas and Saul for the work to which I have called them.' So after they had fasted and prayed, they placed their hands on them and sent them off. (Acts 13:2-3)

This kind of action continues today in our services of ordination and licensing or authorisation to particular ministries.

Any questions or comments before we move on to our final section?

WORSHIP IN REVELATION

Slide 24

Handout 3: Worship in Revelation

Revelation

Slide 25

Our understanding of God and our picture of heaven come by revelation, which means literally something is revealed or unveiled. This is 'a disclosure of knowledge to humankind by a divine or supernatural agency' (definition from the *Reader's Digest Universal Dictionary,* The Reader's Digest Association Ltd, 1986). God takes the initiative here and reveals more about Himself. We've seen this before in the Old Testament with Moses at the burning bush and Isaiah in the temple. Now we see similar revelation to people in the New Testament.

- Paul caught up to a third heaven

  I will go on to visions and revelations from the Lord. I know a man in Christ who fourteen years ago was caught up to the third heaven. This man - whether it was in the body or out of the body I do not know ... but God knows - was caught up to paradise.
  (2 Corinthians 12:1-4)

  In the body? Out of the body? In paradise? This experience was so 'other', Paul had no real idea what exactly was going on. It was so amazing it was inexpressible (v.4). Some commentators think Paul may have been beaten or stoned so severely that he was left for dead and had some kind of near death experience.

- John on Patmos

  I, John ... was on the island of Patmos because of the word of God and the testimony of Jesus. On the Lord's Day I was in the Spirit. (Revelation 1:9-10)

John had been exiled to the island of Patmos for preaching the gospel, and his revelation appears to have come in the context of regular worship, day by day, week by week.

The book of Revelation has been traditionally attributed to John, the Apostle. It is full of evocative and suggestive picture language as it seeks to describe the indescribable.

Rather than treating these next few minutes as a bible study or a teaching session, encourage participants to engage with the biblical texts creatively and to imagine themselves caught up into the supernatural realm of heaven. They may want to have bibles handy, they may want to keep an eye on the PowerPoint, or they may prefer to close their eyes and imagine.

First of all, at the beginning of Revelation, John gives us ...

A revelation of Jesus

Slide 26-27

The faithful witness, the firstborn from the dead, and the ruler of the kings of the earth, coming with the clouds ... the Alpha and the Omega. (from Revelation 1:5-8)

John continues:

On the Lord's Day I was in the Spirit, and I heard behind me a loud voice like a trumpet ... I turned round to see the voice that was speaking to me. And when I turned I saw seven golden lampstands, and among the lampstands was someone like a son of man, dressed in a robe reaching down to his feet and with a golden sash round his chest. His head and hair were white like wool, as white as snow, and his eyes were like blazing fire. His feet were like bronze glowing in a furnace, and his voice was like the sound of rushing waters. In his right hand he held seven stars, and out of his mouth came a sharp double-edged sword. His face was like the sun shining in all its brilliance. (Revelation 1:10-16)

John goes on to describe Jesus as ...

The First and the Last, the Living One, the holder of the keys of death and Hades. (Revelation 1:17-18)

Slide 28

Later in Revelation, John uses titles like ...

The Lion of Judah (Revelation 5:5), the Root and Offspring of David (5:5 and 22:16), a Lamb, looking as if it had been slain (5:6), Conqueror (6:2), Faithful and True (19:11), King of kings and Lord of lords (19:16), Bright Morning Star (22:16).

John's response (Revelation 1:17-19)

Slide 29

- Completely awestruck

  When I saw him, I fell at his feet as though dead.

- Touched by God

  Then he placed his right hand on me.

  Remember this was a man who had suffered persecution and who had been sent into exile.

- **Reassured**

  He said: 'Do not be afraid.'

Easier said than done. According to the writer of Hebrews, it is 'a fearful thing to fall into the hands of the living God' (Hebrews 10:31).

Like so many previous occasions in scripture, Jesus speaks words of encouragement and reassurance, and then goes on to commission a specific task.

- Commissioned

  Write, therefore, what you have seen, what is now and what will take place later.

John's writings in the following chapters of Revelation include some amazing descriptions of what worship is like in heaven.

A revelation of worship in heaven (Revelation 4, 5 and 7)

Slide 30

Participants have already read these passages as part of their preparation but we recommend that the prescribed passages are now read by the course leaders or mentors, so that all the participants can engage fully with receiving those scriptures in a different way. Participants may want to ponder the questions on the handout and jot down one or two thoughts and ideas as they stand out during the readings. Alternatively, they may want to get caught up in the action in their imagination.

Read aloud Revelation 4:2-11; Revelation 5:6-14; Revelation 7:9-17.

Slide 31

It may be pertinent to remain in silence for a few moments at the end of the readings allowing them to make their full impact, or to encourage participants to join in the worship of heaven by singing an appropriate song, such as 'Salvation belongs to our God' by Adrian Howard and Pat Turner or a setting of 'Holy, holy, holy is the Lord God Almighty'.

It may be helpful to reiterate and emphasise some of the key answers to the questions on the handout. This could be done as interactive feedback, but too much participation at this point and the risk of getting side-tracked may cut across the sense of being caught up in it all.

- Who is being worshipped?

Slide 32

One who sits on the throne with the appearance of jasper and carnelian; the Lord God Almighty, who was, and is, and is to come; the Lamb, looking as if it has been slain.

- Who is participating in worship?

Slide 33

Twenty-four elders, dressed in white with crowns of gold, seated on twenty four thrones; four strange living creatures, each with six wings and covered with eyes: a lion, an ox, one with a face like a man, and an eagle; many angels, thousands upon thousands, ten thousand times ten thousand; every creature in heaven and on earth and under the earth and on the sea; a great multitude, dressed in white robes, from every nation, tribe, people and language.

- What is the overall impression?

Slide 34

- Magnificence: royalty - central throne and twenty-four other thrones; precious stones.

- Brilliance: dazzling light; seven blazing lamps; flashes of lightning; the glory of God.

- Colour: jasper, carnelian, emerald; a sea of glass like crystal; a rainbow.

- Loud noises: rumblings and peals of thunder.

- Smell: bowls of incense

- Continual worship: day and night

- Using instruments: harps and trumpets

- Singing: giving glory, honour and thanks; singing a new song

- Shouting: in loud voices

- Movement: standing; holding palm branches; bowing down; laying down crowns; falling prostrate

- Holiness: reverence and awe

- What is our response?

Slide 35

Wow! This is not a static picture. It's a dynamic, evolving picture. We find ourselves wanting to join in the declarations of worship. Encourage everyone to stand. As they come up on the screen, proclaim these statements together with the hosts of heaven:

Holy, holy, holy is the Lord God Almighty, who was, and is, and is to come. (Revelation 4:8)

Worthy is the Lamb, who was slain, to receive power and wealth and wisdom and strength and honour and glory and praise!
(Revelation 5:12)

To him who sits on the throne and to the Lamb be praise and honour and glory and power, for ever and ever! (Revelation 5:13)

We have this amazing revelation, this vision which reveals something of what God is like and what heaven is like and what worship in heaven is like. Paul described it as inexpressible, and yet we are invited to …

Worship on earth as it is in heaven

Slide 36

The worship described in Revelation gives us a vision of what we are aiming for, when we come together to worship here on earth.

- Vision produces passion

'Vision is a picture of the future which produces passion.'
(Bill Hybels, founding and Senior Pastor of Willowcreek Church, Chicago, USA)

Vision is something we look forward to in the future which produces a passion and an enthusiasm in the present. Vision helps us to set targets, and gives us dynamism and energy to move towards and achieve those goals.

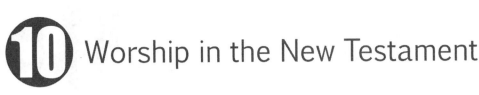 

Where there is no vision, the people perish.
(Proverbs 29:18, Authorised Version)

Without vision, we are in danger of losing our sense of direction and purpose. In time, we can slowly stagnate into routine services which no longer attract or inspire.

We all need vision. Alongside imparting knowledge and developing practical skills, the *Worship4Today* course is all about opening us up to new possibilities and giving us glimpses of what might be. Glimpses can grow into vision; vision can produce passion; and passion can create enthusiasm and energy, which will enable us to serve up inspiring worship 'fit for the King of heaven'.

- **The Lord's Prayer** - Every time we say the Lord's Prayer, we say:

Your kingdom come,
Your will be done,
on earth as in heaven.

Week by week, we pray that God's kingdom would be manifest on the earth in the same way that it is in heaven. This must include our worship, because heaven is a place filled with worship. We are praying that there will be a closer connection between the worship of heaven and the worship of earth. We are all invited to join in the worship of heaven while *still* on earth! We are invited to join in *now!* This is part of the 'now and not yet' of the Kingdom of God, where we live life and worship on earth with an eternal perspective.

- **Worship on earth is a preparation for worship in heaven**

After this I looked and there before me was a great multitude that no-one could count, from every nation, tribe, people and language, standing before the throne and in front of the Lamb. They were wearing white robes and were holding palm branches in their hands. And they cried out in a loud voice: 'Salvation belongs to our God, who sits on the throne, and to the Lamb.'
(Revelation 7:9-10)

One day we will be part of that great crowd. We shall be standing before the throne and in front of the Lamb, wearing white robes and holding palm branches in our hands. If we expect the worship to last an hour, for the music to be at a muted volume and no-one to raise an eyebrow let alone a hand, then we shall be in for a shock! As we worship here on earth, we do well to remember the kind of worship we are preparing for in eternity.

A personal invitation from a relational God

Slide 37

We are offered a personal invitation from our loving God to come and join 'with angels and archangels and all the company of heaven singing: Holy, holy, holy is the Lord God almighty' (see Eucharistic prayers).

The Father, Son and Holy Spirit are all present:

To him who sits on the throne and to the Lamb be praise and honour and glory and power, for ever and ever! (Revelation 5:13)

We are invited into this great community of faith. At the beginning of Revelation, the Holy Spirit invites John to 'come up here' *(Revelation 4:1)* and see. God is always inviting us to see, to listen, to taste, to touch, to smell. All our senses are involved, and we are invited to engage in worship with the whole of our being. What an awesome privilege!

The Spirit and the bride say, 'Come!' And let him who hears say, 'Come!' And let everyone who is thirsty come. Let everyone who wishes take the water of life as a gift. (Revelation 22:17, NRSV)

We come to God with a sense of reverence and awe as befits the King of kings, but we also come to God with a sense of expectancy ready to receive freely the gift of new life.

Slide 38

We suggest that rather than taking any questions it will be more helpful to conclude the teaching by joining together in song.

(Suggestion: 'Crown Him with many crowns' by Matthew Bridges and Godfrey Thring)

20 mins

TEA BREAK

INTRODUCTION TO IMPROVISATION SKILLS

The next part of this session will work best in a worship environment rather than a teaching room. Each person will need a pack of resources, including copies of the music to be used. The pack should include *Handout 4: A new song in my mouth*, but participants should focus on the practical here and refer to the handout after the session. We suggest that proficient musicians and singers demonstrate the various points, encouraging participants to join in wherever possible.

10 mins

Musical improvisation

Also known as musical extemporisation, improvisation speaks of ad-libbing and spontaneity, the art of making things up on the spur of the moment. Many organists will develop this skill out of necessity. When the bride is late for her wedding, it becomes essential to be able to play variations on a theme or to improvise using a basic chord pattern (see the *Additional Handout* to this session).

Demonstrate: A simple version of a well known tune is a good place to start. For example, the theme tune from *Finlandia* by Sibelius. This has a simple chord structure which lends itself to adding a higher descant above the main theme or using the same chord sequence as a basis for a major digression from the theme. The theme has a built-in 'interrupted' cadence, so it is easy to lengthen the piece or draw to a close with the final 'perfect' cadence.

Similarly, we may need to fill in with a short musical interlude for the Gospel procession to return to their places, or extend a hymn or song when the offertory takes a little longer than expected.

Demonstrate: Sing the last verse of 'Praise my soul, the King of heaven'. Then lead back into the final 'Alleluia, alleluia! Praise with us the God of grace!' Some hymns, such as 'Here is love vast as the ocean' or 'In Christ alone', lend themselves to a repeat of the last half of a verse either to extend the length of the hymn or to emphasise a particular set of words. This kind of extension can help both musicians and congregation to develop a degree of flexibility.

131

Also, if we stop the final chord of a hymn or song abruptly, any sense of atmosphere can be cut dead and completely destroyed, whereas lingering on a final chord or playing an extra bar or two can gently maintain the flow. Once the music has stopped, it is very difficult to start up again.

Demonstrate: Using a contemporary worship song, demonstrate a variety of repeats and extensions, using the beginning, middle, refrain or last line. Vary the order and train the musicians and congregation to follow, making it clear either musically or with a voice-over which part we are going to repeat. We used Nathan Fellingham's 'Holy, holy'. We can repeat the refrain *'lift up His name'* several times and then repeat the final line *'for He is worthy to be praised'* several times to build to a climax or we can use the opening *'holy, holy'* with alternative words: *'worthy, worthy is the Lord ..., Jesus, Jesus is the Lord ...'* The use of crescendo (getting louder) and diminuendo (getting softer) can help to create atmosphere and develop a sense of direction.

20 mins

A new song in my mouth

The Old Testament has many references to 'new songs'. Isaiah's encouragement to 'sing to the Lord a new song' (Isaiah 42:10) is a response to God, which follows God's announcement of his intention to restore Israel to its former glory. New songs usually grow out of a response to God in a particular situation.

Personal and corporate 'new songs' in Psalms

- **Sing and play skilfully** (Psalm 33:3) - We respond by building on creative skills we already have.
- **Sing ... and declare his glory to the nations** (Psalm 96:1-2) - These songs are about God not about us! We can respond together and our new song becomes a proclamation of who God is to those around us.
- **Sing ... for victory** (Psalm 98:1) - New songs may be a corporate response to answered prayer, or ...
- **I will sing ... and play ...** (Psalm 144:9) - they may be a personal response to answered prayer.
- **Sing ... His praise in the assembly of the faithful** (Psalm 149:1) - The musicians and singers may take a lead, but the expectation is for the whole gathered congregation to join in.

At significant points on our Christian journey we can experience a new realisation of God's love; then a new desire to praise can emerge from deep within. Here, new songs can grow out of very different extremes of emotion from exuberance and elation to deep pain and despair. This was King David's experience:

Psalm 40 - a psalm of David

I waited patiently for the LORD;
He turned to me and heard my cry.
He lifted me out of the slimy pit, out of the mud and mire;
He set my feet on a rock and gave me a firm place to stand.
He put a new song in my mouth,
a hymn of praise to our God.
Many will see and fear and put their trust in the LORD.
(Psalm 40:1-3)

The song of desperation evolves into a song of deliverance and a proclamation of good news.

New songs of lament grow out of the big questions during the struggles of life. Sometimes it is: Where are you, Lord? How long, Lord? Why, Lord? The honest complaint of lament helps us to break through into a new hymn of praise.

Why new songs? God's Spirit is always active, ever present and ready to release new creativity. We respond to God by expressing our love and, indeed, our pain, to give new depth to our relationship.

Planned or spontaneous? The one leads to the other. New songs are continually being written and published. These published new songs are a composer's expression of an encounter with God. There may be songs for a particular season, reflecting what God is doing in the Church *now*. These are then adopted by the whole congregation to become a tremendous vehicle for new and life-giving worship. From here it is only a small step into the immediate and spontaneous.

Encourage creativity

In our experience, spontaneity does not just happen! Flexibility is a good first step but we need to learn a few more basic skills and prepare ourselves.

Demonstrate: Sing 'O come let us adore Him' with the additional verses *For He alone is worthy* and *We'll give Him all the glory* (see *Songs of Fellowship*, book 1, no.409). Then add a few extra verses prepared beforehand to fit in with the tune. We need a phrase of seven syllables with the main accents on the second and sixth syllable. We can continue on a similar theme with phrases such as *Ascended into heaven, Enthroned in heav'nly splendour, Our Saviour and Redeemer*. The repetition makes the verses easy for the congregation to pick up and join in.

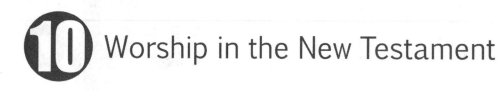

Use different names of God

This is an easy, non-threatening way to extemporise, and most of the congregation are likely to know a few names for God, such as: *Lord, King, Creator, heavenly Father.*

Demonstrate: Sing the Taizé chant 'Adoramus te O Christ'. The 'O' at the beginning of the phrase leaves a helpful space for improvisation. We can improvise both words and melody over the basic chord pattern in the first two bars. The less confident and non-singers can also easily join in by speaking names of God or phrases from the Psalms. A short phrase like *God is my refuge and strength* or *The Lord is my light and my salvation* can be either sung or spoken over the 'O'. Phrases here can be different lengths and a few *Amens* can clearly signal the final time. Individuals can take turns to improvise; or divide the congregation in half with one side singing the chant and one side improvising. We feel less exposed if we are responding as part of a bigger group.

Use the psalms

When we are unsure of what words to use, the Psalms can provide a rich resource with words and phrases to cover every mood and situation.

Demonstrate: Sing 'For Thou, O Lord art high' and then just keep repeating the chorus. Again we can easily substitute alternative words for *I exalt You*, such as *You are worthy* or *Lord, we honour You*, or we can add short extemporary phrases over the long tied notes, such as *Holy, holy, holy*, picking up the picture of heaven we have explored earlier in the session. Alternatively we can add an improvised instrumental obligato against the main melody. The different instruments will alter the style and atmosphere from ethereal flute to plaintive oboe to dancing violin, mellow 'cello to jazzy saxophone to the bright call of the trumpet. Alternatively, we can introduce a rhythmic element with percussion or guitar which can pick up pace and lead us in a new direction entirely. Here we can touch the majestic and triumphant, we can move into spiritual warfare, or we can send people out with renewed vision.

NB. The songs above are only there for guidance, but over the years we have found these particularly useful and readily accessible for teaching improvisation skills.

EXPLANATION OF SMALL GROUP TASK

The small group work now gives participants the opportunity to 'have a go' and try out some improvisation for themselves. We suggest that they begin with all the material that has already been used, building on what they have just experienced.

Encourage participants to use names of God, to choose a psalm, or to adapt some of the worship phrases from Revelation. Reassure everyone that this is a safe place in which to experiment and try out new things.

Each group will need resources packs and Bibles. We also provide writing paper, art paper, pencils, and pastels for each group for those who want to be spontaneously creative in other ways.

45 mins

SMALL GROUPS with mentors in separate worship spaces.

20 mins

WORSHIP TOGETHER

Hopefully, confidence will have been building as participants have been experimenting together in their small groups. At the end of the group time, draw everyone back into the main worship space for a final time of improvised worship together.

Musical improvisation in the context of worship is a creative response in the moment to God, to the immediate environment, to our own inner feelings, and to the other musicians and members of the congregation. We are meant to be IN Christ, joined in love and connected to Him as one. As in any close relationship, words become an inadequate means of expression. We find a deeper level of connecting and communicating from within our very soul. We respond in spirit and truth (John 4:24) so that the whole congregation is built up in truth and love (Ephesians 4:16).

Give permission to experiment freely, both individually and corporately in whatever way seems appropriate. Taking what people learnt in *Session 9*, encourage the use of spontaneous movement - gesture, posture, procession, flags or dance. We may sing in English or our own first language or we may sing 'in tongues', a heavenly language and gift of the Holy Spirit (see 1 Corinthians 14). Remember, we referred earlier to the day of Pentecost, when the disciples found themselves 'declaring the wonders of God in other tongues!' (Acts

2:11), so if anyone feels a new language bubbling up from deep within encourage them to use it and not hold back. Others may want to speak out words of scripture or write or draw or move about. Try to create a safe environment with no holds barred!

Heavenly sounds

Begin worshipping by taking everyone back to the images from Revelation that we considered earlier. Ask a participant to read:

Then I looked, and there before me was the Lamb, standing on Mount Zion, and **with him** 144,000 who had his name and his Father's name written on their foreheads. And I heard a sound from heaven like the roar of rushing waters and like a loud peal of thunder. The sound I heard was like that of harpists playing their harps. And they sang a **new** song before the throne ... (Revelation 14:1-3)

Encourage everyone to use their imagination and join the multitude who were lost in wonder ... caught up in the heavenly praise. Their wonder and awe spilled out into song, a great and glorious spontaneous anthem of praise, completely unrestricted, way beyond the boundaries of language and structure, full of heavenly sounds.

Begin by singing a known song which lends itself to moving into free singing, and then be prepared to go with the flow.

We have used 'Let our praise to You be as incense' by Brent Chambers and 'All who are thirsty' by Brenton Brown and Glenn Robertson. Both of these songs include simple, repeated sections which lend themselves to improvisation over a simple chord pattern. These in turn could blend into one of the simple chord patterns from the *Additional Handout* to extend the music further. The chord patterns can easily be transposed into different keys or adapted rhythmically to suit different time signatures.

NB. Stuart Townend includes a helpful chapter on improvisation in his book *Playing the Keyboard in Worship* (Kingsway, 1995).

10 mins

FEEDBACK ALL TOGETHER

Allow participants to share from their experiences:

What surprised them?
What did they find difficult?
How did they meet with God?

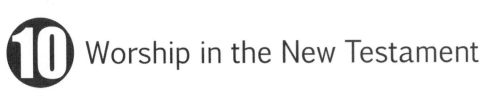 

Finally

Quickly summarise with a few pertinent points:

If we are going to encourage freedom in worship, we must create an appropriate safe worship environment. We must also exercise leadership and discernment. We cannot be so lost in wonder, love and praise ourselves that we have completely lost touch with the congregation. We need to discern what is happening and encourage the congregation to meet with God in it. We should be prepared for a manifestation of spiritual gifts, particularly speaking or singing in tongues and prophecy but also gifts of faith, miracles and healing. Many would testify to being healed within worship without any prayer or ministry of any kind, having been touched by God directly. We also need to discern when to draw worship to a close, and to do so in a sensitive manner.

We can only imagine what worship is like in heaven. According to 1 Corinthians 13, we can only know in part at present. However, every now and again, God gives us glimpses of His heavenly throne. In worship, we move that bit nearer, and when we respond freely during worship, we move nearer still.

CLOSING PRAYER

Draw everyone back together for a final prayer to close the session; and give a brief reminder of the preparation for the next session: *The challenge of all-age worship.*

worship4today

The challenge of all-age worship **11**

Slide 39

worship 4 today

session

Worship in the New Testament

JESUS THE WORSHIPPER

Jesus the Jew (Luke 2: 21-52)

- Grew up in a Jewish culture

- Attended the synagogue as a boy

- Knew his Old Testament scripture

- Made pilgrimages to Jerusalem for major Jewish festivals

- 'Went to church' as an adult following Jewish customs

Jesus the Rabbi

He brought a new dimension:

- Jesus used the Jewish traditions of which he was a part (Luke 4:14)

- He expanded, deepened and revolutionised them (Matthew 5:17)

- Internalisation and relationship (John 15:4a)

- Jesus' leadership was transformed by his relationship with the Father (John 14:10)

- 'The Spirit of the Lord is on me, because he has anointed me to preach good news ...' (Luke 4:18, quoting Isaiah 61:1ff)

Jesus at the Jewish festivals

- Clearing the temple just before Passover (John 2:12ff)

- Healing at the pool of Bethesda (John 5)

- 'I am the Bread of Life' (John 6)

- The Feast of Tabernacles (John 7)

- 'The Father is IN me and I am IN the Father' (John 10:22ff)

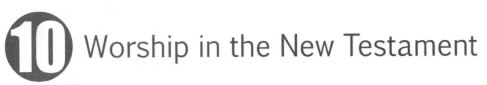 

Beyond the boundaries: the woman at the well (John 4:4-24)

- Jesus was not limited or restricted by Jewish practices (v.7)

- Jesus overturned everything that was *normal,* accepted practice (v.9)

- Jesus explored a whole new concept of worship (v.21ff)

In spirit and truth ...

- The place of worship is irrelevant (v.21)

- God is Spirit and his worshippers must worship *in* spirit and *in* truth (v.24)

- *Proskuneo* (Greek) – to worship; to come towards to kiss in a token of reverence

- *Pneuma* (Greek) - breath or wind; figuratively, spirit (human or divine)

- *Aletheia* (Greek) – truth; not hidden; not concealed; free from falsehood, pretence or deceit

- Worship is accessible to everyone (v.25-26)

The ultimate revolution: the Last Supper

- Jesus began with familiar Jewish traditions

- Jesus took them 'into' himself

- Jesus is 'heir' of the Old Testament covenants

- From external tradition to internal transformation

- Jesus establishes a new pattern ...

  ... of taking, giving thanks, breaking and giving

As one ...

- Communion – to share intimately, feel in close touch – from Latin *communio* meaning sharing in common; also old French *com un* meaning 'as one'

- *Koinonia* (Greek) – fellowship, intimate relationship, partnership, communication

- *Eucharist* (Greek) – thankfulness, gratitude or the giving of thanks; closely related to the Greek words *charis* (grace) and *charismata* (gift)

WORSHIP IN THE EARLY CHURCH

Regular gatherings

- Upper room (Acts 1 and 2)

- The temple (Luke 24:53; Acts 3)

- The local synagogue (Acts 13:13; 17:2; 19:8)

- In homes

  - The believers post-Pentecost (Acts 2:42-47)

  - Lydia (Acts 16:14-15)

  - Priscilla and Aquila (Acts 18:2ff; Romans 16:3-5)

Worship anywhere, anytime

- Mount of Olives (Luke 24:50-53; Acts 1:1-12)

- By the river (Acts 16:13)

- In prison (Acts 16:25)

- In the desert (Acts 8:28-40)

Coming prepared (Ephesians 5:19-20)

- Bring psalms, hymns and spiritual songs
  (v.19; also Colossians 3:16)

- Sing and make music in your hearts to the Lord (v.20)

- Give thanks for everything (v.20; also Philippians 4:4-7)

Proper conduct of worship

- The Lord's Supper (1 Corinthians 11:17-34)

- Orderly worship (1 Corinthians 12-14)

- Sound doctrine (Acts 6:1ff; 2 Timothy 3:16-17)

Encountering God

- A place of conversion (Acts 2)

- A place of transformation (2 Corinthians 3:17-18)

- Offering ourselves and our money (Acts 4 & 5; 2 Corinthians 8 & 9; Romans 12:1)

- Commissioning (Acts 13:2-3)

WORSHIP IN REVELATION

Revelation

'A disclosure of knowledge to humankind by a divine or supernatural agency'

(Definition from the *Reader's Digest Universal Dictionary*, The Reader's Digest Association Ltd, 1986)

• Paul caught up to a third heaven (2 Corinthians 12:2-4)

• John on Patmos (Revelation 1:9-10)

A revelation of Jesus Christ

The faithful witness, the firstborn from the dead, and the ruler of the kings of the earth, coming with the clouds ... the Alpha and the Omega. (from Revelation 1:5-8)

John describes Jesus as:

• Someone like a son of man
• Dressed in a long robe with a golden sash
• Head and hair as white as wool and as white as snow
• Eyes like blazing fire
• Feet like bronze glowing in a furnace
• A voice like the sound of rushing waters
• A sharp double-edged sword coming out of his mouth
• A face like the sun shining in all its brilliance
• The First and the Last
• The Living One
• The holder of the keys of death and Hades
  (from Revelation 1:10-16)

Later in Revelation, John uses titles like:

• The Lion of Judah (5:5)
• The Root and Offspring of David (5:5 & 22:16)
• A Lamb, looking as if it had been slain (5:6)
• Conqueror (6:2)
• Faithful and True (19:11)
• King of kings and Lord of lords (19:16)
• Bright Morning Star (22:16).

John's response (Revelation 1:17-19)

- Completely awestruck

- Touched by God

- Reassured

- Commissioned

A revelation of worship in heaven (Revelation 4, 5, and 7)

- Who is being worshipped?

- Who is participating in worship?

- What is the overall impression?

- What is our response?

Worship on earth as it is in heaven

- Vision produces passion

'Vision is a picture of the future which produces passion.'
(Bill Hybels, founding and Senior Pastor of Willowcreek Church, Chicago, USA)

Where there is no vision, the people perish.
(Proverbs 29:18, Authorised Version)

- The Lord's Prayer

Your kingdom come, Your will be done, **on earth as in heaven.**

We are invited to join in the worship of heaven ... while still on earth!

- Worship on earth is a preparation for worship in heaven (Revelation 7:9-10)

  - A great multitude that no-one can count, from every nation, tribe, people and language
  - Standing before the throne and in front of the Lamb
  - Wearing white robes
  - Holding palm branches in their hands
  - They cry out in a loud voice
  - Salvation belongs to our God ... and to the Lamb

A personal invitation from a relational God

God as community

Father, Son and Holy Spirit are all present

To him who sits on the throne and to the Lamb be praise and honour and glory and power, forever and ever! (Revelation 5:13)

The Spirit and the bride say, 'Come!' And let everyone who hears say, 'Come!' And let everyone who is thirsty come. Let everyone who wishes take the water of life as a gift. (Revelation 22:17, NRSV)

A NEW SONG IN MY MOUTH

HANDOUT 4

The Old Testament has many references to 'new songs'

Isaiah's encouragement to 'sing to the Lord a new song' (Isaiah 42:10)

- A response to God

- God has announced His intention to restore Israel to its former glory

Personal and corporate 'new songs' in Psalms

- Sing and play skilfully (Psalm 33:3)

- Sing ... and declare his glory to the nations (Psalm 96:1-2)

- Sing ... *for victory* (Psalm 98:1)

- I will sing ... and play ... *personal rescue* (Psalm 144:9)

- Sing ... His praise in the assembly of the faithful (Psalm 149:1)

A new realization of God's love prompts ...

- Praise for God's deliverance

- A move from darkness into light

- A new desire to worship God emerging from deep within

Especially Psalm 40: A psalm of David

I waited patiently for the LORD;
He turned to me and heard my cry.
He lifted me out of the slimy pit, out of the mud and mire;
He set my feet on a rock and gave me a firm place to stand.
He put a new song in my mouth,
a hymn of praise to our God.
Many will see and fear and put their trust in the LORD.
(Psalm 40:1-3)

New songs of lament

- New songs can grow out of different extremes of emotion

- People write out of their experience of life

- Sometimes it is ...

  - Where are you, Lord?
  - How long, Lord?
  - Why, Lord?

Joined in love

- We are meant to be IN Christ, connected to Him as one

- As in any love relationship, words become an inadequate means of expression

- We find a deeper level of connecting and communicating from within our soul

  - In spirit and truth (John 4:24)
  - Built up in truth and love (Ephesians 4:16)

Heavenly sounds

Then I looked, and there before me was the Lamb, standing on Mount Zion, and **with him** 144,000 who had his name and his Father's name written on their foreheads. And I heard a sound from heaven like the roar of rushing waters and like a loud peal of thunder. The sound I heard was like that of harpists playing their harps. And they sang a **new** song before the throne. (Revelation 14:1-3)

- The multitude were caught up in the heavenly praise

- They were lost in wonder...

- Their wonder and awe spilled out into song

- A corporate, concerted, spontaneous anthem of praise

- Completely unrestricted

- Way beyond the boundaries of language and structure

- Heavenly sounds

We can only imagine ...

- Now I know in part; then I shall fully know (1 Corinthians 13:12)

- God gives us glimpses of His heavenly throne

- In worship, we move a bit nearer

- When we respond during worship, we move nearer still

Why new songs?

- God's Spirit is always active

- God's Spirit is ever present

- God's Spirit releases creativity

- We respond to God by expressing our love, and indeed our pain, to give new depth to our relationship

Planned or spontaneous?

- One leads to the other

- Published new songs are a composer's expression of an encounter with God

- New songs are adopted by a congregation to become a means of corporate worship

- A tremendous vehicle for the whole congregation to express worship in new and life-giving ways

Musical improvisation (also known as musical extemporisation) speaks of ad-libbing and spontaneity.

- To compose on the spur of the moment

- To perform without prior preparation or practice

- To draw on existing creative skills

- To respond spontaneously to other musicians

- To maintain a sense of direction and flow

Musical improvisation in the context of worship

A creative response in the moment

- To God

- To the immediate environment

- To our own inner feelings

- It might include singing in tongues
  (see Acts 2:4ff and 1 Corinthians 14)

Develop flexibility

- Repeat verse, half verse, chorus, bridge, last line

- Vary the order

- Train the musicians and singers to watch and follow

- Train the congregation to be flexible and follow

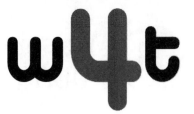

Encourage creativity

- Use significant words or phrases

- Use different names of God

- Use the Psalms

- Use rhythm as well as melody

- Use recognisable chord patterns and riffs

- Use different instruments as well as voices

- Use creative writing or art, not just musical expression

- Use spontaneous movement: gesture, posture, procession, flags, dance

Give permission to experiment freely

- Individually and corporately

- In English

- In other languages or in 'tongues'

Exercise leadership and discernment

- To create a safe worship environment

- To discern what is happening

- To be prepared for the prophetic

- To know when to stop!

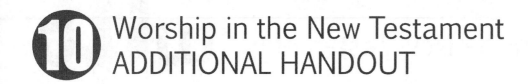

SIMPLE CHORD PATTERNS which can be transposed into any key.

1: A very simple chord extension which can be used at the end of many songs.

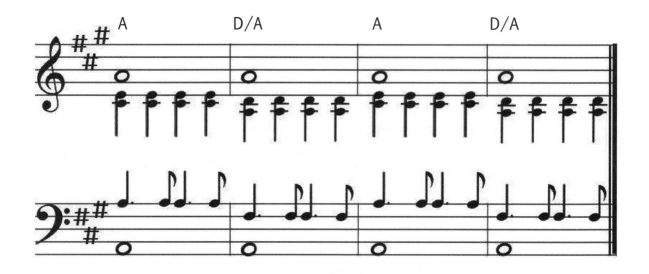

2: A chord pattern which can be gentle and plaintive or rhythmic and upbeat.

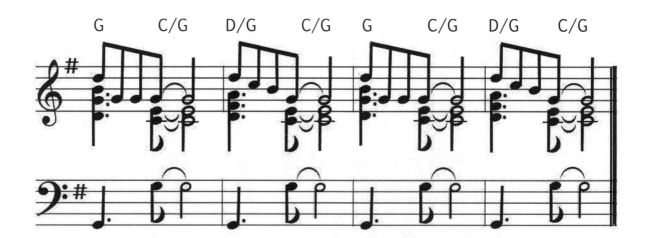

3: A simple and useful chord sequence to fill in gaps. Different repeated melodic ideas can be used and developed.

4: A chord pattern using 7ths to give the chords more interest and open up new melodic possibilities.

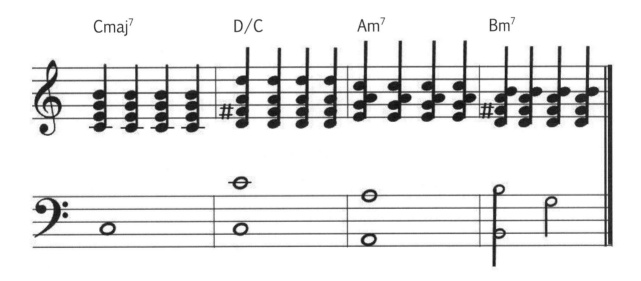

Before or after session 10

KEEP CHECK

Please make sure that you speak to each member of your small group individually either before or after the session or during the tea break.

Did everyone manage a 'link group' meeting between *Session 9* and *10?* Are they beginning to think about their review and what they have learnt during the course?

With the final deadlines rapidly approaching, check that everyone is on target for the completion of their *Personal Project*, which is due to be handed in at *Session 11*. Give plenty of encouragement and reassurance. If anyone is having real difficulties, refer them back to the course leaders.

45 mins

SMALL GROUP PRACTICAL TASK

Improvisation will be completely new to some participants whilst others will already have some experience and skill. Whatever their experience, this is an opportunity to 'have a go' and explore together.

Before you begin, make sure everyone has their resources pack and a bible, and that you have writing and drawing materials available for your group.

Encourage every member of the group to take part in some way.

Reassure them that this is a safe place to experiment and to make mistakes. Reiterate that the creative response does not necessarily have to be musical, but could take the form of creative writing, drawing or movement.

We suggest a repeat of all the material that has been demonstrated already, because this provides some concrete examples as a starting point.

Begin by trying out each of the following to build confidence:

1: Extend the end of a hymn

Suggestion: 'Praise my soul', 'Here is love' or 'In Christ alone'

2: Develop flexibility within a song repeating different parts a varied number of times and experimenting with the order.

Suggestion: 'Holy, holy, holy' *(lift up His name)*

These first two exercises need not take many minutes, but could also be missed out if deemed too basic. Be guided by the small group themselves, so that they get the most out of the time.

Then move on to

3: Use new words to an existing tune - To get everyone started, suggest everyone writes out a phrase with the right number of syllables and then encourage the group to sing each verse in turn.

Suggestion: 'O come let us adore' Him (a phrase of seven syllables with the main accents on the second and sixth syllable).

4: Use the names of God - Now encourage participants to write down the names of God that are especially meaningful to them at the moment. Using the simple Taizé chant, go round the group in turn. Encourage them to sing or speak out the names they have chosen whilst the rest of the group sing the 'O' at the beginning of the chant.

Suggestion: 'Adoramus te O Christe'

5: Use phrases from a Psalm - Encourage participants to choose a Psalm and pick out one or two meaningful phrases. Using the same chant, experiment with psalm words spoken or sung over the 'O'.

Suggestion: 'Adoramus te O Christe'

6: Free improvisation - If time permits, use *For Thou, O Lord (I exalt you)* and allow the group to take the song in whatever direction they wish using alternative words, adding an improvised instrumental melody, or developing a new rhythmic element.

WORSHIP ALL TOGETHER

20 mins

Hopefully, confidence will have been building as participants have been experimenting together in their small groups. At the end of the group time, draw everyone back into the main worship space for a final time of improvised worship together.

1: THE CHALLENGE OF ALL-AGE WORSHIP

Reflect on your own experience of all-age services, as a leader and as a participant:

- Do you have family services or all-age services at your church?
- What is the difference?
- How might we model ways to worship for children and young people?
- What can *we learn* from the worship of children and young people?

You may want to ask different people of different ages in your congregation what they think. You may want to refer back to observations about children and young people in the *Worship Audits*. Jot down any significant thoughts. This is an aid for your own memory (and will not be collected in).

2: ENABLING OUR CHILDREN AND YOUNG PEOPLE TO WORSHIP

Select a worship resource which you feel might be suitable for use with children or teenagers. It might be:

- A musical item – hymn or worship song or song sung at school
- A piece of liturgy
- A drama or piece of puppetry
- A set of intercessions
- An activity or movement
- A film clip or PowerPoint presentation
- Something else!

Come prepared to share your idea with your small group. Bring enough copies for each group member. Consider the time frame, both in your small group and within an act of worship. Items should not be too long!

3: PERSONAL PROJECT: HAND IN AT SESSION 11

Complete writing up and present in an appropriate format for your chosen topic. Please ask if you are having difficulty.

4: PORTFOLIO

Aim to keep up to date by adding to the different sections as you go along.

Remember this too will need to be handed in at the final session (Session 12). With only two months left to the submission date, try not to leave it all to the last minute!

Section 5: Make sure you plan a final church visit before the end of the course.

worship 4 today

session

The challenge of all-age worship

TEACHERS' NOTES

SESSION PROGRAMME

5 mins	**Welcome and introduction to the session** Give reminders about hand-in date for portfolios, end of course reviews and assessments
70 mins	**The challenge of all-age worship** Children and young people in worship What is all-age worship? Building up the 'Body' Meeting different needs Learn from the media and education Planning and leading
20 mins	**Tea break**
70 mins	**Planning all-age worship** Explanation of small group task Small group practical preparation for worship
30 mins	**Sharing worship with other groups**
15 mins	**Feedback all together**

LIST OF MATERIALS NEEDED

- Food and drink
- Flipchart and pens
- Laptop, data projector and screen
- Bibles
- Members' Handouts, including *Preparation Sheet* and *Church Growth Sheet* for Session 12 (we recommend this is printed on different coloured paper to distinguish it)
- All-age worship exercise, adapted from *Leading worship that connects* by John Leach (used with permission of the author). Sufficient for one each.
- For group work, each group member will be providing sufficient copies of their chosen material themselves
- Sufficient copies of *New Patterns for Worship* for one per group
- A few examples of all-age service materials for groups to refer to if they wish. We recommend resources such as copies of *Roots Magazine*, *Living Stones* by Susan Sayers or *All-Age Everything* or *Worship Words* by Nick Harding

ROOM SET-UP

Ensure there are sufficient chairs and tables where everyone can see the screen for the PowerPoint. You will also need separate rooms for small group work with sufficient chairs and, if possible, a keyboard.

The challenge of all-age worship

SESSION AIMS

- To consider how worship is shaped by being in the presence of children and young people
- To discover inclusive ways of engaging the whole congregation in meaningful worship
- To prepare a short act of all-age worship
- To share that act of worship with others

5 mins

WELCOME AND INTRODUCTION TO THE SESSION

Welcome participants and settle them quickly. As this is now the penultimate session, participants will be aware that time together is rapidly running out just when groups are really gelling and firm friendships are forming. Reassure everyone and encourage them to build on these relationships after the end of the course.

If you are intending to run the course on a rolling basis, this is a good moment to raise the issue of mentors for the following course. If participants have gained from the course, they may want to give something back in return. Becoming a mentor is a great way to do this. Mentors have the privilege of walking alongside others and sharing some of their new knowledge whilst benefiting from the whole course again without having to do any homework! During the subsequent year, mentors will develop new skills in leadership, managing small groups and pastoral care. (For more about mentors refer to Appendix 6 in *Worship4Today*, part one)

Deal with other administrative tasks swiftly, including:

- Collect in *Personal Projects*
- Give out *Preparation* and *Church Growth Sheets* for Session 12

Session 12 will take a different format as we look forward to the future beyond *Worship4Today* and share Holy Communion together.

The *Preparation Sheet* also includes some questions for reflection linked to the completion of the *Portfolio* and preparation for the *End of Course Review*.

- *Personal Portfolios:* Remind everyone that these should be completed and handed in at the final session on **(give date)**. If anyone is having difficulties at this stage, encourage them to discuss these with the course leaders.

• *End of Course Reviews*: Remind everyone that there will be an end of course review within the next few weeks. Letters will have been sent to them and to their incumbents inviting them to attend a review and giving suggested dates. It will be helpful to have a list of dates and time slots available, so appointments can be booked now.

The review will take the form of a conversation based on a series of specific questions to enable the participants to reflect on their learning and the way in which their ministry is developing. They are also invited to bring a member of their 'link group' or their 'buddy'.

Slide 2

Quickly run through the aims from slide 2.

Pray

10 mins

TABLE TALK

Slide 3

Up to this point in the course, we have basically been looking at worship from an adult point of view but before we begin to unpack all-age worship, let's spend a few minutes specifically considering children and teenagers and how they might participate in worship.

Dr Rebecca Nye, Consultant in Children's Spirituality, has looked at children's worship from a theological, psychological and educational point of view. She is responsible for introducing Berryman's Godly Play to the UK. Her research has prompted her to ask two key questions:

• How are children shaped by being in the presence of worship?

• How is worship shaped by being in the presence of children?

We could expand this further with two additional questions:

- How are teenagers shaped by being in the presence of worship?

- How is worship shaped by being in the presence of teenagers?

Allow five minutes talking time and five minutes feedback on flipchart.

10 mins

CHILDREN AND YOUNG PEOPLE IN WORSHIP

Handout 1: The challenge of all-age worship

Children in worship

Slide 4

Gone are the days when children were seen and not heard, but when it comes to church worship perhaps as adults we would rather this still be the case. If we are honest, we all prefer worship the way we like it and we have all come across those who choose to stay away on all-age service weeks! However, we would do well to hear Jesus' challenge to his disciples before we go too far down this road:

People were also bringing babies to Jesus to have him touch them. When the disciples saw this, they rebuked them. But Jesus called the children to him and said, Let the little children come to me, and do not hinder them, for the kingdom of God belongs to such as these. (Luke 18:15-17)

- Children naturally know what is important in life – Children grow up with a natural wonder which is able to embrace the mystical and supernatural in an uncomplicated manner. They can be open and highly sensitive to God's presence and have an incredible range of spiritual experiences.

- Children exercise simple faith and trust whereas as adults we tend to overcomplicate belief and like to be in control. We can learn much from children.

Jesus called a little child and had him stand among them. And he said: 'I tell you the truth, unless you change and become like little children, you will never enter the kingdom of heaven.' (Matthew 18:2-3)

- Children recognise authenticity - Children are acutely sensitive to atmosphere, attitudes and non-verbal communication. They can prove remarkably discerning when we try to fob them off. As adults we can be guilty of tokenism, cajoling them to come to the front to do a children's 'action' song or asking them to hold up visual aids rather than encouraging them to engage fully in the worship at their own level. Roger Hart's *Ladder of Young People's Participation* goes further and suggests that tokenism and involving children as convenient stagehands may actually diminish or damage them. (Hart, R. 1992, Florence: UNICEF Innocenti Research Centre)
- Children use mystery as a stimulus to learning - Children grow up not knowing what everything means. They are surrounded at home and at school by words and actions they do not yet fully understand. Mystery is an accepted part of their everyday life and acts as a stimulus to their learning. Rather than becoming suspicious or analytical, their natural curiosity encourages them to explore new things and discover more answers.

Finally, we do well to remember that when we welcome children to participate fully in worship, we welcome Jesus:

Whoever welcomes a little child like this in my name welcomes me. (Matthew 18:5)

Teenagers in worship (Luke 2:41-52)

Slide 5

If we have a problem with children, we are often even more suspicious of teenagers, especially when they hunt in packs! However, many smaller churches will only have two or three teenagers, so their specific needs can easily be overlooked.

- Teenagers look for value and identity - The teenage years are when we begin to discover who we really are for ourselves. It is an interesting fact that in most churches worship is either directed at adults or children but rarely at teenagers. This both undervalues and disempowers young people at a crucial age. A second major growth spurt takes place between the ages of eleven and thirteen, so what happens during this time will have a profound effect on the rest of life. If teenagers connect with worship at this formative age, then it is likely to become a part of who they are.

- Teenagers want to belong and be identified with a bigger group - It is difficult to be a Christian teenager alone. Peer pressure is a potent force, which can affirm or undermine. Teenagers require other Christian teenagers in order to feel relaxed and be full-on with God. They are reassured and empowered by worshipping with others of a similar age; some may feel inhibited by worshipping with their parents. They may look for a style of worship arising out of their own culture, which does not fit comfortably with the rest of the church.

- Teenagers learn through questioning, exploration and discussion - Jesus was just approaching his teenage years when he famously stayed behind in Jerusalem after his parents had left without him.

After three days they found him in the temple courts, sitting among the teachers, listening to them and asking them questions. Everyone who heard him was amazed at his understanding and his answers. (Luke 2:46-47)

Teenagers do not learn passively, even though they may give the impression of being permanently half asleep, bored and unenthusiastic! They are able to reason for themselves, ask perceptive questions, and discuss life-changing issues. This creative interaction can produce some surprising results and genuine deep insights. They may want to plan their own worship in their own way, and discover how to worship for themselves.

- Teenagers begin to take responsibility - This is good for them and allows them to grow and mature, whether it is playing or singing in the music group or choir, becoming a server or helping with the technical stuff of sound desks and data projection. Teenagers frequently develop a strong concern for moral issues and justice, so sometimes we may need to let them have their head and share their passion with us. We also need to let them learn from their own mistakes. Our goal is to see them growing in wisdom and stature like Jesus during his teenage years. (Luke 2:52)

10 mins

WHAT IS ALL-AGE WORSHIP?

Slide 6

Basically what it says! It is worship that includes people of any age. Many churches will designate one particular service a month for all-

age worship but in reality the majority of services will have a portion of time, either at the beginning or during Holy Communion, when all the different ages are present together. To this extent, every service can be considered all-age. What we are trying to avoid is an adult service with a token children's slot, a wholly child-oriented service or, at worst, a service which satisfies no-one.

Together or segregated?

Slide 7

This is a good first question to ask, and there are pros and cons for both. We are ...

- All pilgrims on a journey whatever our age. Remember back to the big Jewish festivals. The whole people of God went up to Jerusalem together. We too are all in this together and so we need time and opportunity to worship together to forge relationships with God and with one another. As adults we model worship for our children and teenagers, but they in turn model worship for us. We learn different aspects from each age group.

However, we are also ...

- All disciples who need to learn in appropriate ways - Sometimes segregation into specific age groups will be helpful so that we can all receive teaching at an appropriate level. Sometimes it will be better for teenagers in particular to worship separately so that they can experiment freely and work things out for themselves.

Family service or all-age worship?

Slide 8

In the past, a family service was seen as the answer but what is the difference between a family service and an all-age service? We asked this question as part of the homework, so everyone should already have some thoughts.

Share BRIEFLY with one another in pairs.

Share any significant thoughts.

- Inclusive or exclusive? In today's fragmented society, 'family service' is no longer a helpful term. With many widows, divorcees, single parents, co-habiting couples and other singles in our congregations, the idea of *family* can easily alienate or exclude those to whom we want to minister. All-age is morally neutral as a term.

  We need to remember what we said about indigenous worship in *Session 7*. To be fully inclusive, not only do we need to understand our biblical heritage and our present culture, we also need to understand the background history and cultural roots of a particular congregation. All-age worship at its best will be indigenous with authentic participation from every age group.

- Worship or entertainment? We can spend a lot of time keeping children entertained and out of mischief rather than developing them as worshippers and disciples. How often do we give out flags or percussion instruments during certain songs without any instruction simply to keep the children occupied and happy?

  There is a fine dividing line between worship and entertainment. Obviously we come to a service primarily to meet with God but if we do not enjoy or benefit from the experience in some way, we are unlikely to keep returning.

- Lowest common denominator? In a family service, we have tended to fall into the trap of aiming the service almost exclusively at the children. This has some advantages: the service is generally shorter; we tend to concentrate on one primary theme; some adults, particularly visitors and enquirers, warm to the simplicity and clarity but again there is a fine dividing line between simplicity and an unhelpful watering down of the content which becomes patronising.

  It is also worth considering from a mission point of view whether a pattern of once a month for all-age is helpful. Does this pattern hinder newcomers from attending services regularly? There may be such a marked contrast in style between the all-age service, which they find enjoyable and easy to understand, and the regular service structure for the rest of the month, which is less accessible, that it therefore puts them off.

All-age 'worth-ship'

Slide 9

We talked about 'worth-ship' in our very first session. Worship is about giving God reverent love, honour and respect because He is worth it.

- Giving God His worth whatever our age - Children learn by copying. If they see older children and adults fully engaged in honouring and worshipping God, they will learn to do the same. Children are also a means of grace for us. They can remind us of things we have lost as we have grown older: simple trust; openness to wonder; eagerness to embrace the new; transparency; freedom of expression without inhibitions.

- Fixing the attention of everyone on God – All-age worship should help everyone focus on God. Too often our focus is on the children or young people 'doing their turn'. Chris and John Leach point out that inviting children up front to 'perform' can be patronising and can become increasingly embarrassing as they approach adolescence. It can detract from any sense of worship. (See *How to plan and lead all-age worship*, Grove Worship Series, 2008, p.19)

- 'Proskuneo' (John 4:21-24) - meaning to come towards or to greet or welcome with profound respect. We talked about this last session. The woman at the well had been focusing her attention on worshipping in a particular place. Jesus re-focused her attention on worshipping someone she could know personally. However, in the context of a service, this coming towards and welcoming Jesus is corporate. In all-age worship it is easy to focus our attention on the different style rather than focusing on our relationship with God. Our main purpose is giving him honour and getting to know Him better – together.

Building up the 'Body'

Slide 10

Some people love all-age; some hate it! In a consumer society where we all want things to suit us, all-age worship is counter-cultural. It requires a spirit of generosity which comes to give and comes to encourage and build up others. Throughout the course, we have kept coming back to this idea of worship as sacrifice and coming to give God our very best whatever the style or context of worship. We also 'speak (or sing) to one another with psalms, hymns and spiritual songs' in an attitude of thankfulness (Ephesians 5:19-20), which blesses God and blesses the rest of the gathered congregation.

- Every part of the body counts (1 Corinthians 12) - We touched on 1 Corinthians 12-14 in the last session, but let us consider these verses for a moment in the context of all-age worship. All-age means that every age is important without exception. Therefore ...

The eye cannot say to the hand, I don't need you! And the head cannot say to the feet, I don't need you! On the contrary, those parts of the body that seem to be weaker are indispensable.
(1 Corinthians 12:21-22)

In the same way we cannot say to the children we don't need them, or to the teenagers we don't need them either! If we minimize their contribution to our worship, then we too become diminished. We know they are equally loved and valued in God's eyes but somehow that knowledge does not always carry through into the way we treat them in worship. Children and young people should be able to give and receive in worship just as much as the adults but we may inadvertently make this difficult. It is so easy to criticize their approach, even though genuine, and to overlook or dismiss issues which are of great significance to them. For example, do we offer prayer to an old lady for her arthritic hips and yet forget to pray for a six year old child's grazed knees? Or do we pray for a marriage which is struggling but fail to take seriously the teenager hurting from a first broken relationship?

- Loving one another (1 Corinthians 13) - We want to build an all-age congregation which is based on mutual love and respect for every age. Perhaps Paul's famous passage about love comes in the context of worship, because he knew we would find love surprisingly difficult in this particular context. We are reminded of the two great commands to love at the beginning of the Holy Communion service: we love God first and our neighbour second, beginning at that moment with the rest of the gathered congregation. If we come to all-age worship valuing every part of the body and ready to give in love, the complaints will cease and we will discover the truth of Peter's advice in his practical pastoral letter to the Church.

Above all, love each other deeply, because love covers over a multitude of sins. (1 Peter 4:8)

- Encouraging all (1 Corinthians 14; Ephesians 4:12) - Early on in the course, we discovered that liturgy literally meant 'the work of the people' for the people; i.e. for the common good of everyone whether young or old, believers or not. During worship, God's people are …

… prepared for works of service, so that the body of Christ may be built up. (Ephesians 4:12)

Children and teenagers are nurtured in their faith, but so too are unbelievers. According to Paul, authentic worship should also make an impact on them, so that they …

… will fall down and worship God, exclaiming, God is really among you! (1 Corinthians 14:25)

All-age can provide a stepping stone towards fresh expressions of church. Not only do different ages worship in different ways, different personality types also respond in a variety of ways. Some personality types will never darken the doors of the church; worship does not scratch where they itch! This is an ongoing challenge which we will pick up in our final session.

- Creating an atmosphere of thankfulness - Worship is no place for selfishness and criticism, which undermines all that we are and do. Paul encourages us to …

Rejoice in the Lord always … Do not be anxious about anything, but in everything, by prayer and petition, **with thanksgiving,** present your requests to God … whatever is true, whatever is noble, whatever is right, whatever is pure, whatever is lovely, whatever is admirable - if anything is excellent or praiseworthy - think about such things. (Philippians 4:4, 6, 8)

If a loving heart covers over a multitude of sins, a thankful heart really lifts the spirits and helps us to appreciate our many blessings. This in turn encourages wholesome thoughts and brings peace to the gathered congregation:

And the peace of God, which transcends all understanding, will guard your hearts and your minds in Christ Jesus. (Philippians 4:7)

If we encourage this attitude of love, generosity, and thankfulness, we will go a long way to meeting the needs of the various different age groups.

20 mins

MEETING DIFFERENT NEEDS EXERCISE

Slide 11

Additional handout: All-age worship grid

(This chart is adapted from one that first appeared in *Leading worship that connects* by John Leach, Anglican Renewal Ministries, 1999, and later in the aforementioned *How to plan and lead all-age worship*. It is reproduced here with permission)

To save time, allocate different parts of the grid per table. The grid can either be divided into age brackets or into the four categories of need. Participants may also want to think about the adults in two separate age groups: 20-45; 45-65.

Allow around ten minutes for discussion on the tables and then take ten minutes feedback, gradually filling in the whole grid by going round each table in turn.

10 mins

PLANNING AND LEADING ALL-AGE WORSHIP

Slide 12

We live in a hi-tech, visual world of sound bites, web cams and *Skype*. Television programmes are full of fast moving images. When we want to find something out, we 'google' it and read up on Wikipedia. When we forget to record a favourite television programme, we log on to *iPlayer* to catch up. The world is literally at our fingertips and we can view almost anywhere around the globe via satellite with *Google Earth*. This is what we are used to now, so what can we learn when it comes to planning worship and how can we use these resources to our advantage?

Learn from the media and education

Handout 2: Planning and leading all-age worship

Learn from the media

Slide 13

- Keep a clear basic theme or story line – Underlying many programmes, there is a simple theme or basic story line whether it is good versus evil or boy meets girl. Our chief aim within a service is to communicate one central idea clearly, so that the congregation will engage with it and remember it, whatever their age. And as we have already said, simpler more accessible styles can provide an easy way in for visitors and seekers.

- Use sound bites – A sound bite is a very short piece from something longer, which acts as an appetite-whetter. This approach holds our attention and leaves us wanting to find out more. Why not video activities and show them on the screen as they happen, or use them at the beginning of the next all-age service? Everyone loves to see themselves!

- 'We don't have to understand everything' – If we do, things can become banal or boring. We can all enjoy programmes like *Top Gear* or *Countryfile* without necessarily being experts on cars or nature. We start where we are and build on the knowledge we already possess. In the same way, curiosity and exploration will encourage us all to discover new things about God. Worship will foster discipleship.

- Engage with different people on different levels – Classics like *The Chronicles of Narnia* and *The Lord of the Rings* can be enjoyed by all ages because they work on different levels. As we grow older, we learn to appreciate the allegory and underlying Christian message that we missed as children. Films like *Bruce Almighty* and *Evan Almighty* provide great family entertainment but again children will completely miss some of the subtleties. There are clear biblical references here and some of the theological insights are profound.

- Finish on a cliff hanger – Writers always leave their audience wanting more. The hero or heroine may be left in a desperate situation; a shock revelation or a new clue to a mystery may be revealed just before the chapter or programme ends. The technique ensures that we read on to the next chapter or switch on for the next episode. The scriptures are full of such stories with the events of Good Friday providing us with the greatest cliff hanger of all time.

 Use modern learning techniques

Slide 14

Current thinking in education recognises that we all learn in different ways. During a service, the congregation will not only engage with God directly but they will also learn about God and about their faith. Therefore, it will be helpful to adopt multiple learning styles within worship.

- **Something to hear** - Auditory learning includes teaching, explaining and storytelling. In years gone by, we have been used to listening to one service leader or preacher at the front. Nowadays, this leadership may be shared by ordained and lay people, giving a variation in voice and approach. However, the educationalists have discovered that listening on its own is not necessarily the most effective way to learn. We can easily lose concentration and become detached from what is happening;

- **Something to see** - We live in a visual age, so we are used to computer images, television and film. In worship, we can play video clips and add images on PowerPoint ranging from old masters to current photographs, as well as putting song words and key points or illustrations from the sermon on the screen. If we combine hearing with seeing, our concentration improves and our learning retention increases. However, unless we choose visual images with care, these may diminish our own imagination and ability to engage with God creatively.

  Demonstration is another important facet of the visual, so sight of the choir or music group giving their all in worship will model worship for others in the congregation.

- **Something to do** - Known as kinaesthetic learning, we collaborate and actively participate in the learning process. This 'inquiry' learning by doing enables us to explore and discover by becoming fully involved in the action. At its simplest level, this might include holding a pebble, lighting a candle, writing a prayer request on a post-it, or physically moving from one part of the church building to another for certain parts of the service. *Messy Church* and many other fresh expressions of church are exploring this activity based worship further.

Research suggests that men learn better by doing, so we may need to take a hard look at our worship style in order to attract more men into the congregation.

- **Something to say** - Singing hymns and songs or saying liturgy and verses of scripture out loud enables us to take in words and commit them to memory. Articulating our thoughts and reflecting back what we have heard helps us to understand and remember. Opportunities to discuss and develop sermon points or share scriptures and prayers enables us to offer our contribution to worship rather than merely having worship done for us. What we have learnt becomes a part of us and shapes us.

We *experience* worship, and that experience makes an impact on us in different ways. As service leaders, we want that experience to be inspiring and rich, so we will do well to incorporate all these different learning styles when appropriate.

Use teamwork

Slide 15

We have already discussed the importance of teamwork in *Session 4* and *Session 8*, so we will not take up too much time here. However, it is worth remembering that we come to the team at a particular age ourselves. It may be difficult to see things from other perspectives unless there is a good age range in the team.

- **Two heads are better than one!** Working in a team aids creativity as we pray together and bounce around ideas. There is also a level of accountability. Everyone is familiar with the building and the local congregation so we can challenge ideas that are not suitable or might not work in this location.

- **Encourage and develop others** - All-age worship requires quite different skills from other styles of worship. Preparation can be time and resources hungry so this may be a good way of involving fringe members with specific gifts. Use the opportunity to draw them in to prepare resources or activities and share the load more widely.

- **Recognise gifts and skills** and choose the best. The usual service leaders may not be great at all-age services, although they can learn and improve. However, one or two - often lay people - will

stand out from the rest as particularly gifted at preparing and leading this style of service.

- Model the Body of Christ - Christians working together in a team can naturally model what it means to be the Body of Christ here on earth. And people notice!

- Include children and teenagers - We so often leave all the planning to the adults, thus making assumptions about what children and young people will find helpful and enjoy. Why not include children and teenagers as part of the planning team, perhaps taking it in turns? We really do need to learn to listen to our kids. They have a voice! We may be surprised by the depth of their spiritual insights and the quality of their contributions, and in time we may discover hidden talent.

Planning and leading

Plan ahead

10 mins

Slide 16

We have touched on much of this material already, so use it to consolidate and reinforce. Rather than going through the material point by point, it may be more constructive to initiate some discussion and use the points to summarise or fill in any gaps.

- Lectionary or themed series? Both of these can work well. Ideally we want to have a long term plan and sense of overall direction, which will promote and nurture a growth in the faith and discipleship of every age group.

- Collect resources - When inspiration strikes, jot it down and then collect the necessary resources. If we need twenty egg boxes for an activity or a hundred cardboard hearts for the prayers, we cannot leave it until the last minute.

- Clearly define roles and responsibilities - Make sure everybody knows who is doing what and is happy with it. Good communication is vital for supportive teamwork. Uncertainty can waste time and either duplicate or leave some tasks undone.

- Leave sufficient time to practise - The use of drama, dance or new music all requires forward planning. To be fair to others, allow adequate rehearsal time - ideally several weeks - for everyone to prepare thoroughly.

Create an atmosphere

Slide 17

We can all sense atmospheres, and some are more comfortable than others! Ask anyone why they like the Christmas carol service and they will almost certainly mention the atmosphere created by subdued flickering light and the waxy smell of candles. Atmosphere and appearance often speak volumes. So can a building.

* Change the venue - Worship does not always have to be in church or even indoors. All-age may work better in the church hall or the local school hall, where there is space and flexible seating rather than being restricted by pews and poor sight lines. Ask: are we doing this in the most effective space at the most effective time? And what about occasionally worshipping outside?

* Change the interior - Why not worship in the round, or café style at small tables? Coloured light bulbs or drapes can be very effective. For example, when our Indian mission partners came to visit, we hung vivid coloured saris from the roof beams and over the windows to create a vibrant display of colour all round the church. This all took time and ingenuity but it was well worth the effort and created a very different atmosphere for the service.

* Change the music - Whether we walk into church to organ music, contemporary worship songs, classical or contemporary music on CD or silence, each will create its own distinct atmosphere.

* Involve the congregation - This is a good ploy to raise expectation and encourage people to prepare for worship beforehand. For example, we might ask everyone to wear something red at Pentecost or to bring a particular object.

Use a simple structure

Slide 18

- *Common Worship* Service of the Word provides a flexible, liturgical framework, which is legal! The outline structure allows for creativity whilst making sure we do not miss out anything vital.

- Keep it short! We cannot emphasise this point enough. Time so often runs away with us. Psychologically it is much better to leave a congregation wishing the service had gone on longer than wondering when it is going to finish. Remember, with a book at least we know when we have reached the last page, but with everything on data projector people have no idea how much longer we have to go.

- Keep it simple! Can we describe what we are trying to do in one sentence? Keep the main theme or aim in view at all times when selecting material. Make every element count. We should keep asking ourselves: will this add or detract?

- Check the flow and try to get a good balance within each service. Where are the high points? Have we included some moments of stillness and reflection? What sort of balance is there between words, music and activity? We are taking people on a journey, leading them into worship and then sending them back out into the world.

Welcome well

Slide 19

What do people think when they first walk into church? We must ask ourselves this question honestly.

- First impressions matter - Newcomers can feel like a fish out of water, so if we are hoping to attract visitors to our all-age service we will need to get this right. Why not help visitors relax on arrival by serving a simple continental breakfast before the service rather than coffee afterwards? Many young families start their Sunday shopping with breakfast out and time to chat or read the paper, so this practical change can help them feel more at home.

- Only essential notices - What is it about church and notices? We can usually narrow the real essentials down to what we all need for the service and the location of the toilets! There is no need to repeat everything on the notice sheet. These could be scrolled through on a PowerPoint before and after the service.

- Permission giving - Begin by introducing yourself if there are newcomers, telling them roughly what to expect and how long it will take. We want everyone to feel as comfortable and secure as possible. Encourage people to join in but also give them permission not to if they don't feel able. We want to promote an authenticity that enables everyone to join in with what they can with integrity and does not alienate them by making them feel conspicuous or put on the spot.

Listen to and learn from one another

Slide 20

- Get to know names - This is incredibly important, because it values us for who we are and helps us to belong. In many churches, there will be an elderly person who has been there for years and yet nobody can remember their name. At the other end of the spectrum, we all remember the bright children and the naughty ones, but there are also the shy, quiet ones who can so easily get overlooked.

- Deliberate involvement of all ages - All-age services provide a great opportunity to invite children and young people to act as welcomers alongside the adults, to act as servers or acolytes, or to come and join the music group and build on musical skills they are already learning at school. This deliberate intention to include and train children and young people then forms a natural stepping stone to integrating young people into the PCC and the decision making of the church. The elderly are often great conversationalists and love to reminisce. They have a lifetime of stories to tell. The elderly may be less active and mobile, but can often develop a real rapport with the young, giving time to listen to their hopes and fears.

- Honour every age group - Worship together which involves activity, discussion and prayer in mixed groups can be illuminating. Adults are encouraged to listen carefully to what children and teenagers have to say and receive their spiritual insights. Children and teenagers are exposed to the Christian experience, wisdom and knowledge of the adults. Together we build mutual respect that values and honours every age group equally.

 Liturgy

Slide 21

This can be a helpful tool, so do not be tempted to throw the baby out with the bath water!

- **Creatures of habit** - We are all creatures of habit, doing certain things in certain ways, day in day out. Elderly people and small children in particular do not like their routine upset, so we need to take this into account in our planning.

- **The three Rs - rhythm, routine, repetition** - Creativity is good but we do not need to reinvent the wheel every time. Every small child has their favourite stories, which they want to hear over and over again without tiring of them. Rhythm and routine bring security and comfort through expectation and predictability. Repetition develops familiarity and enables scriptures and prayers to become a part of us.

- **Learning by heart** - As we repeat familiar liturgy, simple responses and scripture verses, we gradually learn them off by heart. These help to shape our faith now but they will also sustain us in times to come when we face difficulties or can no longer get to church. In the past, congregations would learn the psalms and weekly collects off by heart, together with key texts like the Creed and Lord's Prayer. Nowadays too much variety can make this difficult. This begs the question: what will sustain the coming generations, if we have so much variation that we never learn anything by heart? *Common Worship Rites on the Way* endeavours to address this important issue by highlighting four essential texts which shape our faith. These texts are: Jesus' Summary of the Law; The Lord's Prayer; The Apostles' Creed; and The Beatitudes (*Rites on the Way* can be found in *Common Worship Initiation Services*).

Music

Slide 22

Coming to church can be a huge culture shock, especially if we expect visitors to sing! We need to choose the music with great care.

Although karaoke and television programmes like *The X-Factor*, *Britain's Got Talent* and *The Choir* have helped, we do not take part in communal singing as we once did.

- **Easily singable** - Much of the contemporary worship music most loved by our teens is not designed for congregational use in the traditional sense. It is led from the front by a band with a lead singer, often male, making it too high and too complex for the average congregation.

- **Familiar tunes help** - Or at least good, strong melodies which are easy to pick up and which are well within the vocal range of the congregation.

- **Hymns and songs with refrains** give people something to catch on to quickly even if they just listen to the words during the verses.

- **Action songs** can be effective but increasingly cause embarrassment to everyone whatever their age. Sign language can be a 'cool' alternative, because the actions not only mean something but they add a new dimension to the worship.

- **Secular songs** can be effective in the right context. 'Any Dream Will Do' from the musical *Joseph and His Technicolour Dreamcoat* can be used as part of the Joseph story but it could also introduce a service about vision or a New Year commitment service. Or what about Westlife's 'You Raise Me Up' for a service linked to resurrection, walking on water or God's presence with us in difficulties and distress?

- **Music to listen to** - People outside church are not generally used to communal singing and are often self-conscious, especially if they think others will hear. However, they are used to doing a range of activities from study to shopping accompanied by canned background music. We can introduce music to worship in many creative ways other than singing: to give space for reflection and prayer, or to illustrate a sermon point. We can also reclaim the power of music to minister and restore by focused listening rather than it passing us by almost unnoticed.

Prayers

Slide 23

- **Litanies** - This type of prayer follows a repeated formula of petition followed by a short bidding and response. Simple

memorable responses enable everyone to join in, including the less literate, those with learning difficulties and asylum seekers, who speak little English. Include visuals on the screen as well and we may enable everyone to say 'Amen'.

- Use silence - We underestimate the power of silence, especially in all-age services. We wrongly assume that the children will not handle it. However, in our experience, it is often the adults who struggle more to remain still. Children have times of quiet at school and they are great at playing games like 'dead lions' and 'wink murder'. Adults live in a busy, noisy world with few moments of quiet solitude. As a result, they may find silence uncomfortable. Prepare people for silence and give some indication of how long it will last but do not avoid it. It is a powerful tool. Remember after the frenzied activity of earthquake, wind and fire, God eventually spoke to Elijah out of 'a sound of sheer silence.' (1 Kings 19:12, NRSV)

- 'Doing' prayers - We have already mentioned simple ideas such as holding a pebble, lighting a candle or writing a prayer but this could extend to the use of several prayer stations at different points round the building. This can prove a great way of introducing newcomers to the idea of prayer and enable them to participate easily without embarrassment.

Enjoy!

Slide 24

In our very first session, we learned that ...

'Our chief end is to glorify God and enjoy Him forever.'
(Westminster Shorter Catechism)

- Have fun together - We can enjoy worshipping in God's presence with others without being irreverent. If worship is relaxed and enjoyable, people will want to come back.

- Inspiration to transformation - When we encounter the living God in worship, whatever form that worship might take, we are inspired and spurred on in our faith. When Moses went up the mountain and spent time with God, his face shone and had to be covered with a veil. We too, whatever our age, are in the process of being changed from one degree of glory to another (2 Corinthians 3:18).

Review

Slide 25

It is vital to review all-age services as we go along to keep them vibrant and prevent them growing stale. We can use the worship audit principle to help us ask the right questions at regular intervals.

- **Get feedback** - Ask a good mix of people for feedback, including the children and teenagers. Then evaluate honestly. Good questions to ask might be: Is every age group engaging with God at least some of the time? Are these services meeting the needs of every age group? Is any age group being marginalised?

- **Learn from successes** - A good idea, new song, creative way of praying that worked well, will all be worth repeating in the future. Be discerning about the timing. A new song may need to be used in several services in a row to get it well known, whereas we may want to wait twelve months or more before repeating an activity;

- **Learn from mistakes** - Mistakes can be embarrassing or humiliating for us and for others. They are nearly always painful but they give us a platform to model humility, apology and forgiveness. Mistakes are often the most fertile learning ground for us as leaders, because they force us to reflect and evaluate thoroughly. When everything is going well, it is all too easy to go with the flow and to forget to review.

Vision for the future

Slide 26

Without vision, we will find it difficult to move a service forward or develop it in a new direction. As we plan ahead, we need to keep three areas in mind:

- **Coming to faith** - All-age services can form a good access point for visitors and enquirers, so we need to include opportunities within the worship for decision and commitment on a regular basis.

- Nurture - Just as our children and young people need to be nurtured and encouraged on their way, those new to faith will also need ongoing nurture and encouragement on their Christian journey. We need to include some of the basic building blocks as we go along.

- Discipleship and growth - As we said at the beginning of this session, we are all in this together, all learning to follow Jesus, all in the process of becoming disciples. We are different ages, different personalities and at different stages in our walk with God. During worship we learn and grow together but then we are sent back out into the world to make more disciples. We will be exploring this missional aspect of worship in our final *Worship4Today* session.

Don't forget to ask if there are any further questions.

20 mins

TEA BREAK

10 mins

KISS THE CONGREGATION!

Or to put it another way, Keep It Short and Simple!

A kiss implies welcome, greeting, loving relationship and mutual care. These are all things we want to see embodied in all-age worship. As we learnt in *Session 10*, a kiss (on the hands or feet in reverence) is also implied in the Greek word 'proskuneo' as we come towards God in worship.

Handout 3: Kiss the congregation!

Today's task is designed to channel enthusiasm and make sure we don't use all our best ideas at once. We also want to take into consideration the different needs of our all-age congregation.

Draw on past experience

We don't prepare worship in a vacuum.

- Positives and negatives - We all come to this task with some previous experience whether as leaders of all-age services or as part of the congregation. In the planning, consider what has

worked well in our own church contexts and why. Good ideas are worth repeating. Not all our experiences may be so positive but we can still learn from our mistakes and the mistakes of others. Be honest and discerning about pet hates. They may not all be bad ideas just because we don't like them.

- Build on previous sessions - Think back to planning the Christmas task in *Session 4*. Timing was of the essence to keep the service from over-running. We also learnt about the importance of teamwork and playing to people's strengths as well as using the occasion as an opportunity to involve new people. In *Session 7*, we thought about putting ourselves in the place of the congregation and mentally 'living' the service as it progressed. How might this be extended to consider the needs of each age group?

- Put new teaching into practice - Think particularly about the media and current thinking in education. How might this change the shape of our worship together?

Choose material carefully

- Choose the right starting point - We frequently have either too many bright ideas or none at all. This is a time to benefit from teamwork. As we bounce around ideas, new inspiration strikes. However, we can then easily end up with far too much material. Isolate one key theme or aim for the service and begin there.

- Gimmicks and jokes can be great but they should not be our starting point. We cannot plan a whole service around the latest gimmick or joke. These may excite us or make us laugh but there is no guarantee that others will respond in the same way. At best gimmicks and jokes may complement, expand and illustrate. At worst they may fall flat, be totally irrelevant and distract. As we said earlier, there is a thin dividing line between worship and entertainment.

- Roller coaster ride or smooth journey - In an all-age service, this may be a physical issue as much as an emotional one. If we include creative, activity-based elements within a service, how do we move smoothly from one element to another without them jarring? What can we use as links between elements to ensure a clear direction and a smooth flow? Emotionally, how might we maintain a balance between engaging with an activity or with one another and engaging with God?

Deal realistically with practicalities

- Space - It is great to introduce creativity which utilises the church building to the full but is there enough room for the numbers of people involved? Have we allowed sufficient time for them all to move about? Will anyone feel excluded because movement is difficult? This could apply to a young mum with a child in a pushchair as much as an elderly person with limited mobility.

- Time of day - What worked really well on a dark afternoon in winter may not work at all on a sunny morning in summer.

- Drama is another great way to involve people of all ages, but it requires organisation. Have we allowed enough time for the required number of rehearsals? Will the congregation be able to hear children's voices? This is a common complaint even in these days of hand-held radio microphones.

- Visuals - Can everybody see? The visuals may be fantastic but if two thirds of the congregation cannot actually see them, someone's artistic talent and effort will be wasted. The congregation may even lose interest and disengage.

- Technology - We may be used to using PowerPoint regularly for worship but film clips may require extra cables for the sound track. The sound track also needs to be loud enough. All technology must be tried and tested well in advance. If the technology fails, do we have a plan B?

Health and safety!

Health and safety may be the bane of our present culture but we do need to think about this in the context of all-age worship, especially if people are moving about the building.

Consider any potential hazards:

- Trailing electric cables – fasten down properly;
- Other trip hazards – mark steps with white edges;
- Disabled access for wheelchairs or pushchairs;
- Candles – stand on a glass/metal base or in sand;
- Paint and glue – provide appropriate cleansing wipes;
- Food stuffs – check for anyone with food allergies;
- Any others?

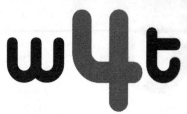

EXPLANATION OF SMALL GROUP TASK

As before, we now have the opportunity to put the theory into practice.

The task

- A ten minute cameo of an all-age service – The ten minute section could be from the beginning, the middle or the end of a service. This can be made clear at the beginning before it is shared with the other groups.

- A typical church context – Imagine a fairly typical small to medium-sized congregation. There are a few families with children ranging from babies and toddlers through the primary years. At present, there are three teenagers, two boys and one girl. Numbers of children and young people can easily fluctuate between two or three and fifteen on any given week.

In this session's task ...

- Consider the needs of all age groups in relation to the given church scenario. Use the results of the exercise on meeting needs to help with the planning.

- 55 minutes to plan, so groups will need to work quickly and efficiently. Share everyone's contribution first before considering how they might fit together. What can be used today? What will need to be left aside for another time? Keep an eye on the timing of items, being realistic about the time it takes to involve a congregation in something interactive especially if it involves them moving round the building.

The tools

- Everyone's contribution
- Possibly inappropriate material
- A copy of *New Patterns for Worship*

Have a few extra resources available if groups are floundering or need to fill in some small gaps.

60 mins

SMALL GROUPS with mentors in separate worship spaces.

30 mins

SHARING WORSHIP

As before, visit groups in their own location rather than moving instruments back to a central space.

Encourage everyone to fully participate in the worship.

15 mins

FEEDBACK ALL TOGETHER

Take each group in turn and invite positive feedback. Encourage and build up as much as possible. Focus on issues of suitability of material for all-age and how the needs of every age have been addressed.

Reflect back on the experience

- How were the needs of each age group met?
  - What was easy and straightforward?
  - What proved more difficult?
- What would they do differently another time?
- Who seems particularly gifted at *planning* this type of service?
- Who seems particularly gifted at *leading* this type of service?
- Was there any other material that participants brought that is worth a particular mention? Why did they decide not to use it?

Encourage everyone to continue to reflect on the experience:

- How did you personally respond to this task?
- What was the most helpful/exciting aspect?
- What was the most difficult/distracting aspect?
- What have you learned from the experience?

CLOSING PRAYER

Draw everyone back together for a final prayer to close the session; and give a brief reminder of the preparation for the next session: *Worship in a mission context.*

worship4today

Worship in a mission context **12**

Slide 27

185

worship4today

session

The challenge of all-age worship

CHILDREN AND YOUNG PEOPLE IN WORSHIP

HANDOUT 1

Some important questions to ask

- How are children shaped by being in the presence of worship?

- How is worship shaped by being in the presence of children?

- How are teenagers shaped by being in the presence of worship?

- How is worship shaped by being in the presence of teenagers?

Children in worship (Luke 18:15-17; Matthew 18:2-5)

- Naturally know what is important

- Exercise simple faith and trust

- Recognise authenticity

- Use mystery as a stimulus to learning

Whoever welcomes a child welcomes Jesus.

Teenagers in worship (Luke 2:41-52)

- Look for value and identity

- Want to belong and be identified with a bigger group

- Learn through questioning, exploration and discussion

- Begin to take responsibility

Grow in wisdom and stature like Jesus.

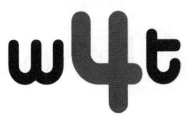

WHAT IS ALL-AGE WORSHIP?

Together or segregated?

- All pilgrims on a journey

- All disciples who need to learn in appropriate ways

Family service or all-age worship?

- Inclusive or exclusive?

- Worship or entertainment?

- Lowest common denominator?

All-age 'worth-ship'

- Giving God His worth whatever our age

- Fixing the attention of everyone on God

- 'Proskuneo' (John 4:21-24)

Building up the 'Body'

- Every part of the body counts (1 Corinthians 12)

- Loving one another (1 Corinthians 13)

- Encouraging all (1 Corinthians 14; Ephesians 4:12)

- Creating an atmosphere of thankfulness (Philippians 4:4-9)

PLANNING AND LEADING ALL AGE WORSHIP

Learn from the media and education

Learn from the media

- Keep a clear basic theme or story line

- Use sound bites

- 'We don't have to understand everything'

- Engage with different people on different levels

- Finish on a cliff hanger

Use modern learning techniques

- Something to hear

- Something to see

- Something to do

- Something to say

Use teamwork

- Two heads are better than one!

- Encourage and develop others

- Recognise gifts and skills

- Model the Body of Christ

- Include children and teenagers

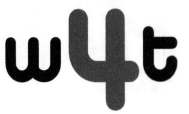

Planning and leading

Plan ahead

- Lectionary or themed series?

- Collect resources

- Clearly define roles and responsibilities

- Leave sufficient time to practise

Create atmosphere

- Change the venue

- Change the interior

- Change the music

- Involve the congregation

Use a simple structure

- *Common Worship* 'Service of the Word'

- Keep it short!

- Keep it simple!

- Check the flow

Welcome well

- First impressions matter

- Only essential notices

- Permission giving

Listen to and learn from one another

- Get to know names

- Deliberate involvement of all ages

- Honour every age group

Liturgy

- Creatures of habit

- The three Rs - rhythm, routine, repetition

- Learning by heart

Music

- Easily singable

- Familiar tunes

- Hymns and songs with refrains

- Action songs - but exercise caution

- Secular songs

- Music to listen to

Prayers

- Litanies

- Use silence

- 'Doing' prayers

Enjoy!

- Have fun together

- Inspiration to transformation

Review

- Get feedback

- Learn from successes

- Learn from mistakes

Vision for the future

- Coming to faith

- Nurture

- Discipleship and growth

KISS THE CONGREGATION!

Or to put it another way,
Keep **I**t **S**hort and **S**imple!

Draw on past experience

- Positives and negatives

- Build on previous sessions

- Put new teaching into practice

Choose material carefully

- Choose the right starting point

- Gimmicks and jokes

- Roller coaster ride or smooth journey

Deal realistically with practicalities

- Space

- Time of day

- Drama

- Visuals

- Technology

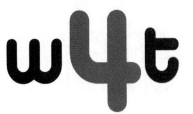

Health and safety!

Consider any potential hazards:

- Trailing electric cables - fasten down properly

- Other trip hazards - mark steps with white edges

- Disabled access for wheelchairs or pushchairs

- Candles - stand on a glass/metal base or in sand

- Paint and glue - provide appropriate cleansing wipes

- Food stuffs - check for anyone with food allergies

- Others?

Reflect back on the experience of the small group task

- How were the needs of each age group met?

  - What was easy and straightforward?

  - What proved more difficult?

- What would you do differently another time?

- How did you personally respond to this task?

  - What was the most helpful/exciting aspect?

  - What was the most difficult/distracting aspect?

- How do you feel about planning and/or leading all-age services?

  - Gifted?

  - At sea?

  - With potential?

- What have you learned from this experience?

What do you think each age group needs in worship?

	Physical needs — How will people be made comfortable?	Spiritual needs — How will people engage with God?
Babies		
Toddlers		
Children		
Youth		
Adults		
Retired		
Elderly		

196

The challenge of all-age worship
ALL-AGE WORSHIP EXERCISE

	Babies	Toddlers	Children	Youth	Adults	Retired	Elderly
Intellectual needs How will people learn about God?							
Emotional needs How will people know God loves them?							

Taken from *Leading worship that connects* by John Leach (Anglican Renewal Ministries, 1999, p.23)
Used here with permission of the author.

197

Before or after session 11

KEEP CHECK

Please make sure that you speak to each member of your small group individually either before or after the session or during the tea break.

Has everyone finished and handed in their *Personal Project* or are some having difficulties? Are they on track with writing up their *Portfolios?*

Encourage everyone to meet up with their 'link group' or buddy within the next few weeks to help them prepare for their *End of Course Review.*

60 mins

SMALL GROUP PRACTICAL TASK

Get organised as quickly as possible.

Share resources

Everyone should have brought a contribution suitable for use with children or young people. Encourage them to share their contribution briefly with the group. The material may be a motley selection of great ideas but may not all dovetail together. What are the implications for the other age groups in using this particular material in an all-age context?

Leading all-age worship is a real gift so a new leader may surprise us and suddenly emerge from the shadows. This may be just the opportunity someone has been waiting for.

The task

- **A ten minute cameo of a service** - The ten minute section could be from the beginning, the middle or the end of a service. What resources can be used today? What will need to be left aside for another time?

- **A typical church context** - Remind everyone of the context. Imagine a fairly typical small to medium-sized congregation. There are a few families with children ranging from babies and toddlers through the primary years. At present, there are three teenagers, two boys and one girl. Numbers of children and young people can easily fluctuate between two or three and fifteen on any given week.

198

In this session's task

- **Consider the needs of all age groups** in relation to the given church scenario. Use the results of the exercise on meeting the needs to help with the planning.

- **Put new teaching into practice** - Think particularly about the media and current thinking in education. How might this change the shape of our worship together?

- **Short and simple** - Choose one clear theme or aim and stick to it. Work in sound bites, keeping an eye on the length of each element.

- **Links and logistics** - What will help this service to flow smoothly and avoid becoming a series of disjointed items, especially if it involves movement around the building? How can we take people on a worship journey with direction and flow?

The tools

- Everyone's contribution;
- Possibly inappropriate material;
- A copy of *New Patterns for Worship*.

There are a few extra all-age resources available if the group is floundering or needs to fill in some small gaps.

30 mins

Sharing with other groups

Again to save time, visit each group in their own location rather than moving instruments back to a central space.

Encourage everyone to fully participate in each act of worship.

Feedback all together when every group has contributed.

1: WHAT IS MISSION-SHAPED WORSHIP?

- How do we keep a mission focus in our regular worship?
- How do we develop worship that is welcoming and transforming?
- How do we model authentic worship for visitors and enquirers?
- If you have visited any Fresh Expressions of worship, consider: who is attracted to these acts of worship? Why?
- You may want to ask some friends who don't go to church: what might attract them to come to a service? What might put them off?

You may like to jot down a few notes. This is an aid for your own memory (and will not be collected in).

2: IS YOUR LOCAL CHURCH GROWING?

Please answer the questions on the *Church Growth Sheet* in preparation for *Session 12.*

3: MOVING ON

As we approach the end of the course, look back through your *Portfolio* and ask yourself the following questions:

- Where was I when I started the course? Where am I now?
- What new things have I learnt? How have my skills developed?
- How am I already putting this learning into practice?
- How can I share my new knowledge and skill with the rest of the church?

Reflect on these questions as you prepare for the *End of Course Review.*

Look back through your Worship Audits:

- Where was my church when I began the course?
- Where is my church now? What, if anything, has changed?
- How might worship develop in the future?
- What would help this to happen?

These issues relating to the worship life of the local church as a whole are particularly important. These questions will be discussed together with course tutors, your incumbent and a member of the 'link group' at the *End of Course Review.*

4: PERSONAL PORTFOLIO - HAND IN AT SESSION 12

- Please make sure this is up-to-date.
- Section 6: Plan a monthly meeting with your 'link group' or 'buddy' to help you prepare for the *End of Course Review.*

Your incumbent will also want to have a look at your *Portfolio* before the *End of Course Review.* Please ensure that this happens.

IS YOUR LOCAL CHURCH GROWING?

In the last ten years, how has your local church changed?

1. How has the liturgy/music/style/content/presentation of the services changed?

2. How has the building or the use of the building changed?

3. Has this facilitated growth?

    *   Do more or less people attend Sunday services?

        - New Christians?
        - Births?
        - Moving into area?
        - Transfer to or from another church?
        - Deaths?
        - Moving out of area?

    *   Are there midweek ... (please give details)

        - Services?
        - Fresh expressions?
        - Home groups?
        - Prayer groups?
        - Bible studies?
        - Alpha/Start courses?
        - Other small groups?

    *   Are there social or community events? If so, what?

4. Has there been a shift in age-range of those attending?

    *   In what age group(s)?

5. Can you identify any specific 'pockets' of growth?

    *   Why here?

    *   Why now?

worship4today

session

12

Worship in a mission context

TEACHERS' NOTES

SESSION PROGRAMME

5 mins   **Welcome and introduction to the session**
Explain the different format with a teaching session, pointers
for moving on from the course, and a final act of worship together.

85 mins   **Worship in a mission context**
Church growth or church decline?
Going beyond words
Engaging with current culture
Non-believers but not non-worshippers
Helps and hindrances to encountering God
Emerging worship and fresh expressions

15 mins   **Tea break**

20 mins   **Moving on**
Where are we on the journey?
What next?

10 mins   **Preparation for closing worship**

60 mins   **End of course worship – Holy Communion**

15 mins   **Thanks and farewells**

LIST OF MATERIALS NEEDED

- Food and drink
- Flipchart and pens
- Laptop, data projector and screen
- Post-it notes in two different colours
- Bibles
- Members' Handouts, including the additional handout with the results of the 'all-age exercise' from *Session 11*, based on our observations over five years of the course. This is a Word document on the CD-Rom to enable additions and alterations
- Orders of service for the final Holy Communion service
- Prayer cards - one for each participant with an appropriate encouraging scripture prayerfully prepared by the mentors

ROOM SET-UP

Ensure there are sufficient chairs and tables where everyone can see the screen for the PowerPoint. The main worship space will need to be prepared for Holy Communion beforehand. We recommend using a visual centrepiece to create atmosphere and give focus.

SESSION AIMS

- To consider our current mission context and how we model worship for others, particularly seekers and the unchurched
- To explore encounters with God through emerging worship and fresh expressions
- To set a new vision for moving on from the course
- To share Holy Communion together

5 mins

WELCOME AND INTRODUCTION TO THE SESSION

Welcome participants and settle them quickly. There will be a sense of anticipation and excitement, achievement and satisfaction as the course draws to a close. However, there may also be a certain sadness and disappointment that the course is already ending. Reassure participants that this is not the end, but in fact the first stage on a longer journey. All that has been learnt during the past year will be slowly assimilated and passed on to the worship team and congregation within each parish. This is a process that takes time and should not be rushed. There will also be regular opportunities to meet together in the future through Continuing Ministerial Education and diocesan worship.

Deal with administrative tasks swiftly, including:

- Collect in *Portfolios*
- *End of course evaluation* - Feedback forms were included at the back of the course syllabus. Hopefully, participants will have been keeping a record as they went along. Underline the importance of this evaluation process. It is vital for the course leaders to receive some kind of feedback so that a thorough review of the course can take place before it begins again. This is an important discipline every year, even when the course is well established. The course evaluation form is included on CD-Rom, so that it can also be sent out electronically.
- *End of course reviews* - Give a quick reminder for anyone who has not yet had their review.
- *Mentors* - Again, flag up the request for mentors for the following course. This is a great way to consolidate learning by working through the course again with a whole group of new people representing different churches.

Slide 2

Quickly run through the aims from slide 2. This session will take a slightly different format after the tea break as we look forward to the future beyond *Worship4Today* and share Holy Communion together.

Pray

10 mins

WORSHIP IN A MISSION CONTEXT

Handout 1: Worship in a Mission Context

We are now coming full circle to pick up some threads from our very first session together.

Slide 3

'Our chief end is to glorify God and **enjoy Him** forever.'
(Westminster Shorter Catechism)

And Jesus' first call to us is:

'**Love the Lord** your God with all your heart and with all your soul and with all your mind. This is the first and greatest commandment. And the second is like it: **Love your neighbour as yourself**.'
(Matthew 22:37-39)

Our love for God is inextricably linked to our relationship with those around us. How can we use all that we have learned and discussed on the course to enable others to come to this place of enjoyment – the place of knowing and loving Jesus as Lord? And taking it a stage further, how can we 'make disciples of all nations' (see the Great Commission in Matthew 28:19) and bring others to the throne of God as well? If we can't, then we will all have had a really nice time but to no avail.

This session poses more questions than it answers but hopefully it will expand our awareness of our context and give us some pointers as to where to start with worship and mission. We have seen some rapid changes in culture and social norms over the past decade, so we want to focus more on overriding principles rather than on time-specific detail.

How will it all fit?

Slide 4

What can we do in a world of rapid change and the (apparently) declining numbers of people attending church?

- **Are we 'scratching where society itches'?** Where is society today? What cultural influences are holding sway?

Share BRIEFLY with one another in pairs.

- **How do we 'do worship' in our current culture?** What are the aspects of our society that the Christian church can tap into and where can connections be made?

Share BRIEFLY with one another in pairs.

Then take brief feedback on flipchart.

This is a huge subject, so we can only hope to skim the surface. Be alert to the temptation to make assumptions (sometimes wholly inaccurate) about what others think both inside and outside the church, in our own neighbourhood, nationally or further afield.

15 mins

In the last fifty years

Slides 5-6

Let us think back to what we have learnt about the liturgical and musical development in the Church of England over the last fifty years.

Liturgically, developments can be summarised as follows:

- 1960s and 1970s   Series 1, 2, 3
- 1980   Alternative Service Book
- 2000   Common Worship

The 1958 Lambeth Conference also set out principles for liturgical change across the Anglican Communion. During the same period, we find similar experimentation in other countries in the 1960s leading to revised liturgies and prayer books in the 1970s and 80s: for example, *The New Liturgy* (1966) in the Episcopal Church, USA, *The Book of Alternative Services* (1985) in the Anglican Church of Canada, and *The New Zealand Prayer Book* (1989).

Alongside these liturgical changes there have been other significant developments:

- **Huge amounts of new and varied music** for worship.

- **The growth of the 'family service'** which has then gradually evolved into 'all-age' worship.

- **Experimentation with 'alternative' worship** - Starting with the 'Nine O'Clock Service' in Sheffield in 1986, there has been a conscious effort made to attract young people to a different kind of worship that might suit them better than traditional services.

- **The ordination of women** has brought with it a move towards inclusive language and new models of priesthood.

- **Fresh expressions of church** have taken alternative worship in many new directions in an attempt to reach out more effectively to the unchurched.

- **Multi-faith influences** - Many of our communities now have an international flavour with representatives of several different faiths. This can foster a healthy respect for spirituality and belief but may marginalise Christianity as it becomes one among many equals.

- **Pilgrimage – sacred and secular** - Youth Pilgrimages to Taizé or the Shrine of Our Lady at Walsingham have become popular alongside pilgrimages to Iona or Holy Island in the footsteps of the Celtic saints. The unchurched journey along the Great Wall of China or rediscover the Incas of Machu Picchu in Peru as they search for the next great adventure and chase the desire for self-fulfilment.

- **And now?** The landscape is continually changing, challenging the Church to keep up!

Reflecting back over this melting pot of change and challenge, we have to ask ourselves some hard questions:

Has our church grown as a result?

Slide 7

- Have the changes of liturgy, music, style, or a reordering of the building led to growth?

- Or have we just created new traditions for the regulars?

We asked these questions as part of the preparation for this final session. Participants may wish to refer to their *Church Growth Sheet* here. We are not in competition with one another. Now is the time for some honest appraisal.

Share BRIEFLY with one another in pairs.

Then take brief feedback on flipchart.

Draw this section to a close by asking some further questions. Have any changes to worship attracted new Christians or have they attracted transfer growth from other churches? Have changes 'held' the congregation or have people simply drifted through?

10 mins

How do we learn?

Additional Handout: The needs of worshippers

As we think about whether the Church is 'connecting' with the needs of today's people, let us take a quick look back at the results of the 'all-age' exercise from last time. These have now been summarised onto a handout together with results over a longer period of time.

Give everyone time to look through the additional handout. Ask for any immediate comments and observations.

Across the age groups, we find considerable common ground and overlap but we also find some important differences, especially when it comes to spiritual and intellectual needs. How we engage with God and how we learn about God are closely affected by current culture and social trends.

Spiritually, nothing can take the place of a genuine encounter with God. Worship, which is relevant and connects with current culture, may provide a healthy environment for such an encounter to take place.

The love of God is expressed to babies through a loving church family, toddlers come with an authentic sense of wonder at the world around them, children are naturally questioning, whereas young people want to explore spirituality 'in their own way'. For the 20s-45s today, there is a spiritual vacuum waiting to be filled whereas the over-45s and retired may be seeking space from a busy world. The elderly may connect best with God through more traditional elements.

We can explore faith, share personal stories and experiences, and learn from others. However, our learning styles may vary even more dramatically depending on age. The biggest differences are seen here. A huge sea change has taken place during the past twenty years or so mainly due to growth in technology, internet innovations and globalisation. Generally our attention span is getting less, so we need learning styles in worship which connect well.

Slide 8

In 2013

- Under 45s were thought to need:
  - Interactive, visual, sensory, activity-based learning

They want to get involved and be an essential part of what is happening. This could bring renewed energy into the church.

- Over 45s and older people were thought to need:
  - Sermons, teaching, Bible study, discussion

The inclination here is more passive. This can lead to an unhealthy introspection and inertia in terms of moving with the times, although this age group often makes up the largest numbers of volunteers in churches.

Is this still the case or have things moved on again?

Going beyond words

10 mins

Slide 9

In 2002, Peter Craig-Wild in *Tools for Transformation* argued:

'For the past 500 years we have lived in a word/mind based culture ... That culture is now breaking down rapidly, but the church and its worship is still locked in it. If we are to relate to the people of our emerging post-modern age, we need to find ways of worshipping that reflect the multi-dimensionality of human nature and move beyond the word-based mentality of the past 500 years.' (Peter Craig-Wild, *Tools for Transformation*, 2002)

By way of encouragement, many churches have come a long way during the past ten years, but there has been a huge and very quick change in the nature of learning, communicating, relating and inter-acting, which churches are struggling to get to grips with.

Slide 10

- **Visual images** – The McDonald's golden arches are recognised world-wide.

- **Universally recognised signs** – There are other universally recognised signs used for the common good.

- **Sound bites** make us listen out for train announcements and memorable jingles and phrases in advertising remind us of particular products.

- **'Hands on' museums** invite us to live in the past using all our senses: e.g. at the Jorvik Centre in York, we are invited into history with sounds, sights and smells.

- **Taste and see** – Nowadays we can taste food from all over the world and be tempted into the ultimate heavenly combination of rich, dark Belgian chocolate!

Slide 11

- **Experience** – Life today is all about sensory experience. We no longer want to simply learn *about* things. We want to do them and experience them to the full whether it is the latest extreme sport or a relaxing pamper day to escape for a while.

This can all lead to an unhealthy consumerism, which leaves us hungry for the next adrenalin rush or self-indulgence. Peter Craig-Wild argues that despite efforts to introduce changes, many churches have remained mostly word-based in the way they do worship on a week-to-week basis. Is he right?

The increasing popularity of prayer stations and the introduction of data projection are part of the response to update the Church and move with the times. Researcher, Lynda Barley, puts it another way as she describes ...

The 'Diana' phenomenon

Slide 12

'Roadside shrines, bouquets and teddies, and the widening appeal of prayer stations, labyrinths and beads are all indications that **images** are the new words for people today ...'

(Emphasis ours, from *Christian Roots, Contemporary Spirituality* by Revd Lynda Barley, CHP, 2006, ch.4. Lynda Barley was Head of Research and Statistics for the Church of England. She is now Truro Diocesan Secretary and Canon Pastor at Truro Cathedral)

These physical symbols are also indications of a spiritual void and the need for something tangible when life is unravelling. As St Augustine put it: 'Our souls are restless until they rest in You' (from the *Confessions of St Augustine of Hippo).*

Authenticity

Slide 13

Changing boundaries – a changing sense of duty, commitment and rightness – have led to the 'if it's right for me now, I'll do it' approach. This in turn leads to a lack of moral absolutes and a kind of pick 'n' mix spirituality. People experiment with different forms of spirituality, a bit of this and a bit of that, but only what suits them. Thus, when asked whether he wanted his child baptised, footballer David Beckham

could say, 'Yes, but I'm not sure into what religion.' Jesus has become just one of many valid truths. Yet, in the midst of all the change, there is a growing hunger for the 'real thing'.

A desperate need

We have lost our former belief that science and materialism have the power to solve all our problems. We are unable to save the planet and halt global warming. More disposable income has not made any of us happier. In fact, family and community breakdown has increased and with it the loss of personal identity and value. Suicide rates are slowly and steadily increasing worldwide, especially amongst the under 45s, reflecting a desperate need and sense of hopelessness. As Christians, we are people with hope! We have good news on offer:

Find rest, O my soul, in God alone; my hope comes from Him.
(Psalms 62:5)

Virtual reality and isolation

Slide 14

Not only has family breakdown led to isolation, but also hi-tech communication, which means that we no longer have to talk to one another. Even people within the same office will send emails rather than have a conversation face-to-face. Our social networking now takes place in cyberspace through *Facebook* and texting on mobiles. Even in a crowd, we can be in our 'own little world' listening to our own choice of music on *iPod*, texting or talking to someone elsewhere on a mobile. Virtual reality and fantasy games provide other worlds in which to escape but these may encourage people to lose touch with reality and serve to isolate individuals even further. We can even find 'internet church' and 'virtual worship' online, which enable us to fit in church at our convenience without reference to anyone else. We might ask whether we can really have 'virtual reality' worship, where we never meet face-to-face and we don't have to work out relationships with real people or ever say we're sorry.

These are broad brush strokes, which suggest ...

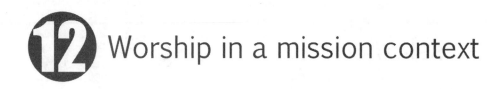

A growing need for transformation

Slide 15

Our current television programmes, whether they uncover unrecognised talent, give us a personal makeover, or revamp a house or garden, reveal a growing dissatisfaction with life as it is. We are observing:

- **A genuine search for meaning** - Life is uncertain and insecure; immorality and scandal undermine trust. Many people are longing for something bigger and beyond themselves. Fifty years ago Christian values still formed the bedrock of British society, but nowadays many people do not know what to base life on. This in turn is leading to ...

- **A rethinking of core values and the meaning of life** as many people decide: 'there must be more to life than this'.

In June 2009, a sobering article appeared in *Christianity* magazine. Then editor, John Buckeridge, wrote: 'According to *Christian Research* the recession has caused three quarters of UK adults to rethink their core values and reconsider the meaning of life, but hardly any have turned to the church. The search for meaning is occurring among young and old, in both genders and across all social grades.'

- Many want to spend time with family and friends, or renew old friendships.
- 14% said they had tried praying.
- 12% found it worthwhile.
- 3% said they had considered going to church.
- 1% actually went.
- NONE said they would go again.

This is what we are up against. There is ...

- **A desire for a complete life change** and a genuine hunger for something more but church is not necessarily seen as part of the answer.

This presents us with a huge challenge. St Paul writes:

Do not conform any longer to the pattern of this world, but be transformed by the renewing of your mind. (Romans 12:2)

Slide 16

Questions *(to ponder at greater length after the session)*:

- How should the Church respond to the current culture?
- How can transformation take place?
- What will a mission-shaped church look like?
- What will worship look like in a mission context?

Now the Lord is the Spirit, and where the Spirit of the Lord is, there is freedom. And we, who with unveiled faces all reflect the Lord's glory, are being transformed into His likeness with ever-increasing glory, which comes from the Lord, who is the Spirit.
(2 Corinthians 3:17-18)

Fortunately, God is in the transformation business!

SHAPING WORSHIP FOR MISSION

10 mins

Slide 17

Handout 2: Shaping worship for mission

We have included a few noteworthy quotations at the beginning of this handout, so we may wish to pick out the salient points:

'Good worship is converting.'
(Revd Simon Reynolds, Succentor of St Paul's Cathedral)

The Liturgical Commission also picked up this idea of change and transformation by entitling its 2007 Report (GS 1651), *Transforming Worship: Living the New Creation*. Its companion booklet for use by small groups, PCCs and worship groups bore the similar title: *Worship changes lives*. We should rightly expect individuals and congregations to be changed as they engage with God in worship.

215

Slide 18

'Worship is the wellspring (source) of evangelism. We need to rise to the challenge of seeing worship as part of our evangelistic strategy in a society that has a genuine thirst for something spiritual.'
(The Rt Revd Stephen Cottrell, Bishop of Chelmsford)

We commented back in *Session 7* that worship should have a mission focus. Unexpected visitors do drift into services, and these visitors frequently recognise God's presence during authentic worship even though they may not fully understand what is happening. We don't need to dumb down our worship for visitors. Many are searching for something 'other'.

Slide 19

'A healthy church will have worship which is an **inspiring** experience for the participants. When worship is inspiring, it draws people **all by itself**.' (Christian Schwarz, *Natural Church Development*)

We should be aiming for excellence, so that a congregation is giving its best and visitors can experience both authentic and inspiring worship. Life is busy, so time is short. If people are going to come to worship, they will want to come to something worthwhile. If worship is not engaging and uplifting, why should people come back?

Worship is for non-believers ...

Slide 20

... as well as believers and it should be:

- A welcoming experience

    - I am allowed to be here
    - I am wanted by these people
    - I am accepted by God

- An eye-opening experience

  - So this is God
  - So this is what Jesus is like
  - So this is what the Christian life is about

- A drawing experience

  - I want more of this
  - I want to find out more about Jesus
  - I want to come again

Non-believers … but not non-worshippers!

Our final quotation comes from Sally Morgenthaler, an American worship consultant, speaker and writer. God has created us to be worshippers, so Sally puts forward the following hypothesis:

Slide 21

'It is impossible to categorize people into two categories, *worshippers* and *non-worshippers*. Indeed, everyone worships something because that is the way we are made … Therefore if we do not worship God, we will worship something else.'
(From an article 'Is Worship Evangelistic?' by Sally Morgenthaler)

We are now competing with so many other things on a Sunday morning. We find clues to our worship priorities amongst the things to which we devote most time.

What does the world worship?

Slide 22

We flagged this up in our very first session:

- Football or another sport
- Job
- House
- Children or grandchildren
- Status
- Holidays and worldwide travel

We could also add to this an enthusiasm for retail therapy and a fascination for celebrity. Church now competes with sport, shopping and a whole variety of leisure activities. After a full week at work, Sunday may be our only family day or opportunity to tidy the house. Many feel compelled to work on Sundays for fear of losing out on employment.

The worries of this life, the deceitfulness of wealth and the desires for other things (Mark 4:19) truly crowd in leaving no time for belief and worship of God.

Modelling authentic worship for others

Slide 23

Nevertheless, people do come into church occasionally for the important rites of passage: baptisms, weddings and funerals. In these situations, worship remains a vital shop window for the church, and a shop offers its best lines in the window to attract shoppers. We have a big responsibility on such occasions.

We have already said we do not have to dumb down just because there are visitors present. However, worship needs to be accessible to people, who may well find themselves like fish out of water. Worship should also be a potentially inspiring and life-changing experience. *Natural Church Development* suggests '*inspiring* worship' is one of its eight key factors leading to church growth. *Inspiring* comes from in-spiratio (from Latin) literally meaning 'to breathe into', and implies that true inspiration and life come from the Spirit (breath or wind) of God.

On the day of Pentecost (see Acts 2), the Spirit breathed on the gathered disciples with a mighty wind and tongues of fire. And although this Spirit-inspired worship occurred in the Upper Room, it still attracted a crowd, who heard the works of God praised in their own languages. Inspiring worship happened and people got curious.

There are three important points to draw out here:

- **No watering down** - The crowd witnessed the 'real thing', and then Peter went on to explain what was happening.

- **Caught and taught** - The passion and enthusiasm of the worshippers was so infectious that others caught on. Worship is caught as much as taught, but it must also be authentic and genuine otherwise visitors will see through us.

- **Move outside the building** - Worship spilled out of the Upper Room into the local community and 3000 came to faith that day! Worship was not confined to one designated place.

Mission-shaped worship will not solve all our evangelism and outreach problems. Since writing her book, *Worship Evangelism: Inviting unbelievers into the presence of God* (Zondervan, 1995), Sally Morgenthaler has been rethinking her own paradigm. She is promoting *'celebrated'* worship inside the church and *'lived'* worship outside.

Mission-shaped worship in the church has its place, but we cannot use it as an excuse for not taking the gospel out into our local communities and doing the hard work of getting to know people there. Some do drift into worship and stay, but the majority come because of regular contact and friendships with others within the congregation.

ENCOUNTERING GOD

Slide 24

Visitors to worship will often comment on a sense of peace or they may find themselves close to tears. They might not be able to fully articulate what is going on within, but these are the first stirrings of encounter.

We worship an 'invitational' God, who is always encouraging us to come and see, to taste, to smell, to touch, to hear what the Spirit is saying to the churches.

5 mins

Brainstorm

Slide 25

How do people encounter God?

In worship, what might help people to encounter God and what might get in the way and hinder?

Ask people to call out their ideas. These can then be written up in two columns on the flipchart and in the box on the handout.

Some possible suggestions might be:

Helps	Hindrances
A sense of God's presence; a sense of awe	Too many different books or pieces of paper
Permission giving	Religious jargon
Feeling welcomed, accepted and included	Unsure what to do when
Accessible music and liturgy	Inappropriate song lyrics - both old and new
Different styles and different times of service	Lack of anticipation, expectancy and enthusiasm

Of course, many of these helps and hindrances will actually apply to the regular congregation as well, and not just to visitors. Encourage participants to give more thought to their list after the session.

10 mins

What about the men?

Slide 26

This is a whole subject in its own right (see suggestions for CME in the final section of the manual), but we want to flag it up briefly here because it is so important to the future health of the church.

There has been much talk of the feminisation of the church. Our first Parish Worship Audits revealed that at best most churches are 60% women to 40% men, but some can be as imbalanced as 80% women to 20% men. If this trend continues, gloomy researchers suggest that by 2030 there will be no men left in the church.

How might unchurched men respond to the following aspects of church services?

- Singing?
- Words of hymns and songs?
- Style of music?
- Perceived image of Jesus?
- Prayer?
- Robes?
- Styles of leadership?
- Technology?

What changes should we consider to make worship more accessible to men?

Take some quick feedback on flipchart.

For those who want to find out more, we recommend as a good starting point David Murrow's book *Why men hate going to church*, (Nelson Books, 2005); and the organisation *Christian Vision for Men*, headed up by Baptist minister, Carl Beech (www.cvm.org.uk).

We may need to recast the language of worship not only for men but for everyone. We could arguably ask all these questions on behalf of the existing congregation or any visitors to worship. What is appropriate? And what about the personality types who have never yet darkened the doors of a church?

Some biblical encounters

Slide 27

Quickly run through the following encounters between men and God in the Bible. In each case, a transformation took place and the men in question went out from worship to make a difference.

- **Jacob dreams of the ladder up to heaven** - Jacob is on the run, having just cheated his brother out of his birthright and his father's blessing, when God directly intervenes:

  When Jacob awoke from his sleep, he thought, 'Surely the LORD is in this place, and I was not aware of it.' (Genesis 28:16)

221

Jacob responds in worship and sets up a stone pillar, naming the place Bethel. Here he makes a commitment to God that will help to shape the rest of his life and the life of his family. Some of us may have significant places where we have met with God. When we return, we are more sensitive to God's presence there than elsewhere.

- **Moses and the burning bush** (Exodus 3) - Moses is out in the desert tending sheep when he sees the burning bush. The bush is not consumed, so he goes to investigate.

  'Do not come any closer,' God said. 'Take off your sandals, for the place where you are standing is holy ground.' (Exodus 3:5)

  Out of this encounter in the wilderness, Moses is sent to rescue the Israelites from Pharaoh. The Israelites will retell the story again and again. We are still retelling this story of a God who rescues desperate people.

- **Isaiah in the temple** (Isaiah 6) - Isaiah is already inside a place of worship, and there he has an encounter with God that blows him away.

  Then I heard the voice of the Lord saying, 'Whom shall I send? And who will go for us?' And I said, 'Here am I. Send me!'
  (Isaiah 6:8)

  Through confession and forgiveness, he is equipped and sent out to prophesy. What prophecies! Isaiah's words continue to speak into our lives today.

- **Wise men follow a star** (Matthew 2:1-11) - Eastern astrologers discover a new and unknown star. Curiosity aroused, they set out on a lengthy quest to discover its significance.

  On coming to the house, they saw the child with his mother Mary, and they bowed down and worshipped him. Then they opened their treasures and presented him with gifts of gold and of incense and of myrrh. (Matthew 2:11)

  Their quest ends in an act of worship accompanied by gifts of extravagant generosity, and then they disappear off the radar again. Yet, they have been remembered ever since and we retell their story every Christmas.

- **Philip and the Ethiopian** (Acts 8:26-39) - The Ethiopian has travelled up to Jerusalem to worship, probably as a pilgrim at one of the traditional festivals, but he does not really understand what

it is all about. That is until Philip comes and shares his 'car'. We've talked about this story before. Philip explains the scriptures, the penny drops and an impromptu baptism ensues:

And he gave orders to stop the chariot. Then both Philip and the eunuch went down into the water and Philip baptised him.
(Acts 8:38)

Then the newly baptised eunuch returns home with a new mission imperative and the gospel spreads to Africa. The Christian Church in Africa continues to grow today.

Consider

Some people meet with God directly and unexpectedly, some are searching for something more, some are already inside the church. Each of these biblical encounters resulted in worship, and yet four out of five of these encounters between men and God took place *outside* designated places of worship. What impact might this observation have on the way we shape worship for mission and mission to men in particular?

. 15 mins

EMERGING WORSHIP AND FRESH EXPRESSIONS

Slide 28

We cannot talk about shaping worship for mission without mentioning emerging worship and fresh expressions of church.

Have we got any examples of fresh expressions within the participants' churches? Ask one or two to share BRIEFLY a little of their story.

Slide 29

According to the *Fresh Expressions* website:

'A fresh expression is a form of church for our changing culture established primarily for the benefit of people who are not yet members of any church.'

This is first and foremost church for the unchurched in communities where people already belong. Here an appropriate style of worship for this community grows up from the grassroots. New congregations are planted alongside more traditional ones with the idea that these new congregations will become 'church' in their own right rather than being seen as a stepping stone into more established church services.

The term 'fresh expression' has come into use in recent years to describe a congregation 'with a different ethos and style from the church that planted it' (see Fresh Expressions website). There are lots of examples and stories on the website, so we are simply going to give a few broad brush strokes here to open up the subject and get participants thinking.

Fresh expressions of church do not just suddenly appear out of a vacuum. In fact, many churches already have completely separate congregations meeting in the same building: e.g. an eight o' clock Holy Communion clientele who never go to the later 'main' service; and perhaps a once a month Night Prayer or Compline service, which is popular because it is peaceful, reflective and short! As we listen to the promptings of God's Spirit, we may discern an opening for a completely new form of worship which is geared to another entirely different group of people.

Emerging worship must come out of ...

Slide 30

- **A tradition** - Many fresh expressions of church use a potent mix of ancient, contemporary and future resources for their worship: catholic sacraments and prayer, plainsong, traditional icons and old masters all combine with contemporary language, ambient beats, and multi-media presentation. The resurgence and popularity of Celtic imagery and prayers sit alongside Eastern Orthodox traditions and a new monasticism with its rule of life and passion to reach out to the poor. There may be a certain amount of formal ritual with robed service leaders.

- **A context** - Local neighbourhood plants may be based around a local community centre, coffee shop or pub, or they may begin on deprived housing estates with an informal approach to worship. Alternatively, church may evolve out of an existing network or

common interest. Thus, the surfer church in Polzeath began with surfing. *Sorted* in Bradford began with skateboarding, but soon went beyond to form a new youth church. The worship here will reflect the nature of the group, so the *Goth Eucharist* in Cambridge will make connections in its worship with Goth culture.

- **A particular pastoral need** - These fresh expressions too can vary greatly according to the need. The *Focus Church* in Sheffield, for those with learning disabilities, has a relaxed and chaotic style of worship, where everyone is invited to participate as fully as possible. A growing number of 'haven' services meets the need for a restful environment in which to find peace and solace from the stresses of life in the fast lane. And *Messy Church* taps into the missing generation of 20s to 45s attracting whole families to come to worship together, focused around activity-based learning, worship and a meal together.

Generally there is a great variety in approach appropriate to the context rather than cloning something that works elsewhere. *Messy Church* may be an exception to this, as variations on this theme have sprung up right across the country. Eating together as an integral part of the worship is also a repeated theme across fresh expressions, reflecting the model of Jesus in the Gospels:

The Son of Man came eating and drinking, and they say, 'Here is a glutton and a drunkard, a friend of tax collectors and sinners.'
(Matthew 11:19)

Jesus' life of worship, devoted to glorifying the Father, rubbed off on those with whom he ate, inspiring them to greater things.

It is worth noting that a 'fresh expression' of church in one context may be 'old hat' in another, and some may not be as radical as the initiators think. If a person has never been to a traditional church, cathedral worship can be radical, mysterious and awesome, especially when experienced anonymously from a dimly lit nave.

Facing the challenges

Slide 31

- **High maintenance resource hungry worship** - By their very nature, most fresh expressions of church require huge amounts of

planning and preparation, and a constant input of inspiration and new ideas. Sufficient resources may need to be collected for weeks in advance of a service. The combination of multi-media and hands-on can make these types of worship services high maintenance, especially if they include food as well. Therefore ...

- **Team work is essential** - This has come up again and again throughout the course and we want to reiterate its importance one more time. Whatever location is used, fresh expressions frequently require considerable setting up, especially if they are hi-tech. However, the same group of people does not have to do everything. One group may prepare interactive materials whilst another prepares the venue and the technical side. A further group may look after the catering.

- **Develop indigenous leadership** - We talked about this back in *Session 7*. If we take seriously the definition of liturgy as the work of the people, then we will allow the style of worship to evolve gradually from the bottom up, so that it is truly shaped and owned by the people who come. This can be a risky and uncomfortable process, where some of us will have to sacrifice our preconceived ideas and familiar ways of doing things for the benefit of the newcomers.

- **Becoming settled and established** - Sooner or later the issue of sacraments comes up, specifically baptism and the Eucharist. Here we have a rich heritage to fall back on to help us formulate something suitable to the context.

  - Baptism: If a fresh expression is seen as 'church' for this particular congregation, then it is only right and proper for baptisms to occur within their usual worshipping context, whatever form that might take. The essential elements of the rite (presentation, decision, signing with cross, profession of faith, and baptism) should remain, but the format will be shaped by that particular fresh expression.

  - Eucharist: For fresh expressions in a sacramental tradition, the Eucharist may well be their starting point, so it is not a problem. However, within less sacramental fresh expressions, sooner or later they must address the issue of how to introduce the Eucharist as part of the ongoing nurture and discipleship of the new worshipping congregation. Holy Communion was first instituted in the context of a celebration meal of remembrance. Can we therefore blend the sacrament creatively with a meal on a regular basis (as we might on Maundy Thursday)? Does *café church* also give a natural connection with its welcoming tables? Alternatively, the *Goth Eucharist* may connect with the darker dimensions of

blood and death and a taste for the theatrical. It will be important to look creatively for the natural links.

- **Retaining Anglican identity** - The evangelists among us will not be bothered by this one as long as we are successfully reaching the unchurched and developing appropriate styles of worship that connect. For others it will be a much bigger issue. If fresh expressions are not rooted in the liturgy, they may be in danger of being hijacked by consumerism. As a helpful benchmark, it may be useful to remind ourselves of the undergirding principles which mark out our worship as recognisably Anglican. Cranmer's original idea was one of 'common' prayer and worship, which could be understood and accessed by everyone. Within this, he emphasised the central place of scripture, the importance of Holy Communion and the building up of the Body of Christ. *Common Worship* may herald the greatest revolution within worship since Cranmer, giving us clear structures and a huge library of resources from which to legally explore new forms of worship whilst still fulfilling Cranmer's original criteria.

  NB. Those of other denominations may wish to draw out alternative distinguishing features.

- **Avoid reinventing the wheel** - We have inherited rich patterns of worship stretching back over hundreds of years. For this very reason, *Worship4Today* has sought to provide sound biblical knowledge and understanding coupled with a good grasp of church history and tradition. We are able to come to the preparation of worship in whatever context with a good working knowledge of what has gone before. Hopefully this will enable us to dip into a vast tool bag of ready resources and draw on different strands of Christian spirituality to give a depth and rootedness to our planning.

BIG QUESTIONS

Slide 32

Although in many ways, we have come full circle to where we began in *Session 1*, we are well aware that we are leaving a whole range of new questions to be pondered at greater length and to be picked up in Continuing Ministerial Education in the future.

227

Worship in a mission context

How do we attract those who never come to church?

- The missing men
- The missing 20s to 45s age group

If we attract these groups, then we are also likely to increase the numbers of children and young people in church.

How do we address ...

- A desperate need for quiet space in a busy stressful world?

Throughout the *Worship Audits*, we have discovered so many who have valued the peace of a quiet space. This applies to people outside the church too.

- The needs of different personality types?

Although pigeon-holing people is not always helpful, there is significant evidence using the Myers Briggs Type Indicator, which suggests that certain personality types are completely missing from the church. (See *Knowing me knowing you* by Malcolm Goldsmith and Martin Wharton, SPCK, 1993, part 3; these findings are confirmed by more recent research by Canon Professor Leslie J. Francis of Warwick University)

The harvest is plentiful

Then Jesus said to his disciples, 'The harvest is plentiful but the workers are few. Ask the Lord of the harvest, therefore, to send out workers into his harvest field.' (Matthew 9:37-38)

This is a sobering verse. The problem is clearly not the harvest. We are called to pray for the workers. If we read *Purpose Driven Church* by Rick Warren (Zondervan, 1995), we will find that they chose their style of worship at Saddleback deliberately to connect with their surrounding community. Otherwise few would have come. This may mean some losses, but also some gains. We cannot always retain worship just the way we like it at the expense of others. At rock bottom, that is selfish. However, as we modify our approach to accommodate the unchurched, we will also discover new riches. Look back prayerfully through the *Worship Audits* and then prayerfully compare the findings with the needs of the local community.

- How appropriate is our worship to the mission task?
- How can we enable worship without getting in the way?
- What kind of worship will sustain our community ...
  - Now?
  - In 5 years?
  - In 10 years?

As worship leaders, we are charged to enable the kind of worship that will glorify God and edify the people. Any people, anywhere, any time. All people.

This is the ultimate challenge for mission-shaped worship.

Finally ...

Slide 33

Worship is not just a place we go, it is a way of life. (Romans 12:1-2)

We want to finish this teaching session with a final quote from Sally Morgenthaler. It leaves us in a good place from which to reflect and move on. As it is a long quote, we suggest getting someone else to read it:

'Jesus himself spent crucial time in synagogues and the temple. He affirmed that the worship of God is central to what it means to be a disciple. But here's the catch. He did not make the building - or corporate worship - the destination. His destination was the people God wanted to touch, and those were, with few exceptions, people who wouldn't have spent much time in holy places. Jesus' direction was always outward. Centrifugal. Even in death, he was broken and poured out for the sake of a needy world. God's work may not be "all outside," but if we look at where Jesus spent his time, I think we can safely say that most of it is ...

'May you and the Christ-followers you serve become worshippers who can raise the bar of authenticity, as well as your hands. And may you be reminiscent of Isaiah, who, having glimpsed the hem of God's garment and felt the cleansing fire of grace on his lips, cried, "Here am I, send me."'

(From an internet article on www.rev.org where Sally Morgenthaler rethinks her own paradigm of 'worship evangelism'.)

Keep a few moments of stillness ending with a short prayer before breaking for refreshments.

15 mins   **TEA BREAK**

12 Worship in a mission context

MOVING ON

Slide 34

Handout 3: Moving on

Participants have already started addressing the whole question of moving on as part of their preparation for the end of course review. It is helpful to look back at where we started nearly twelve months ago and reflect on the journey so far.

5 mins

Post-its

Slide 35

Where are we personally on the journey now?

Ask everyone to write down on one colour post-it three key things that they have learnt in the last twelve months. On the second colour post-it, ask everyone to jot down what they considered the best part or highlight of the course.

Then allow 2-3 minutes sharing in pairs.

The post-its can become part of offering ourselves to God for ministry during the closing worship, but they can also be an uplifting encouragement for the course leaders at the end of the course!

10 mins

How will we continue to maintain momentum?

Slide 36

- Consolidate the learning by slowly going back through all the handouts and notes session by session. Information has been given out thick and fast. Some things have already been tried out

for the first time or put into regular practice whereas others can barely be remembered. Still the participants may feel as though other things have gone straight over the top of their heads. In reality, everyone will have taken in much more than they realise, and this knowledge and expertise will gradually permeate through, shaping the worship life of the individuals and their parish worship in the months and years to come.

- **Share learning with others** - A good way to find out how much we have really taken in is to pass it on to others. As we articulate our learning it takes root in us at a deeper level, but we can only share it a little at a time. This can be frustrating, especially if we are full of enthusiasm and new ideas. We should be prayerful and discerning: introduce the wrong new song or creative idea and it can put a congregation off new creativity for some time; choose wisely and they will be eager for more.

Build up a wider worship team

Slide 37

We've already said this once this session, but it is actually a good way to maintain momentum. A team finds it easier to generate new ideas and resources and more importantly, it creates an environment of accountability.

- **Who might we include?** Musicians and singers, other service leaders, technical people, PCC members, new Christians, teenagers and children. What about running a *Worship4Today* course within the parish? This has the advantage of including people who would never have the confidence to join a central diocesan course, and it helps people to recognise and appreciate the breadth of worship styles and experiences already present within their own congregation.

- **Foster good communication and joined up thinking** - The end of course review with the incumbent and a member of the parish 'link group' could be a good starting point for this process. This is not just about communicating well with the people involved in a particular service, but also about building trust across the whole congregation. If we foster openness and honesty it will be much easier to share common goals and deal with difficulties as and when they arise. Relationships take time and effort, but they are well worth the investment.

- **Look for potential leaders** - We should always be on the lookout for those we can start nurturing now, who might be potential leaders and course participants in the future.

  Remember Jesus: he demonstrated, he did stuff alongside, he let the disciples have a go while he was there, he sent them off in twos and then took feedback and reviewed, and finally he gave them responsibility and left them to get on with it.

  Ideally, we want to gradually work our way out of a job. This is important, because none of us knows what is round the corner. Many churches have been left in the lurch, when the key leader is suddenly ill or moves away.

- **Rejoice in others' successes** - Some of our potential leaders may gradually become better than us. This is a good test of our character and our security in God. It is a time to rejoice even if we feel somewhat threatened. Shared leadership is good to temper pride with humility and it shares the load. If we always have to lead or play, then we may have a problem.

Gently move forward

GENTLY MOVE FORWARD

Listen to God
Develop a vision
Be prophetic not nostalgic
Develop a strategy
One step at a time

Slide 38

- **Listen to God** - There is no way around this one. It should always be our first priority, although in the busyness it can easily get relegated to well down the list. We should listen as individuals, as a worship team and as a congregation. Hopefully, this way everyone will be fully involved and 'own' the worship.

- **Develop a vision** together with the incumbent and other worship leaders in the parish.

  Without a vision, the people perish. (Proverbs 29:18, KJV)

  Bill Hybels, pastor of Willowcreek Church in the States, has said: 'Vision is a picture of the future which produces passion.'

  Vision not only gives us direction, but it also gives us energy and enthusiasm.

- **Be prophetic not nostalgic** - We may think the course has been great, but doubt what can be implemented in our own situation.

  Forget the former things; do not dwell on the past. See, I am doing a new thing! Now it springs up; do you not perceive it? I am making a way in the desert and streams in the wasteland.
  (Isaiah 43:18-19)

  We are so good at nostalgia, looking back to the good old days whilst forgetting the not so good parts. We can respect our history and traditions without being bound by them. We worship a God who is always doing something new and who makes a way in the most unlikely places. God wants to communicate these new things to us if we will only listen. We are invited to listen to what the Spirit is saying to the Church and to *see* prophetically what might be coming.

- **Develop a strategy** - We have to plan if we are going to move forward, so be intentional. Long term plans involve dreaming dreams and seeing the big picture. Medium term plans form the interim stages to achieve the vision. Short term goals map out what to do first. Alongside intent, we also need wisdom. Godly wisdom is essential but often in short supply. Listening to God is not only the beginning of the process but also a necessity throughout as vision is shaped into reality.

- **One step at a time** - There is a wise saying which has been a great encouragement to us during the revision and publication of *Worship4Today:* 'Inch by inch is sinch; yard by yard is hard.' It has kept us going in tough times. The important factor is the steady, forward momentum no matter how slow. As we are faithful in the small things, God gives more. May we encourage you to be faithful and never limit God's vision.

5 mins

MOVING ON: WHAT NEXT?

Handout 4: Moving on: What next?

This handout can be found in *Appendix 1* to this session. We have given an outline for the content, but the information will need to be adapted for local use. It is included as a Word document on the CD-Rom.

If this course has been run within a deanery or parish setting, then please refer to pages 267 and 268 of the document *Assessment and CME* in the *Assessment* section of this book.

Very briefly run through the appropriate information.

Slide 39

Immediate

- **Reviews** - Give reminders of dates for any still to come. The discussion from the review forms the basis of the overall assessment together with the observations of the course leaders and mentors throughout the year.

- **Assessments** - There will be three written assessments:

  - Personal Project
  - Portfolio
  - Overall assessment and recommendation

  Projects and portfolios will be returned together with the written assessments as soon as possible after marking. The overall assessment also includes a recommendation that the participant should be authorised (or not as the case may be) as a worship leader within the diocese. The final assessment and recommendation will be sent by post to the participant. A copy is also sent to the incumbent. Depending on the size of the group and the speed of marking, this notification is usually sent out four to six weeks after the end of the course.

- **Recommendation** - Participants are recommended to be authorised as worship leaders within the diocese in recognition of their studies and their role within the worship ministry of the local church. From time to time, they may also be invited to lead or participate in worship elsewhere.

- **Authorisation** - Arrangements for this will vary from diocese to diocese, but it is anticipated that worship leaders will be authorised by the bishop alongside readers, parish evangelists, pastoral workers and children's ministers. Give appropriate diocesan details.

- **Ministry Agreement** - Copies of this simple document are sent to the participant and incumbent together with the final assessment and recommendation. The ministry agreement sets out some helpful parameters at the beginning of this new phase of ministry. It enables participants and their incumbents to agree duties and a

realistic time commitment. It also encourages ongoing support and accountability as well as a commitment to further training and ministerial development. It is hoped that the ministry agreement will be reviewed annually.

Slide 40

Future

- **Continuing Ministerial Education (CME)** for authorised worship leaders will be organised regularly:

  - Twice a year
  (Add appropriate diocesan details here)

  If there are particular requests regarding suitable subjects for CME, these should be taken into account in the planning.

- **Oversight** - Over a period of years, the group of authorised worship leaders will increase. We recommend appointing a warden (from amongst the authorised) specifically to oversee the group.

  (Add appropriate diocesan details here)

- **Worship teams for use around the diocese** - The growing number of authorised worship leaders gradually builds up a group of people with varied gifts scattered throughout the diocese, who can be called upon to support and facilitate worship at parish, deanery or diocesan level as and when required. As a result, worship at larger events can truly reflect the nature of worship across a whole diocese rather than simply representing the flavour of the hosting church.

- *Worship4Today* network - In Sheffield we have run the course on a rolling annual programme. Over time, relationships and networks have developed within and beyond the diocese, creating a fertile ground for sharing ideas and resources.

Slide 41

Local

(Add appropriate details here)

National

Keep informed at www.worship4today.co.uk

10 mins

PREPARATION FOR CLOSING WORSHIP

This short comfort break marks a definite change of mood and pace to give everyone adequate time to prepare themselves for the Eucharist. Remind everyone to take their post-it notes with them.

60 mins

HOLY COMMUNION

(In a different space if possible)

Finish this session with a service of Holy Communion. An outline of what has been used in previous courses can be found in *Appendix 2* to this session. This service includes personal prayer for each participant, the offering of our post-it notes, and a final act of commitment.

15 mins

THANKS AND FAREWELLS

We hope and pray that everyone has enjoyed the course and found it a fruitful and worthwhile experience.

Finally, thank all those who have contributed to the course in any way during the year: thank all the course leaders and teachers, acknowledging the contribution of those not present; thank mentors for their hard work and support of all the participants; and thank the participants themselves for engaging so enthusiastically throughout the course.

worship 4 today

session

Worship in a mission context

WORSHIP IN A MISSION CONTEXT

'Our chief end is to glorify God and enjoy Him forever.'
(Westminster Shorter Catechism)

But how?

- How will it all fit?

- Are we 'scratching where society itches'?

- How do we 'do worship' in our current culture?

In the last 50 years

Liturgically ...

- 1960s and 1970s   Series 1, 2, 3
- 1980   Alternative Service Book
- 2000   Common Worship

Alongside ...

- Huge amounts of new and varied music
- Growth of 'family service' then 'all-age'
- Experimentation with 'alternative' worship
- The ordination of women
- Fresh expressions of church
- Multi-faith influences
- Pilgrimage – secular and sacred
- And now?

Has our church grown as a result?

Have the changes of liturgy, music, style, or a reordering of the building led to growth?

Or have we just created new traditions for the regulars?

How do we learn?

In 2013

- Under 45s were thought to need:
  - Interactive, visual, sensory, activity-based learning

- Over 45s and older people were thought to need:
  - Sermons, teaching, Bible study, discussion

Is this still the case or have things moved on again?

Going beyond words

- Visual images
- Universally recognised signs
- Sound bites
- 'Hands on' museums
- Taste and see
- Experience

The 'Diana' phenomenon

'Roadside shrines, bouquets and teddies, and the widening appeal of prayer stations, labyrinths and beads are all indications that **images** are the new words for people today …'

(Emphasis ours, from *Christian Roots, Contemporary Spirituality* by Revd Lynda Barley, CHP, 2006, ch.4. Lynda Barley was Head of Research and Statistics for the Church of England. She is now Truro Diocesan Secretary and Canon Pastor at Truro Cathedral.)

Filling a spiritual void:

'Our souls are restless until they rest in You.' (from the *Confessions of St Augustine of Hippo*)

Authenticity

- Changing boundaries
- Lack of moral absolutes
- Pick 'n' mix spirituality

A desperate need

- Financial crises
- Save the planet
- Family and community breakdown
- Loss of personal identity and value
- Increasing suicide rates worldwide
- Hopelessness

Yet we have a hope ...

Find rest, O my soul, in God alone; my hope comes from Him.
(Psalms 62:5)

Virtual reality and isolation

- Hi-tech communication
- Social networking in cyberspace
- 'Own little world' even in a crowd
- Virtual reality and fantasy games

A growing need for transformation

- A genuine search for meaning
- Rethinking core values and the meaning of life
- A desire for a complete life change

Do not conform any longer to the pattern of this world, but be transformed by the renewing of your mind ... (Romans 12:2)

Questions:

How should the Church respond to the current culture?

How can transformation take place?

What will a mission-shaped church look like?

What will worship look like in a mission context?

Now the Lord is the Spirit, and where the Spirit of the Lord is, there is freedom. And we, who with unveiled faces all reflect the Lord's glory, are being transformed into his likeness with ever-increasing glory, which comes from the Lord, who is the Spirit.
(2 Corinthians 3:17-18)

SHAPING WORSHIP FOR MISSION

'Good worship is converting.'
(Revd Simon Reynolds, Succentor of St Paul's Cathedral)

'Worship is the wellspring (source) of evangelism. We need to rise to the challenge of seeing worship as part of our evangelistic strategy in a society that has a genuine thirst for something spiritual.'
(The Rt Revd Stephen Cottrell, Bishop of Chelmsford)

'A healthy church will have worship which is an 'inspiring' experience for the participants. When worship is inspiring, it draws people 'all by itself." (Christian Schwartz, *Natural Church Development*)

Worship is for non-believers

- A welcoming experience

- An eye-opening experience

- A drawing experience

Non-believers ... but not non-worshippers!

'It is impossible to categorize people into two categories, *worshippers* and *non-worshippers*. Indeed, everyone worships something because that is the way we are made ... Therefore if we do not worship God, we will worship something else.'
(From an article, 'Is Worship Evangelistic?' by Sally Morgenthaler)

What does the world worship?

Modelling authentic worship for others (see Acts 2)

- No watering down

- Caught and taught

- Move outside the building

ENCOUNTERING GOD

How do people encounter God?

Helps and hindrances to encountering God

In worship, what might help people to encounter God and what might get in the way?

Helps	Hindrances

What about the men?

How might unchurched men respond to the following aspects of church services?

- Singing?
- Words of hymns and songs?
- Style of music?
- Perceived image of Jesus?
- Prayer?
- Robes?
- Styles of leadership?
- Technology?

What changes might we consider to make worship more accessible to men?

Some biblical encounters

- Jacob dreams of the ladder up to heaven (Genesis 28:11-22)

- Moses and the burning bush (Exodus 3)

- Isaiah in the temple (Isaiah 6)

- Wise men follow a star (Matthew 2:1-11)

- Philip and the Ethiopian (Acts 8:26-39)

EMERGING WORSHIP AND FRESH EXPRESSIONS

Emerging worship must come out of ...

- A tradition

- A context

- A particular pastoral need

Facing the challenges

- High maintenance resource hungry worship

- Team work is essential

- Develop indigenous leadership

- Becoming settled and established
  - Baptism
  - Eucharist

- Retaining Anglican identity

- Avoid reinventing the wheel

For further information: see www.freshexpressions.org.uk
Fresh Expressions in the Sacramental Tradition, ed. Steven Croft and Ian Mobsby, Canterbury Press, 2009.

BIG QUESTIONS

How do we attract those who never come to church?

- The missing men
- The missing 20s to 45s age group

How do we address ...

- A desperate need for quiet space in a busy stressful world?
- The needs of different personality types?

The harvest is plentiful

- How appropriate is our worship to the mission task?
- How can we enable worship without getting in the way?
- What kind of worship will sustain our community ...
  - Now? In five years? In ten years?

Finally ...

Worship is not just a place we go, it is a way of life. (Romans 12:1-2)

'Jesus himself spent crucial time in synagogues and the temple. He affirmed that the worship of God is central to what it means to be a disciple. But here's the catch. He did not make the building - or corporate worship - the destination. His destination was the people God wanted to touch, and those were, with few exceptions, people who wouldn't have spent much time in holy places. Jesus' direction was always outward. Centrifugal. Even in death, he was broken and poured out for the sake of a needy world. God's work may not be "all outside," but if we look at where Jesus spent his time, I think we can safely say that most of it is ...

'May you and the Christ-followers you serve become worshippers who can raise the bar of authenticity, as well as your hands. And may you be reminiscent of Isaiah, who, having glimpsed the hem of God's garment and felt the cleansing fire of grace on his lips, cried, "Here am I, send me."' (From an internet article on www.rev.org where Sally Morgenthaler rethinks her own paradigm of 'worship evangelism'.)

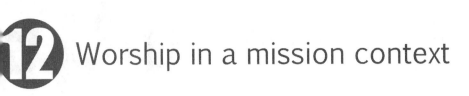

MOVING ON

Where are you personally on the journey?

- What are the three key things that you have learnt in the last twelve months?

- Highlights?

How will you continue to maintain momentum?

- Consolidate your learning

- Share your learning with others

Build up a wider worship team

- Who might we include?

- Foster good communication and joined-up thinking

- Look for potential leaders

- Rejoice in others' successes

Gently move forward

- Listen to God

- Develop a vision

- Be prophetic not nostalgic

- Develop a strategy

- One step at a time

245

THE NEEDS OF WORSHIPPERS

Physical needs: how will people be made comfortable?

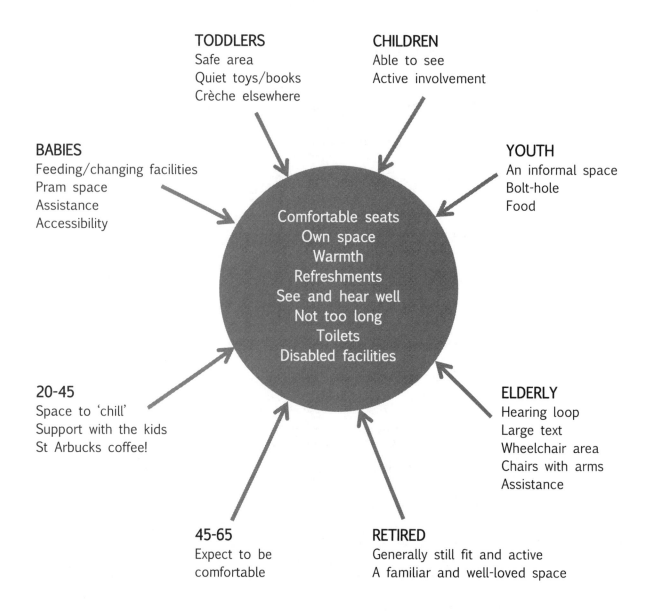

TODDLERS
Safe area
Quiet toys/books
Crèche elsewhere

CHILDREN
Able to see
Active involvement

BABIES
Feeding/changing facilities
Pram space
Assistance
Accessibility

YOUTH
An informal space
Bolt-hole
Food

Comfortable seats
Own space
Warmth
Refreshments
See and hear well
Not too long
Toilets
Disabled facilities

20-45
Space to 'chill'
Support with the kids
St Arbucks coffee!

ELDERLY
Hearing loop
Large text
Wheelchair area
Chairs with arms
Assistance

45-65
Expect to be
comfortable

RETIRED
Generally still fit and active
A familiar and well-loved space

There are subtle differences between age groups.

246

Spiritual needs: how will they engage with God?

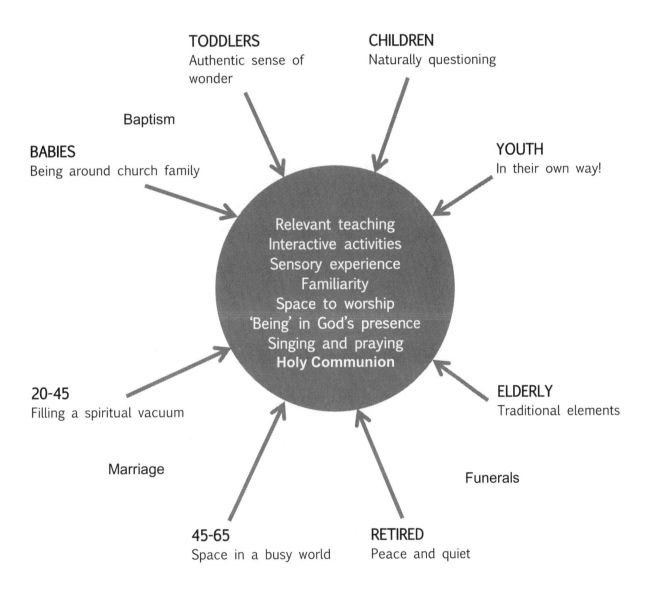

We cannot assume that spiritual age and faith experience is the same as actual age.

Intellectual needs: how will they learn more about God?

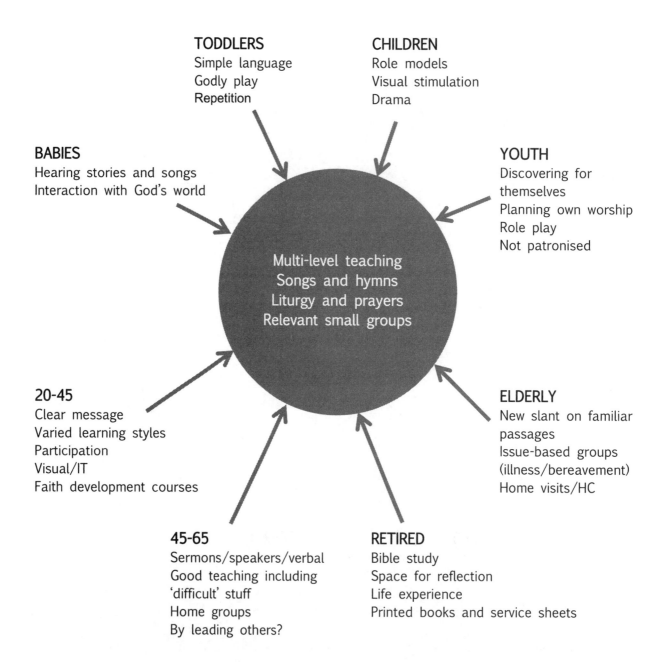

TODDLERS
Simple language
Godly play
Repetition

CHILDREN
Role models
Visual stimulation
Drama

BABIES
Hearing stories and songs
Interaction with God's world

YOUTH
Discovering for themselves
Planning own worship
Role play
Not patronised

Multi-level teaching
Songs and hymns
Liturgy and prayers
Relevant small groups

20-45
Clear message
Varied learning styles
Participation
Visual/IT
Faith development courses

ELDERLY
New slant on familiar passages
Issue-based groups (illness/bereavement)
Home visits/HC

45-65
Sermons/speakers/verbal
Good teaching including 'difficult' stuff
Home groups
By leading others?

RETIRED
Bible study
Space for reflection
Life experience
Printed books and service sheets

Our attention span is generally getting less, so there is a growing need for interactive (kinaesthetic) learning.

248

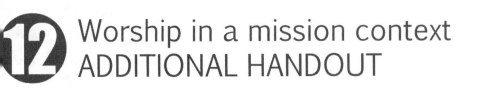

Emotional needs: how will they know they are loved?

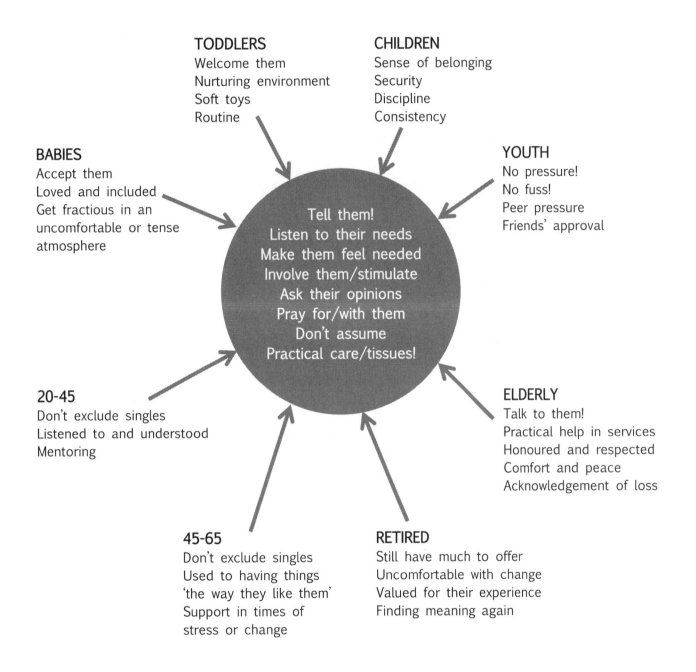

TODDLERS
Welcome them
Nurturing environment
Soft toys
Routine

CHILDREN
Sense of belonging
Security
Discipline
Consistency

BABIES
Accept them
Loved and included
Get fractious in an
uncomfortable or tense
atmosphere

YOUTH
No pressure!
No fuss!
Peer pressure
Friends' approval

Tell them!
Listen to their needs
Make them feel needed
Involve them/stimulate
Ask their opinions
Pray for/with them
Don't assume
Practical care/tissues!

20-45
Don't exclude singles
Listened to and understood
Mentoring

ELDERLY
Talk to them!
Practical help in services
Honoured and respected
Comfort and peace
Acknowledgement of loss

45-65
Don't exclude singles
Used to having things
'the way they like them'
Support in times of
stress or change

RETIRED
Still have much to offer
Uncomfortable with change
Valued for their experience
Finding meaning again

We need to tell people that God loves them to affirm, encourage and reassure.

MOVING ON: WHAT NEXT?

Immediate

- Reviews

- Assessments

  - Personal project
  - Portfolio
  - Overall assessment and recommendation

- Recommendation

  - Notification 4-6 weeks after the end of the course

- Authorisation

  (Add appropriate diocesan details here)

- Ministry Agreements

Future

- **Continuing Ministerial Education (CME)** for authorised worship leaders

  - Twice a year
  (Add appropriate diocesan details here)

- Oversight

  (Add appropriate diocesan details here)

- **Worship teams** for use around the diocese

- *Worship4Today* network

  - **Local**   (Add appropriate diocesan details here)
  - **National** - keep informed at www.worship4today.co.uk

CLOSING WORSHIP OUTLINE: HOLY COMMUNION

This will need to be prepared in advance. We recommend a special order of service, so that participants can take it away with them as a reminder of their promises to God at the end of the course. Mentors should also prepare a prayer card for each member of their small group.

We suggest that the course leaders and mentors make up the worship team for this service, so that participants can focus on God with no other responsibilities.

Simple introduction

- Short liturgical greeting – suggestion: *New Patterns for Worship* (NPfW) A22

- A verse of scripture - suggestion: Psalm 33:1, 3

Hymn/song

Liturgy

- Simple Kyrie Confession and Absolution – suggestion: NPfW B55 & B78

The Gloria

The Collect

Reading

- Suggestions:

  - Isaiah 6:1-8
  - Ezekiel 47:1-12
  - Acts 1:1-8
  - Philippians 1:1-11
  - Colossians 3:12-17

Psalm or contribution from a member of the course

This might be an appropriate moment for someone to present an element from their personal project such as a dance, drama or composition.

Gospel Acclamation

Alleluia, alleluia.
I chose you and appointed you, says the Lord,
that you should go and bear fruit that will last.
Alleluia

Gospel

- Suggestions:

    - Luke 4:14-22a
    - John 4:5-24
    - John 7:37-39

Reflection

- Very brief

Optional song of invocation

- Asking for the coming of the Holy Spirit to lead into prayer

Prayers

- For each participant

We suggest that each mentor moves to a suitable point and each mentee comes in turn for prayer. This discreetly creates personal space and respects privacy.

Mentors will have come to know the members of their small group well over the months. They should prepare a card for each person including an encouraging scripture. We suggest that they begin their prayer with this verse.

The Peace

Offertory hymn/song *during which the post-it notes from the earlier session may be collected and offered.*

Eucharistic Prayer

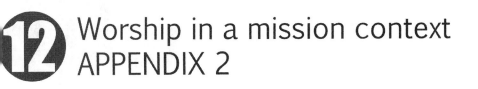

Giving of communion

Communion hymn/song *to be sung during the distribution.*

Act of commitment and commissioning

Leader	You are called to be true worshippers, who worship the Father in spirit and truth. Will you seek after God with all your heart, with all your mind, with all your soul and with all your strength?
All	**With the help of God, we will.**

Leader	Will you bless the Lord at all times with His praise continually in your mouth, as you lead skilfully and sing to Him a new song?
All	**With the help of God, we will.**

Leader	Will you weep with those that weep, and minister through music, creativity and prayer to the hurting and sorrowing?
All	**With the help of God, we will.**

Leader	Will you lift high in praise the name of Jesus, that all people may be drawn into His kingdom?
All	**With the help of God, we will.**

Leader	May God be gracious to you and bless you as you sing of what He has done. May He make His face shine upon you as you worship and adore Him. May God be gracious to you as you minister His grace to others, and may you be filled with His peace.
All	**Amen.**

Helen Bent, 2005, originally written for the licensing of the Bishop's Adviser in Music and Worship, Sheffield Diocese.

Song

• To send out

Blessing

The dismissal

Strengthened for the journey,
go in peace to love and serve the Lord.
In the name of Christ.
Amen.

PARTICIPANT FEEDBACK FORM

Please record any comments here session by session so that we can learn from what worked well and also learn from our mistakes. Please fill it in as thoroughly (but as briefly!) as you can. Thank you.

Session one

Introduction: Expectations and boundaries of confidentiality

Teaching: The theology of worship

Closing worship

Session two

Teaching: Who is the God we worship?

Practical: Worship in small groups

Session three

Teaching: Worship in the Old Testament

Practical: Basic worship skills; overcoming weak spots – work in small groups

Session four

Teaching: Leadership skills

Practical: Building a team (part one) - work in small groups

Session five

Teaching: The role of music in worship

Teaching/practical: A historical overview – English Choral Tradition

Practical: Rehearsal techniques

Session six

Teaching: Worship in the Psalms

Practical: Setting Psalms to music - work in small groups

Session seven

Teaching: Anglican worship - choosing appropriate material

Practical: Balance, direction and flow in worship - work in small groups

Session eight

Teaching: Building a team (part two)

Teaching/practical: Music theory for worship leaders – beginners; intermediate; advanced

Practical: Vocal coaching workshop – men; women

Session nine: practical worship day

Workshop one: Leading up front

Workshop two: Posture and movement

Workshop three: Using technology in worship

Workshop four: Leading corporate prayer and creating prayer stations

Workshop five: Signing in worship (or alternative)

Closing worship

Session ten

Teaching: Worship in the New Testament

Practical: Improvisation skills – work in a large group and small groups

Session eleven

Teaching: The challenge of all-age worship

Practical: Exploration of all-age materials - work in small groups

Session twelve

Teaching: Worship in a mission context

Envisioning: Moving on

End of course Holy Communion service

Homework

Please indicate on the scale what you thought:

Too much   Too little

  1   2   3   4   5   6   7   8   9   10

How appropriate was the homework to the next session?

Any other comments about the types of homework set?

Any other comments you would like to make about the course as a whole?

Any comments you would like to make about the venue and practical arrangements?

Signed (optional):

Please complete this form soon after the final session. This will help us to review the year and make any necessary adjustments before the re-running of the course.

Please return to (Name)
(Address)
or email to (Email address)
no later than **(Add date)**

258

worship4today

Assessment

Assessment and
Continuing Ministerial Education

Assessment and Continuing Ministerial Education

Thorough assessment is a vital part of any course if participants are to reap the maximum benefit from their learning. Assessment is time consuming but worthwhile. It respects and values the effort and commitment that participants have made during the year, acknowledging the sacrifices and struggles, achievements and successes.

This process is directly linked to our original learning outcomes. Upon successful completion of the course, participants will be able to:

- **Understand** the theology of worship and music in worship.
- **Recognise** the biblical and historical foundations of contemporary worship.
- **Identify** a range of forms of worship across the church traditions.
- **Demonstrate** skills for planning and leading acts of worship.
- **Develop** pastoral skills for building a worship team in the local church.
- **Discover** possible ways to facilitate worship in a mission context.

We offer a process of review, assessment and recommendation. This is a two-way process. Participants receive verbal and written feedback at the end of the course from the tutors but the tutors also receive written feedback from the participants. As course leaders, we want to evaluate the overall success of each course and monitor the effectiveness of our own teaching, delivery and management.

REVIEW AND ASSESSMENT AT DIOCESAN LEVEL

Ongoing assessment

Assessment comes in various guises during the course, providing constructive critique tempered with huge amounts of encouragement. We want every participant to develop an honest and realistic self-awareness but we cannot emphasise strongly enough the need for ongoing encouragement and affirmation in order to build secure, confident leaders. We also want participants to develop good habits of reflecting and questioning that will stimulate a desire to learn more.

- **Written assessment:** Through the preparation sheets for each session and those pieces of work which have been submitted for comment as the course has progressed, we have already been building up a picture of each person's ability to learn and question theologically. Written feedback in the form of comments and further questions for consideration aids understanding and develop critical reflection.

- **Practical assessment:** Worship leading is often 'up front' and visible. Through the practical sessions and group work, we observe how participants develop their people skills for working with a worship team. We see how they present themselves and their material when leading from the front. We also see how their particular creative skills and abilities are developing and finding an outlet. Common weaknesses can often be challenged and tackled openly, but specific personal blind spots should be addressed discreetly one-to-one.

- **Long term assessment:** There will be three separate assessments at the end of the course. The completed personal project is handed in at *Session 11* and the completed portfolio is handed in at *Session 12*. Thorough written feedback is given. A final overall assessment is then written based on discussion at the end of course review.

Throughout *Worship4Today* we have set the bar high, whilst being sensitive to the less academic. This is equally true of assessment. Marks and grades often lead to unhealthy comparison with others, so these are deliberately avoided. The *Worship4Today* assessments are more about personal development and growth rather than achieving a fixed academic standard. All assessments include individual comments alongside suggestions for future exploration and development. This is primarily about releasing talents, encouraging development, and inspiring participants to even greater things.

Assessment of the personal project

The format of the project will vary depending on the nature of the content. We suggested four possible formats:

- **Improving specific practical skills**
- **Composition** of liturgy, hymns or worship songs
- **Practical exploration** of a particular area of worship in the local church or a new area of interest
- **Research** of a specific topic of interest

We gave guidelines for each of these types of project in the *Additional Handout* to *Session 5*, and we recommend that markers refer back to this sheet. We want to see how the project has affected the participant's personal worship life and whether it has made any impact on the worship life of the church. Lastly, we want to encourage further exploration.

A generic blank assessment form for the personal project is included in *Appendix 2*, but we have also included some ready worked examples, covering the four different types of project. These are genuine assessments, but fictitious names have been substituted.

Assessment of the portfolio

The portfolio by its nature is a very personal document and should be treated as such. This changes the nature of the assessment. Our chief aim here is to build up and affirm the person. We have asked participants to reflect on their learning as they have journeyed through the course. In our written comments, we want to commend honest insights and growing self-awareness. We not only recognise and rejoice in strengths but also encourage participants to acknowledge and address their weaknesses. This fosters an ongoing life of transparency and accountability.

The course has not been done in isolation, so personal reflection should naturally interweave with reflections on worship in the parish. Participants should have related their learning to the key skills required by a leader of public worship, reassessing previous expertise in the

light of new experiences encountered on the course. There is also opportunity to draw out more from the *Parish Worship Audits*, comparing the findings of all three.

We have recommended at least one church visit per term, so the portfolio should contain feedback from a minimum of three visits. These feedback sheets can be illuminating. Church visits are important to widen experience of other churchmanship, traditions and worship styles. Affirm helpful observations and turn any negative criticism into more challenging personal reflection. Encourage regular church visits in the future to prevent a narrow, insular approach and to help keep ideas fresh.

The section on meetings will reveal how much interaction and support there has been from the parish, especially from the incumbent and parish 'link group'. These are vital relationships, if all that has been learnt on *Worship4Today* is going to be properly disseminated throughout the church.

How participants use the final sections of the portfolio will vary from person to person. Some will include additional worship activities or experiences from *Spring Harvest* or *Greenbelt*. Others may include additional training opportunities. Participants should not be penalised if they have not included anything here.

After the course, the portfolio becomes a valuable resource to accompany the life-long learning journey into the future. It is also a useful way of introducing the participant to the discipline of keeping a journal and prayerfully reflecting on their spiritual growth and walk with God. We encourage mentors to continue with their portfolio throughout their second year of the course. It is quite different experiencing the course from this new perspective and important to reflect on the new skills of leadership, managing groups and pastoral care.

A generic blank assessment form for the portfolio is included in *Appendix 2*, but we have also included a ready worked example. This is a genuine assessment, but a fictitious name has been substituted.

Projects and portfolios should be returned together with the written assessments as soon as possible after marking.

The training review process

Towards the end of the course, a review of training takes place. Each participant is invited to meet together with course tutors, their incumbent and a representative from their parish 'link group'. This process should be set in motion about two months before the end of the course, when letters of invitation are sent out to all participants and their incumbents.

These letters briefly explain the purpose of the review and should include optional dates. A separate training review document gives a fuller rationale. The incumbents are invited to give some preliminary written feedback prior to the review date. This enables them to raise any issues of concern confidentially before the review. Sample letters are included in *Appendix 1* of this section.

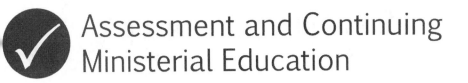

We recommend that 30-45 minutes are allowed for each review. Participants from the same church should be encouraged to come at consecutive times so that the final question about vision for the future worship life of the church may be addressed to all the participants together as a group rather than each individual separately.

Review

The review takes the form of a conversation to enable the participant to reflect together with others on the way in which their ministry is developing. This conversation is shaped by a number of prescribed questions, set out on a *Training Review Record* form for easy use. This sheet is also included in *Appendix 1*. We usually conduct all interviews and reviews in pairs, so that important information is not missed and the conversation is noted down thoroughly on the form.

We explore:

- **Personal growth:** The aim of *Worship4Today* is to nurture a foundation of personal worship, leading to encounter with God and personal development and growth.
- **Worship ministry:** For some, this will be a confirmation or re-affirmation of ministry that they have already been exercising but for others this will be an opportunity to explore how their sense of call to a ministry of worship leading is developing. Some will remain team members rather than upfront leaders but they will now be able to play their part with greater knowledge and understanding. Affirm this warmly and do not underestimate the positive influence such people can have within a worship team and congregation. Still others may now sense a call to continue on to reader training or ordination.
- **Feedback from the parish:** The review enables focused conversation between the participant, their incumbent, and a representative from the parish 'link group'. Hopefully this builds on dialogue that has already been happening within the parish for the duration of the course. We want to discover what impact the course has made on the individual and how this has already started to affect the worship life of the parish. This is an opportunity to affirm the benefits and blessings and raise any areas of concern.
- **Future development:** Finally the review provides an ideal opportunity to reflect on the worship of the parish more broadly to gain new perspective and insight. This can act as a catalyst for renewed vision, direction and momentum. We suggest that where there is more than one participant from the same church, this final area is discussed with everyone together.

It is the expectation that the training review will provide an encouraging, stimulating and constructive experience, which should affirm the participants as they look forward to commencing their new ministry and role. However, this is not a selection interview and it is intended to take place in a relaxed atmosphere in which challenging questions may be asked and difficult issues can be faced in safety.

The discussion from the review forms the basis of the final overall assessment together with the observations of the course leaders and mentors throughout the year.

Attendance

As part of the review, attendance must be taken into account. Every session of *Worship4Today* contributes a different element to the course. The course is incomplete without attendance at all twelve. Inevitably, some participants will miss a session through unavoidable clashes of dates or illness, but we strongly advise individuals to catch up missing sessions the following year. Where several sessions have been missed, a recommendation may be made on condition that those sessions are completed.

Choosing new mentors

If you are intending to run the course on a rolling basis, the review provides a good forum to raise the issue of mentors for the following course and enables course leaders to handpick those they think may be suitable for this role. This is less risky than asking for volunteers and can prove a valuable part of the ongoing learning process.

If participants have gained from the course, they may well want to give something back in return. Becoming a mentor is a great way to do this. Mentors have the privilege of walking beside others and sharing some of their new knowledge whilst benefiting from the whole course again without having to do any homework! During the subsequent year, mentors will develop new skills in leadership, managing small groups and pastoral care. (For more about mentors refer to *Appendix 6* in *Worship4Today*, part one)

Final Assessment

Although it would be possible to share the marking of personal projects and portfolios with others, ideally the main course leader(s) will write the final assessments. They will have observed the participants throughout the course and be most aware of their strengths and weaknesses. They should have been present at the final reviews.

We want to evaluate:

- **Learning:** How much has the participant actually learnt? What key insights have they gained? Have all the set tasks been completed to a reasonable standard, bearing in mind the individual's starting point and academic ability.
- **Role:** How has the sense of calling developed? What direction might this take in the future? Does the participant need to be referred to anyone else to explore further training?
- **Practical skills:** How have these skills developed through the small group exercises? Has the person fully participated in each exercise? Where are the weak spots that need further work?
- **People skills:** How has the participant communicated with others on the course? How readily do they accept and respect the leadership of others? How self-aware are they?
- **Church input:** How is the participant exercising their ministry back in the parish? Of what benefit is this to the wider congregation?

This overall assessment includes a recommendation that the participant should be authorised (or not as the case may be) as a worship leader within a diocese.

Again, a generic blank form for the final assessment is included in *Appendix 2* together with a worked example. This is a genuine assessment, but a fictitious name has been substituted.

Recommendation

Participants are recommended to be authorised as worship leaders within the diocese in recognition of their studies and their role within the worship ministry of the local church. The final assessment and recommendation is sent by post to the participant. A copy is also sent to the incumbent. Depending on the size of the group and the speed of marking, this notification is usually sent out four to six weeks after the end of the course. Sample letters can be found in *Appendix 3.*

In the majority of cases, the final assessment and recommendation will confirm the expectation of the parish. Occasionally it may be appropriate to defer recommendation and authorisation to the following year. If the reviewers make a different recommendation from the parish's expectation, the reasons for this will be clearly stated. If the parish wishes for the recommendation to be reconsidered, a further meeting will be arranged at which the individual, their incumbent and parish 'link group' co-ordinator can present their case again.

Authorisation

Most dioceses hold an annual service to celebrate lay ministries and to authorise those who have recently completed a lay ministry training course. Worship leaders may be authorised alongside new readers, pastoral workers, parish evangelists and children's ministers during a service at which the bishop presides. Certificates of authorisation and badges may be given.

A sample certificate can be found in *Appendix 3.* Details of the *Worship4Today* badge are available from info@worship4today.co.uk. The name of the local diocese can be added.

N.B. Where clergy have studied on the course, they have received a certificate to mark completion of the course and their ministry as a leader of public worship has been affirmed by the Bishop within the service, but they are obviously already licensed within the diocese.

Ministry agreement

The ministry agreement is a useful tool, which sets down some helpful parameters at the beginning of a new phase of ministry. Hopefully, it will underpin good working relationships in the future. Copies of this simple document are sent to the participant and their incumbent together with the final assessment and recommendation. A sample document can be found in *Appendix 3.*

The ministry agreement enables authorised worship leaders and their incumbents to affirm particular expertise and to clarify roles and responsibilities. Designated duties can be clearly listed and a realistic time commitment established to avoid overwork or burnout. Although this is not a formal job description, the ministry agreement specifies lines of authority and encourages ongoing support. It should be completed by worship leader and incumbent soon after the course has finished. As part of this discussion, it may be pertinent to set in place regular meetings with the incumbent and the wider worship team to develop a vision and strategy that is shared and owned by everyone. This group can consider how worship fits into the mission and ministry of the parish and ensure that all the different strands weave together to form a unified whole. The parish 'link group' may also continue in a supporting capacity.

We anticipate that all authorised worship leaders will take part in *Continuing Ministerial Education* (CME). The ministry agreement not only records what further training has taken place, but also enables requests to be made for future training sessions. Authorised worship leaders should also be encouraged to make a contribution to the worship life of the wider diocese whenever the opportunity arises. We want to foster healthy relationships of openness, trust and accountability both inside and outside the parish, so that skills and expertise can be shared with confidence.

Finally, there is space for reflection and comment at the end of each year. The ministry agreement should be reviewed annually by the authorised worship leader and their incumbent. This short section can form the basis of this in-house review. Over time, skills and expertise develop. These can be further affirmed, and roles and responsibilities adjusted accordingly. Areas of weakness and things that have not gone well can be discussed honestly, so that we learn from mistakes and nurture further growth. Sometimes personal circumstances can also change, affecting ministry in the church. We do not want to make matters worse by leaving difficulties unresolved or adding extra pressure; nor do we want anyone to feel trapped in a job because there is nobody obvious to take over. The ministry agreement can help here by facilitating an objective re-examination of the designated duties and time commitments until a constructive resolution is found.

In Sheffield, all lay ministries are reviewed at diocesan level every five years. The five annual ministry agreements form the basis of this central review. After a satisfactory review, worship leaders are then re-authorised for a further five years. This robust process helps to maintain a high quality of ministry offered by our lay volunteers.

Course evaluation

Review and assessment at the end of a course is a two-way process. It is vital for the course leaders to receive some kind of feedback so that a thorough review of the course can take place before it begins again. This is an important discipline even when the course is well established.

Feedback forms were included at the back of the course syllabus. Hopefully participants will have been keeping a record as they went along. The data can be detached and submitted in this raw state in hard copy. Alternatively, the form can be made available electronically. A

course evaluation form can be found in *Appendix 3* to *Session 12* on the CD-Rom. Although we underline the importance of this evaluation process to everyone on the course, in reality we only expect to get about 50% of the forms back. This still gives a good overview.

We also arrange an end of course debrief with the mentors for each year. This not only values the contribution and commitment of the mentors, but also allows them to feed back valuable insights from a different perspective. Together with the course leaders' own reflections, we can then build up a comprehensive picture of the overall effectiveness of the course.

After several years of running *Worship4Today* centrally, it is possible to measure the effectiveness of the course across the diocese as we see diocesan worship invigorated and new creativity bubbling up in parishes. We have discovered that worship is caught as much as taught! Enthusiastic people are by far the best advertisement for any course. They naturally inspire others and inspirational worship helps to grow the Church.

REVIEW AND ASSESSMENT AT DEANERY OR PARISH LEVEL

In publishing *Worship4Today,* it has been our intention to produce all the materials and resources necessary to run the course at deanery level or at parish level as well as at diocesan level.

A deanery course may be run as an outpost of the diocesan course in exactly the same way as a central diocesan course. The course will be run by teachers who are qualified and experienced worship practitioners, so that the quality of delivery is maintained at the highest level, fulfilling all the course criteria and leading to diocesan authorisation by the bishop.

Some participants on a central *Worship4Today* course will want to take the course back to their own deaneries or parishes to equip the rest of their worship teams at a local level. There will always be people in every parish who would never dream of joining a central diocesan course but who may be persuaded to come to a parish course. This provides an opportunity not only to encourage and equip existing worship team members but also to discover new talents hidden within the congregation.

Where *Worship4Today* is taught locally we recommend that at least one of the main leaders has already done the course centrally. This is a great way of enabling participants to continue to study and learn, and to encourage them to grow in new areas of leadership; but the quality of delivery will vary - good worship leaders are not automatically good teachers. In a parish setting, it may be necessary to take the course more slowly over a much longer period of time, and it may be more difficult to maintain a consistent level of attendance. The larger the group the easier it becomes for people to opt in and out of sessions.

In a parish setting, everyone is already used to the style of worship within that parish, and there is a tendency to think that this is the right way or the only way to worship. A parish course may not contain the breadth of churchmanship, traditions and styles to challenge this thinking, putting the group at a further disadvantage. There is clearly a place for running *Worship4Today* at a parish level, but when it comes to review and assessment all these factors must be taken into account.

For these reasons, whilst teaching the course at a local level has the advantage of making the course readily accessible to a wider group, it does raise questions of validation, with authorisation of a locally run course likely to be only at parish level rather than at diocesan level.

At parish level, we encourage everyone to work with a buddy. At the end of the course, it may be helpful for the participant to have an informal review, rather than a formal assessment, together with the incumbent, course leader and buddy. This enables reflection on the individual's growth and learning and how they see themselves contributing to the worship life of the church in the future. What are the key areas of growth and learning? In what ways has their role changed and developed? Is there a new sense of direction? Have there been any difficulties during the course? This is a time to rejoice in the achievements and address any areas of concern or unresolved issues.

At the end of a parish course, we suggest that a special service, focusing on the ongoing worship life of the parish, may be an appropriate means of public recognition and acknowledgement. This may include prayer for each participant and the giving of a certificate, recognising that this person has successfully completed *Worship4Today* within the parish (a sample certificate can be found in *Appendix 3*). For the reasons outlined above, this certificate will not carry the same weight as an authorisation by the Bishop.

Worship4Today is primarily a ministry of encouragement, where we are looking for potential and wanting people to grow. Even within a parish course, new talents will begin to emerge. Some will have had their appetites whetted and will have grown in confidence, so that the parish course becomes a stepping stone to a central diocesan course; others with more experience may attend certain key sessions on a central course to fill in gaps and consolidate their learning. All this should be done in consultation with the central course leaders and diocesan training team.

CONTINUING MINISTERIAL EDUCATION (CME)

The end of the course marks the beginning of a new phase of ministry. All participants are encouraged to re-visit the course materials at regular intervals to consolidate their learning. However, the best intentions can easily become squeezed out in the busyness of everyday life. For this reason, we strongly advise that *Continuing Ministerial Education* is taken seriously and a programme is planned for each year to maintain momentum and stimulate further development. If there have been particular requests regarding subjects for *CME*, these should be taken into account in the planning.

In Sheffield, we encourage every authorised worship leader to attend two *Worship4Today CME* sessions each year (in spring and autumn) and to take part in the music and worship of at least one diocesan or deanery service/event during the year. We regularly ask authorised worship leaders what further training would be helpful, so that what is offered matches the needs.

Within *CME* we endeavour to maintain the same balance of theory and practice, building on the solid foundation of *Worship4Today*. We always allow some time for review, because it is so encouraging to see how much each person has grown and how parish worship has developed. Sharing testimony is a great way to enthuse others and pass on good ideas and resources. We also try to include some practical work back in small groups. The main subject matter is varied, sometimes re-visiting a particular aspect from *Worship4Today* in more depth, sometimes exploring a completely new area of worship.

Suggestions for CME

Below we have given a range of suggestions for *CME* sessions. New suggestions are regularly added to make sure the journey of discovery continues. A few sessions have a specific musical emphasis, but many subjects will comfortably accommodate everyone.

Transforming worship

We were aware that our final session asked more questions than it answered. Taking our title from the *Liturgical Commission* report of July 2007, we made our first follow-up session another full session on worship and mission to follow on from *Session 12*. Here we were able to tackle many unanswered questions and take participants to a new level of understanding.

'Worship changes lives'

During the same year we also ran a *Diocesan Development Day*, attended by over 400 clergy and laity in the diocese, exploring the same theme of mission-shaped worship. This large scale event offered a choice of twenty workshops covering different aspects of mission-shaped worship.

Walking the tightrope

This looked at maintaining balance in worship, building mainly on *Session 7*. We considered various areas:

- **Theology:** Transcendence and immanence; divinity and humanity; all three persons of the Trinity
- **Structure:** Eucharistic and non-Eucharistic; liturgical frameworks and freedom
- **Music:** Hymns and songs; traditional and contemporary
- **Balanced doctrine:** Raising awareness of nuances in the liturgy and dominant strands of doctrine in song lyrics

Called to be not just called to do

We wanted to explore being and doing in relation to being worship ministers, not just organisers and providers of services. Using *Romans 12:1-2* as a starting point, we began to unpack the idea of living the whole of life as an act of worship. This made helpful connections with the Levites in *Session 4*, the life of the psalmists in *Session 6*, and the worship of Revelation in *Session 10*.

Fresh expressions

We were fortunate here to tap into another *Diocesan Development Day* with all the rich resources that a large scale event can bring. Keynote speakers and leaders of several workshops were members of the national *Fresh Expressions* team, so we were able to learn from the experts.

How would Jesus lead worship?

Building on what we had learnt about Jesus as a Jewish worshipper and as a leader from *Sessions 4* and *10*, we unpacked this at a deeper level. Helpful resources here are:

- Sam and Sara Hargreaves, *How would Jesus lead worship?* BRF, 2009
- Marty Haugen, *To serve as Jesus did*, GIA Publications, 2005

Exploring the prophetic in worship

Here we were able to consider a working definition of prophecy in relation to biblical examples. We explored how we listen to God and how we discern what God might be saying to the church, and how that might happen within different traditions and churchmanship. Building on experiences in the improvisation workshop of *Session 10*, we were then able to put in place some safeguards for good practice in a congregational setting.

Rooted in the Word

Inspired by the 400th anniversary of the *King James Bible*, we held a session based on the creative use of the Word of God in worship. This included three separate strands, which flowed from one to the other. *Singing Scripture* explored improvised chant over a simple drum beat, building on from the drum workshop and the improvisation workshop of *Session 10*. We then moved on to look at *Lectio Divina* as a way to plan worship, building on learning from *Session 7*. Finally, we experimented with 'body prayer', responding to the *Lectionary* for the day through posture and gesture, expanding learning from the workshop in *Session 9*.

Helpful resources can be found on the *Contemplative Fire* website (www.contemplativefire.org).

Exploring the Eucharist

Although the Eucharist is discussed at various points during the course, notably in *Sessions 2, 5, 7* and *10*, we never have time to study the liturgy in any real depth. Taking the different titles of Eucharist, we have looked at different aspects:

- **Eucharist:** Developing a culture of thanksgiving and nourishment.
- **Mass:** Using the Eucharist as part of our mission strategy.
- **The Lord's Supper:** Exploring the significance of memorial and remembering.
- **Holy Communion:** Considering 'sharing in common' around the table as the people of God and a more sacramental approach to being 'set apart' and 'holy'.
- **Breaking of bread:** A recurrent theme in the Gospels.
- **Agape:** Rediscovering an informal Eucharist in the context of a meal.

Men and worship

We flagged this up briefly in *Session 12*, but it really needs a session all of its own. With so much talk of the feminisation of the Church, this subject is crucial to the health of the church present and future.

Jesus called men to follow him and become actively involved as kingdom builders, but this is not always expressed in our worship. Intimate worship song lyrics reflect the language of contemporary love songs, presenting Jesus as the 'boyfriend' or 'lover'. This can be uncomfortable and inappropriate language for women let alone men! We have lost the *Church Triumphant* and the *Church Militant* from our phraseology and with it we have been in danger of losing the gritty and gutsy.

Surprisingly, Matthew Bourne's *Swan Lake* may prove insightful here. He has completely reworked the graceful, delicate, feminine swans as arrogant, aggressive, energetic males. Not only is this portrayal more swan-like, it makes ballet more accessible to a wider audience. We have important lessons to learn if worship is to be readily accessible to twenty-first century men.

In the future

We are already planning to have sessions on the following subjects, which appear in no particular order:

Rehearsal skills

This was covered in *Session 5*, but it is always a helpful subject to re-visit at regular intervals to keep us on our toes and to help us make the best of our resources. We want to allow time for experiences to be shared, so that we can establish good rehearsal patterns that work. This kind of session can give the confidence needed to take the bull by the horns and change a pattern that is not working. Working back in small groups can remind us again of typical weak spots and how to overcome them. Rehearsing drama, reading aloud, dance or puppetry may also be included alongside music.

Explorations in time and space

With much church reordering at the present time this is another significant area, which is not really addressed during the *Worship4Today* course itself. The physical layout and decoration of a building will tell us something of the theology and ecclesiology of the church. Every building, no matter how well ordered, brings its own constraints and limitations to the worship. We can ask: what does the space say to us? What does the atmosphere say to us? How can we utilise the physical space to the full in our worship? Alongside these, we can ask other questions about creating safe space: for visitors; to listen and encounter God; to receive prayer ministry, including practical dos and don'ts. We may also want to consider how we create sacred worship space outside the church building.

We recommend reference to the work of Richard Giles and his books *Re-pitching the tent* (Canterbury Press, 1999) and *Creating Uncommon Worship* (Canterbury Press, 2004).

Liquid worship

This could be a useful follow-on from the exploration of God in *Session 2*, the prayer stations of *Session 9* and the missional aspects of *Sessions 11* and *12*. We can include helpful reminders about forward planning and the importance of team work in choosing themes and generating creative and interactive ideas. We can discuss ways of including all the necessary elements for a balanced act of worship, making the best use of the space available, and how technical we should be.

Some may want to specifically allow time to look more closely at prayer labyrinths. This ancient practice of walking slowly and prayerfully along a single path has become popular as a spiritual exercise and form of pilgrimage. Many video games use mazes and labyrinths, so this may build a useful bridge of accessibility between church worship and contemporary culture especially if it can be offered in a suitable space outside the church building.

Developing creative skills

All participants on *Worship4Today* have a go at writing their own psalms in *Session 6*. There is also another opportunity to experiment with creative skills in the improvisation workshop in *Session 10*. Several participants have gone on to write meditations and pieces of liturgy, compose new hymns and songs, produce a series of paintings, or put together a multi-media presentation as part of their personal projects. This session is designed to develop these skills further, or allow participants to 'have a go' at something different.

This workshop could readily combine theory and practice:

- A theological approach to doctrinally sound liturgy and song lyrics
- A literary approach for writing good prose and poetry
- A musical approach to assist with the writing of good melody and arranging material for choir, music group or congregation
- An artistic approach to explore the use of symbols and images, traditional and contemporary
- A multi-media approach following on from the technology workshop in *Session 9*

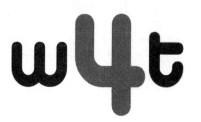

The resulting smorgasbord could be shared as 'works in progress' in an act of worship at the end of the session.

OVERSIGHT OF AUTHORISED WORSHIP LEADERS AND CME

Over a period of years, the group of authorised worship leaders will increase. We recommend appointing a warden (preferably from amongst the authorised) specifically to oversee this growing group. The warden of worship leaders will not only share the *Worship4Today* vision, but also share in the day-to-day organisation and administration of the annual review, the CME programme and the re-authorisation of leaders every five years or if they move to another parish. The warden should be officially commissioned for this role by the bishop.

In Sheffield, our first warden has been fully involved with the course from the outset. The warden was part of the original working party, a student-mentor during the first *Worship4Today* course, a mentor on the second *Worship4Today* course, and has since been involved in the teaching of subsequent courses and certain CME sessions. Alongside wardens of readers, pastoral workers and parish evangelists, the warden of worship leaders is also a member of the *Lay Ministry Oversight Group*. This ensures good communication and joined up thinking across the various disciplines. The warden works closely with the *Bishop's Adviser in Music and Worship* to support worship across the whole of Sheffield Diocese.

SUPPORTING WORSHIP WITHIN A DIOCESE

During their year on the *Worship4Today* course, individuals have been stretched and challenged, and skills have been developed and honed. Many participants respond to all that they have received with a willingness to offer their gifts and talents back to the diocese. The first opportunity for this is often the authorisation service in which the most recent *Worship4Today* cohort is invited to make up a worship group for that service.

The growing number of authorised worship leaders gradually builds up a pool of people with varied gifts and skills, scattered throughout the diocese. These people can be called upon to support and facilitate worship at parish, deanery or diocesan level as and when required. In Sheffield diocese, this has involved providing a music group for the *Archdeacons' Visitations* or a choir and music group for large diocesan events such as the annual *Diocesan Development Day*. Alternatively, it could involve the writing of new liturgy for a special service, or the creation of prayer stations or a prayer labyrinth for a particular occasion such as the *Week of Prayer for Christian Unity* or *Pentecost Praise in the Park*. Through participation in these diocesan occasions, the worship life of the diocese is enriched and the worship at larger services and events can truly reflect the nature of worship across a whole diocese rather than simply representing the flavour of the hosting church.

273

WORSHIP4TODAY NETWORK

After several years of running *Worship4Today*, it is possible to measure its effectiveness in the lives of individuals, parishes and a diocese. Many new services and congregations have been planted, new initiatives have been started, and many flagging choirs and music groups enthused. During long clergy vacancies, we have seen worship not only sustained but gaining new life and dynamism. The course has proved a catalyst in many churches for renewed vision and direction in worship, and we have seen diocesan worship as a whole greatly enriched.

We should always be on the look-out for potential leaders, people who we can start nurturing now, who might make good worship leaders in the future. It is a good principle to enable leaders at least ten years younger than ourselves in order to provide continuity in the future worship life of the church.

As we have run the course each year, relationships have developed within and beyond the diocese, creating fertile ground for sharing ideas and resources. Through the growing *Worship4Today* network we are able to keep one another up to date not only with other worship training and events on offer in the area, but also with what is happening in the wider worship scene and with training available from other denominations and organisations.

Like St Paul, our best method of advertising is by word of mouth from enthusiastic participants and supporters of the course. These people are themselves ...

... our letter, written on our hearts, known and read by everybody. They show that they are a letter from Christ, the result of our ministry, written not with ink but with the Spirit of the living God, not on tablets of stone but on tablets of human hearts. (2 Corinthians 3:2-3)

We are continually amazed by what God does in the lives of the participants on the course, both as individuals and as a growing body. This is a gift from God, for which we are truly grateful. With the publication of *Worship4Today*, the network is stretching further. The course is now being used in other dioceses within the Church of England and the wider Anglican Communion.

We have included the *User Feedback Form* again at the end of this section. Please use this form to tell us how the *Worship4Today* material is being used. We would be pleased to hear any comments or suggestions from course participants as well as course leaders elsewhere, so that we can continue to encourage the development and nurture of worship and worship training in the future.

We will keep everyone up to date with any new developments through the *Worship4Today* website. Visit us at www.worship4today.co.uk.

POSTSCRIPT

After this I looked and there before me was a great multitude that no-one could count, from every nation, tribe, people and language, standing before the throne and in front of the Lamb. They were wearing white robes and were holding palm branches in their hands. And they cried out in a loud voice: 'Salvation belongs to our God, who sits on the throne, and to the Lamb.' All the angels were standing round the throne and around the elders and the four living creatures. They fell down on their faces before the throne and worshipped God, saying: 'Amen! Praise and glory and wisdom and thanks and honour and power and strength be to our God for ever and ever. Amen!' (Revelation 7:9-12)

We hope that you have enjoyed the course and found it a rich experience, as you have studied and worshipped and encountered God together. We have the immense privilege of joining a great crowd of worshippers, past, present and future, from every nation, tribe, people and language. Together with the angels and archangels and all the company of heaven, we participate in an unending dialogue.

Worship is the interface between us and God; the place where Christians engage with the Almighty. Whilst the biblical truths and history of worship will remain the same, we are part of a changing culture and a changing church. Our worship will evolve and develop as we change, as our context evolves and as our understanding of God deepens.

The God we worship does not change. He is the same yesterday, today and forever. However, God is always doing a new thing, if we only have eyes to perceive it. For this reason, worship leaders need to remain firmly rooted in the scriptures and in our inherited traditions whilst at the same time being ever open to the movement of God's Spirit and the changing world in which we live.

Together, here on earth, we are being prepared for the worship of heaven, caught up in a never-ending stream flowing out from the throne of God into eternity.

When we've been there ten thousand years,
bright shining as the sun,
we've no less days to sing God's praise
than when we'd first begun.

John Newton

A Course for Worship Leaders and Musicians

USER FEEDBACK FORM

Please tell us how you are using *Worship4Today* by answering the questions below.

Name		
Address		
Tel	Mobile	Email
Diocese, deanery or parish		
Role		

Course type (Central diocesan, deanery or parish)
Year W4T started
Number of participants
Total number of W4T courses run
Total number of participants to date

SPACE FOR YOUR COMMENTS

Copies of this form can be found on the website www.worship4today.co.uk and returned to email address: info@worship4today.co.uk

APPENDIX ONE

Review materials

Sample letters of invitation
To be sent to each course participant and their incumbents

To use this sample, you will need to reproduce the letter yourself,
inserting the details that are highlighted in brackets.

Training review
Sample review form with questions

All these materials are available on the CD-Rom

(Include an appropriate Diocesan/parish letterhead)

Dear (Insert name of course participant)

Worship4Today: End of Course Training Reviews

A review of training for those currently participating in *Worship4Today* takes place towards the end of each course.

The purpose of the review is to enable you to reflect on the way in which your ministry is developing. It will take into account the new insights you have gained during the course as well as the work you have been doing with your parish 'link group' to discern your gifts. We will consider together how these gifts may best be used in the worship ministry of the parish in the future.

The training review will take the form of a conversation between yourself and two or three others. This conversation is a significant part of the evaluation process, providing information for the final assessment and recommendation. We believe it will be helpful for both you and the review process if you attend the review accompanied by your incumbent and, if possible, the co-ordinator of your parish 'link group'.

You should be prepared to talk informally about the things you have learned about yourself and your ministry whilst doing the course. We suggest that you use your portfolio in this process, not only to help you to have it up to date ready for the hand-in date at Session 12, but also to help you to identify any issues you may wish to raise at the review.

The dates for the review meetings have now been finalised as follows:

(Give several options including daytime as well as evening meetings

Date Option 1	Morning, afternoon or evening	Venue
Date Option 2	Morning, afternoon or evening	Venue
Date Option 3	Morning, afternoon or evening	Venue
Date Option 4	Morning, afternoon or evening	Venue)

Please arrange a suitable date with your incumbent and 'link group' co-ordinator as soon as possible, using the contact details above. We will then allocate you an appropriate time. Please allow half-an-hour per review. Where there is more than one candidate from the same church, reviews should be at consecutive times so that we can spend some time with both/all candidates and incumbent.

I look forward to meeting with you in the near future.

Yours sincerely,

(Your name)

(Include an appropriate Diocesan/parish letterhead)

(Date: approximately two months
before the end of the course)

Dear (Insert name of incumbent)

Worship4Today: End of Course Training Reviews

A review of training for those currently participating in *Worship4Today* takes place towards the end of each course. The purpose of the review is to enable participants to reflect on the way in which their ministry is developing. It will take into account the new insights they have gained during the course as well as the work they have been doing within the parish with you, their incumbent, and with their parish 'link group' to discern their gifts. Together we will consider how these gifts may best be used in the worship ministry of the parish in the future.

The training review will take the form of a conversation between the participant, the incumbent, the co-ordinator of the parish 'link group' and the course tutors. This conversation is a significant part of the evaluation process, providing information for the final assessment and recommendation.

The dates for the review meetings have now been finalised as follows:

(Give several options including daytime as well as evening meetings

Date Option 1	Morning, afternoon or evening	Venue
Date Option 2	Morning, afternoon or evening	Venue
Date Option 3	Morning, afternoon or evening	Venue
Date Option 4	Morning, afternoon or evening	Venue)

Please arrange a suitable date with your candidate(s) as soon as possible, using the contact details above. We will then allocate you an appropriate time. Please allow half-an-hour per review. Where there is more than one candidate from the same church, reviews should be at consecutive times so that we can spend some time with you and the candidates all together.

In preparation for the training review, please could you send a brief report about the candidate(s). We need to know:

- How do you consider the candidate's ministry has been developing in the life of the church?
- How is the candidate's ministry received by the congregation?
- How might the candidate's ministry continue to develop in the future?
- Any concerns?

I look forward to meeting with you in the near future.

Yours sincerely,

(Your name)

279

TRAINING REVIEWS

Training Reviews take place during the final few weeks of the *Worship4Today* course. A number of mornings, afternoons and evenings are set aside for these interviews.

The review provides an opportunity to evaluate how each participant's personal growth and understanding of their call to ministry has developed during their year of training.

It is the expectation that the training review will provide an encouraging, stimulating and constructive experience, which should affirm the participants as they look forward to commencing their new ministry and role. However, this is not a selection interview and it is intended to take place in a relaxed atmosphere in which challenging questions may be asked and difficult issues can be faced in safety.

Participants should remember that they have been accepted for training on the understanding that their parish is already committed to their authorisation. The purpose of the training review is to encourage them and their parishes to reflect on their experience of the course and their growing understanding of themselves and their ministry.

When participants attend their training review, they should be accompanied by their incumbent and preferably their 'link group' co-ordinator. The 'link group' co-ordinator will be expected to report on the progress of the parish 'link group' in identifying the participant's gifts, and their thinking about how these may be effectively used in the ministry of the parish.

Participants and their clergy will be notified of the outcome of the training review by post. In the majority of cases the final assessment and recommendation will confirm the expectation of the parish. However, if the reviewers make a different recommendation from the parish's expectation, the reasons for this will be clearly stated. If the parish then wishes for the recommendation to be reconsidered, a further meeting will be arranged at which the participant, incumbent and parish 'link group' co-ordinator can present their case again.

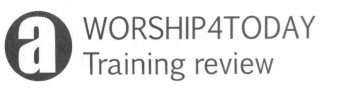

TRAINING REVIEW RECORD

COURSE PARTICIPANT		REVIEWER 1	
PARISH		REVIEWER 2	

Notes for reviewers

Participants should be encouraged to reflect on their experience and articulate their own views. Time and space should be allowed for them to do this. The incumbent and 'link group' co-ordinator should be included in the discussions but should not be allowed to dominate it. Each will have their own opportunity to give their specific comments during the review.

Where there is more than one course participant from the same church, the final question about vision for the worship of the church in the future may be addressed to all the participants together as a group rather than each individual separately.

Pre-review

1: Incumbent's feedback

2: Parish Worship Audit feedback

3: Observations from the practical sessions

4: Any particular areas of concern to discuss at the review?

Questions for the review

1) What has the participant gained from the course?

Any particular highlights?

2) How has the sense of call to this ministry deepened over the course?

3) What have been the main challenges or difficulties of the course?

4) What aspects of the course have you been able to share in the parish context?

5) How are relationships forming in the parish, with other worship leaders, with the musicians and the congregation?

6) Any particular areas of concern?

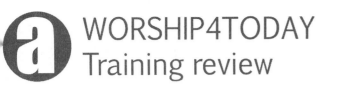

7) Incumbent's feedback

8) Parish 'link group' feedback

9) Are there any other issues which you would like to discuss in more depth, or any questions or comments you would like to explore with us now?

Where now? (The final question may be discussed with all participants from the same church together as a group)

10) How do you see the worship of the church developing in the future?

Recommendation

Recommendation

Any conditions of recommendation

Any specific suggestions for the future

APPENDIX TWO

Assessment sheets

Blank assessment sheets

Personal project
Portfolio
Final assessment

Worked samples:

Personal projects:
Practical skill
Composition
Practical exploration
Research

Portfolio assessment
Final assessment

All these materials are available on the CD-Rom

Personal project assessment

Name of candidate		Academic year	(Add year)
Title of personal project		Date submitted	

Learning outcomes	Individual comments	Areas for future exploration and development
Acquire or develop particular skills Or … Develop a particular area of interest Benefit to the individual Benefit to the parish		

Presentation	Individual comments	Areas for future exploration and development
Appropriate choice of format Clear aims and objectives Clear structure Clear practical application		

Personal project assessment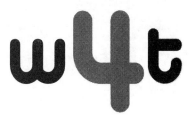

Communication	Individual comments	Areas for future exploration and development
Planning and organisation Clarity and coherence Creativity and insight Use of media		

Tutor signatures	Date of assessment	Overall comment

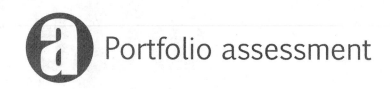

| Name of candidate | | Academic year | (Add date) | Date submitted | |

Learning outcomes	Individual comments	Areas for future exploration and development
Record of learning experiences Reflection on learning Benefit to the individual as a potential leader of public worship Benefit to the worship life of the parish		

Presentation and communication	Individual comments	Areas for future exploration and development
Planning and organisation Clarity and coherence Creativity and insight Use of media		

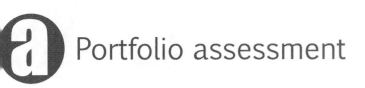

Specific areas	Individual comments	Areas for future exploration and development
Parish audits		
Church visits		
'Link group'		
Additional activities		

Tutor signatures	Date of assessment	Overall comment

| Name of candidate | | Academic year | |

Learning outcomes: Theology and history	Individual comments	Areas for future development
Theology of worship Worship in the Bible and church history Anglican patterns of worship Liturgical formation Mission-shaped worship		

Learning outcomes: Leadership skills	Individual comments	Areas for future development
Skills for leading worship Pastoral skills for building and leading a worship team Enabling a congregation to worship		

Learning outcomes: Practical skills	Individual comments	Areas for future development
General musical or other skills Specific creative gifts Introducing and teaching new material to a congregation Running effective rehearsals		

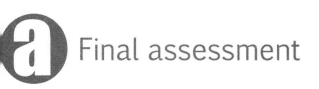 

Group work	Individual comments	Areas for future development
Participation Creativity Clarity of communication Confidence		

Review feedback	Individual comments	Areas for future development
Tutors Mentors Incumbent Parish 'link group'		

Recommendation
We recommend that (Name) should be authorised as a worship leader in the Diocese of (Name).

Tutor signature		Date	

worship 4 today

Assessment

Worked samples

Personal project assessment (practical skill)

Name of candidate	Peter White	Academic year	Any year
Title of personal project	Learning to play guitar	Date submitted	June

Learning outcomes	Individual comments	Areas for future exploration and development
Acquire or develop particular skills Or … Develop a particular area of interest Benefit to the individual Benefit to the parish	Building on previous music skills, you set off on this project with a self-help DVD. You quickly discovered that this method is only satisfactory in part. We need contact with other guitarists who can actually explain and demonstrate skills whilst we watch and copy. The real highlight was to see the learning in action at the final *Worship4Today* communion service, where you were able not only to play as part of a group with Sue and Angela but sing as well. It is always a great joy to hear what God has done through personal testimony.	Continue to seek out more proficient guitarists to pick up more technique and tips. There is no need to beat yourself up over difficult hymns with too many obscure chords. Traditional hymns are not designed for guitar, so often it is better to simply leave these to the organist or sing them with CD backing track or unaccompanied if there is no keyboard player. Keep developing your testimony in song. It could prove a valuable tool for outreach and mission in the future to both adults and young people.

Presentation	Individual comments	Areas for future exploration and development
Appropriate choice of format Clear aims and objectives Clear structure Clear practical application	You have written in the form of a diary with your usual blunt honesty and humour. The diary reveals determination, commitment and a certain stubbornness that will not give in easily. A diary can never do justice to the hours and hours of practice you have put in over the past months, or the significant worship experiences which have occurred.	Practice is often more effective in frequent short bursts rather than longer sessions when concentration goes and fingers get sore. Focus in on the difficult bits rather than wasting time on the stuff that you can play easily. There have been many ups and downs during the year, but remember that most of the growth comes in the valleys not on the mountain tops!

Personal project assessment (practical skill)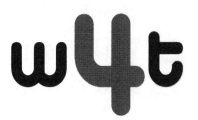

Communication	Individual comments	Areas for future exploration and development
Planning and organisation Clarity and coherence Creativity and insight Use of media	The DVD gave a certain amount of structure, and easy goals to work towards. By February, your chord and song repertoire had expanded considerably and by April, you were playing in church for the occasional service. You have wisely built up confidence gradually by playing for the small Wednesday evening gathering. You have set the bar high, but attainable with lots of practice.	Keep adding on chords one by one. Also develop your sense of rhythm, so you can begin to play in a variety of different styles. Spend time with other *Worship4Today* guitarists and benefit from their expertise. Pace yourself carefully and don't be tempted to run before you can walk! Better to do something you can manage well than be a bit too ambitious and fall flat. Take it one step or target at a time.

Tutor signatures	Date of assessment	Overall comment
Helen Bent *Liz Tipple*	June/July	Your self-discipline and dedication are admirable. The enjoyment is obvious. You have a genuine desire to lead and accompany worship and to give God your best. Your enthusiasm is infectious. There is great potential at St Mary's. Work towards a shared vision with the vicar and the rest of the worship team and channel your enthusiasm into that vision.

Name of candidate	John Smith	Academic year	Any year
Title of personal project	An exploration of lyrics and songs for both personal ministry and congregational use.	Date submitted	June

Learning outcomes	Individual comments	Areas for future exploration and development
Acquire or develop particular skills Or … Develop a particular area of interest Benefit to the individual Benefit to the parish	You have explored the important relationship between our intellect, emotions and experience as we recognise and encounter the presence of God through song. You also consider the importance of using lyrics which contain biblical truths and theological substance. You have explored what is personal, what will minister when sung to others, what is congregational. You are aware of the need for good lyrics and an easily singable but interesting tune for congregational use.	Lyrics need considerable work if they are going to be good quality and easily remembered as well as theologically sound. Graham Kendrick has said that a good song is 10% inspiration and 90% perspiration. It is well worth spending extra time carefully crafting lyrics, but also get feedback from others regularly along the way. Try to decide from the outset what kind of hymn or song you are writing: a song to be sung to others or a congregational piece. This will help to shape the composition appropriately.

Presentation	Individual comments	Areas for future exploration and development
Appropriate choice of format Clear aims and objectives Clear structure Clear practical application	You set out with clear aims, to which you have given careful thought and reflection supported by appropriate reading. There are obvious links with other learning on the course, especially poetry and music and use of 'I' as a corporate identity in the Psalms. The analysis of the songs of others is helpful in honing down your own skill as a singer/songwriter but also as a potential writer of congregational material.	Keep reading round your subject, and continue to study the Psalms in particular. Remember that the Psalms were Israel's hymnbook and therefore all designed to be sung. How might you develop the different strands of lament and praise? Continue to engage critically with the material of other songwriters. What makes a good hymn? What makes a good song for ministry or reflection? Are there any features common to both? How do we encounter God through song? What is actually going on?

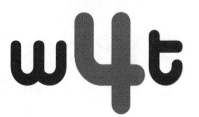
Communication	Individual comments	Areas for future exploration and development
Planning and organisation Clarity and coherence Creativity and insight Use of media	You have an appreciation of how metre works poetically and musically so that several verses will fit neatly to the same melody. Themes lead to jottings, which develop into lyrics, which you have then reflected on and critiqued. 'Doubting Thomas' explores something of story as well as giving us permission to question and work through doubts. You recognise the power that comes from keeping closely to scripture. 'I was young and unaware' puts yourself in the place of one of the first disciples, allowing engagement with the biblical text alongside the use of imagination and poetic licence. 'Broken' stands out as a potential congregational song.	The first verse often comes easily, but the subsequent verses take real hard graft to get them to follow the same metre successfully. The more you write the easier this will become. Some Ignatian spiritual exercises may be a helpful way of exploring scripture and reflecting on the relationship between the biblical text and the use of imagination. This is a valid way of writing but it does have its pitfalls – we can never think exactly like someone else, so our material may contain hidden assumptions and unhelpful biblical inaccuracies.

Tutor signatures	Date of assessment	Overall comment
Helen Bent *Liz Tipple*	June/July	This project is clearly a work in progress. This is only the beginning of your career as a Christian singer/songwriter. You show real talent and insight and an ability to critique your own work honestly. You are also touching on something wider: ways of using music to express inner thoughts without engaging in communal singing. Your personal songs may help those who find response (especially emotional) to God difficult and who struggle to articulate their thoughts.

#
ⓐ Personal project assessment (practical exploration)

Name of candidate	Jane Hill	Academic year	Any year
Title of personal project	Iona worship with reference to inner city issues and congregational singing	Date submitted	June

Learning outcomes	Individual comments	Areas for future exploration and development
Acquire or develop particular skills Or … Develop a particular area of interest Benefit to the individual Benefit to the parish	This is clearly an area which God has laid deeply on your heart. Your concerns and desires come through very strongly. You have clearly benefitted a lot from your research, and have begun putting it to good use in your community. You have discovered new things about yourself and your Scottish roots as well as wrestling with very real issues. You recognise a need for authenticity and integrity in worship if it is to connect with people in inner city situations.	This is an on-going journey of discovery with lots of potential for transforming both your personal approach to worship and that of your parish. It has been proven that singing does us good and uplifts the spirit. How can we ensure communal singing is readily accessible to an inner city congregation? You are tapping into the search for wholeness and the desire to be fully human – we so need a safe place to address issues of insecurity, loneliness and brokenness in our worship. How might this be developed further?

Presentation	Individual comments	Areas for future exploration and development
Appropriate choice of format Clear aims and objectives Clear structure Clear practical application	I like the 'diary' approach – it was good to see how your thoughts evolved from your varied research. You set out with two clear aims, connecting with two important issues. Your diary is helpful and insightful, recognising that mission in the inner city is problematic and singing can be an alien and uncomfortable pursuit for many, especially the unchurched.	You have done lots of thinking and reflecting on both your work and church situations already. Your reading has been balanced by practice as you have been able to try different things out with the congregation. Getting regular feedback from the congregation has led to genuine ownership. You may only be 'scratching the surface', but keep going!

298

Personal project assessment (practical exploration)

Communication	Individual comments	Areas for future exploration and development
Planning and organisation Clarity and coherence Creativity and insight Use of media	You demonstrate good insight into important issues. Your juxtaposition of Iona with your inner-city situation is very interesting and quite profound.	You have touched on an area which is so often neglected, or even denied, in British worship, but which is so important. Keep touching those places!
	You identify Columba as a bridge between different parties and realms of interest. It is interesting to note his dedication to the Psalms, something we are in danger of losing from our contemporary worship.	How might we write and use psalms to connect with 21st century people to give voice to the hurting?
	'Encircling prayers' have made an impact and you have already put them to good use in a variety of contexts. The Big Sing sheets are informative – it's good to see others keeping a balance between new repertoire and some tried and tested favourites.	How might you use these 'encircling prayers' more to hold and enfold the struggling and broken in order to facilitate healing? Is there a place for a specific service of healing – perhaps with anointing?

Tutor signatures	Date of assessment	Overall comment
Helen Bent *Liz Tipple*	June/July	You have asked some serious questions which show that you are thinking deeply about what we are really doing as we worship. You clearly have a heart for people's pain and struggle. This, together with your mature approach to music and worship, will undoubtedly develop into an important area of ministry. You recognise singing as active rather than passive, and you understand how it shapes what we believe. Music and song also minister to the hurting. You are seeing something of the Father's heart; God rejoices over us with singing and He invites us to join in with His song. This in turn will minister to the lost and broken of our inner city communities. What a privilege!

a Personal project assessment (research)

Name of candidate	Sarah Jones	Academic year	Any year
Title of personal project	Worship through the ages: using our history to shape our today.	Date submitted	June

Learning outcomes	Individual comments	Areas for future exploration and development
Acquire or develop particular skills Or … Develop a particular area of interest Benefit to the individual Benefit to the parish	This project does exactly what it says in the title, and then puts it into practice in the parish. It is rooted in scripture, history and tradition, and yet it looks forward to 21st century Sunday worship and fresh expressions of worship at other times and in other places. You show how much you have learnt during the course, but take it on to a deeper level. You understand something of the private and corporate nature of worship and how that works itself out in practice.	Tracing your biblical, historical and Anglican roots have given you a vast amount of knowledge on which to draw in the future. Keep referring back, but also looking forward. Dare to take a few risks with resources, particularly within the new 'Haven' mid-week service. Remember the worship cycle from Sessions 1 and 2? Learning is also a cycle. As we reflect, so we learn more. Keep worshipping, keep learning, keep going and you will venture into even greater intimacy with God. This in its turn will spill over into the lives of others.

Presentation	Individual comments	Areas for future exploration and development
Appropriate choice of format Clear aims and objectives Clear structure Clear practical application	You have presented your material clearly with academic rigour, depth and insight. Your project is a mine of information. You put time and care into everything you do. Services are well crafted and service sheets are well laid out. From the feedback, services are well received.	Begin a file of useful ideas and resources. Add things when inspiration strikes, or you discover a new piece of liturgy, music, artwork, etc. Also, gradually build up your own image library of suitable pictures for service sheets. This can save hours of searching on the internet.

Personal project assessment
(research)

Communication	Individual comments	Areas for future exploration and development
Planning and organisation

Clarity and coherence

Creativity and insight

Use of media | There is amazing breadth of creativity, using the best of the old and the new from the Trisagion to Redman.

You recognise that people arrive at worship from all kinds of situations, both positive and negative. You want to draw them in and take them on a journey in worship where they will encounter God as you have done.

You understand our need for exuberant praise, space and stillness, comfort and healing, as you have ably demonstrated in the juxtaposition of praise and lament.

Seasonal services display an appropriate use of seasonal liturgy. | I shall be on the look-out for 'nChant' on CD! Keep learning more about the old traditions and using them creatively in a contemporary way.

Having grasped the concept of taking the congregation on a worship 'journey', how might you develop this further? How might the journey vary? Do we always want to journey? How might we 'rest' in God's presence and enable people simply to 'be'?

Familiarise yourself further with the Common Worship liturgical resources, but also explore liturgy from other parts of the Anglican Communion, monastic traditions, Iona, the alternative worship scene, etc. |

Tutor signatures	Date of assessment	Overall comment
Helen Bent
Liz Tipple | June/July | You display a maturity of faith, which has grown in a relatively short period of time.

I am impressed with the quality and depth of the academic study, but also the practical outworking of your learning in preparing and leading services in the parish. Profound! |

Name of candidate	John Smith	Academic year	Any year	Date submitted	July

Learning outcomes	Individual comments	Areas for future exploration and development
Record of learning experiences Reflection on learning Benefit to the individual as a potential leader of public worship Benefit to the worship life of the parish	Your portfolio reveals a growth in discipleship as well as musicianship and worship. This is very much about the whole person. Here you have bared your soul to some painful personal self-examination. You have grown in confidence as a musician, and have clearly collected a broad repertoire of musical resources to draw on in the future. Your learning has been complemented and backed up by various related experiences and plenty of background reading. The course has obviously proved more rigorous than you initially anticipated, but you have matched the challenge with your own commitment to the task.	Continue to 'journal.' It is an invaluable daily personal discipline, which will deepen your faith as well as encouraging you to be a 'life-long learner.' You are passionate about 'new music'. Remember to introduce new material slowly and methodically, so it can take root in the hearts and minds of the congregation. And check your enthusiasm. Don't be tempted to use all your best ideas in one service! Keep reading, keep observing, keep participating, keep learning. There is always something new and exciting to discover.

Presentation and communication	Individual comments	Areas for future exploration and development
Planning and organisation Clarity and coherence Creativity and insight Use of media	You have a thorough, prayerful approach, rooted in scripture. You are methodical and rigorous. You have not only reflected on each session as it happened; you have then gone back and re-engaged with tutors' comments. Your learning has been earthed in practice in the parish. You have discovered the difficulties in handling silence sensitively, so that everyone can use it creatively. There is an honest appraisal of personal strengths and weaknesses.	Revisit your handouts at your own pace during the coming year to consolidate your learning. Keep reading, and keep sharing any good resources with others in the *Worship4Today* group. Silences are usually too long for some and too short for others. How can you set clear boundaries to enable everyone to feel at ease? Work on both strengths and weaknesses. Both can always be improved further.

302

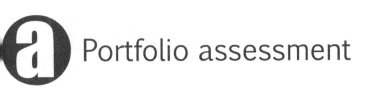 Portfolio assessment

Specific areas	Individual comments	Areas for future exploration and development
Parish audits	Audit 1 was very thorough. Audits 2 and 3 less so. These are helpful overviews to go back to at regular intervals to monitor developments in worship as you go.	Keep reflecting on your findings throughout this next year. How can services be developed and improved on? How can Christmas and Easter services be developed with a clearer missional intent?
Church visits	These have been varied and highlight how scary it can be to visit an unfamiliar church for the first time. You have combined your observations of historic church buildings with your experience of the actual 'living' worship of the place.	What does this have to say to you about mission? Always keep in mind the worshipping congregation. There can be a tendency amongst DAC/architects to see the church empty and forget its chief purpose.
'Link group'	The 'link group' has met regularly and have clearly been supportive throughout the year.	It will be important for you and Janet to build up similar support systems as you settle in a new place.
Additional activities	*Myers Briggs* is always fascinating in understanding ourselves and others better. Participation in church conference – this flags up an interesting teaching/learning dilemma. We usually expect to come away from a conference with some answers and some directives as well as plenty of questions for further reflection.	Every congregation is made up of different personality types, but some types never darken the doors of the church. How might we provide worship which would attract these people? If we don't come away with some answers, we may wonder why we bothered. How can we balance input from the front with discussion? How prescriptive should we be?

Tutor signatures	Date of assessment	Overall comment
Helen Bent *Liz Tipple*	July/August	This portfolio is deeply moving at many points, as you have made yourself vulnerable to God and to others. You have put a huge amount into the course. The one who sows generously will also reap generously. (*2 Corinthians 9:6*)

ⓐ Final assessment

Name of candidate	Sarah Jones	Academic year	Any year

Learning outcomes: Theology and history	Individual comments	Areas for future development
Theology of worship Worship in the Bible and church history Anglican patterns of worship Liturgical formation Mission-shaped worship	This has been such a rich year for you, as you have gained a new appreciation of Anglican tradition and church history. The church calendar and the liturgical year have come alive in a new way. You came spiritually hungry for more of God, and God has given a good measure, pressed down and running over! You have grown in confidence as well as biblical knowledge and you have enjoyed learning from the experiences of others.	W4T has given you a safe place to learn and experiment. Although you began with a lack of knowledge, you never felt intimidated by others. Revisit the handouts at your own pace to consolidate your learning. You are eager to learn and still hungry for more. You realise that it is okay to make mistakes and learn by doing as you go along. In all the doing *for God*, remember to make space for simply being *with God* in personal prayer and worship.

Learning outcomes: Leadership skills	Individual comments	Areas for future development
Skills for leading worship Pastoral skills for building and leading a worship team Enabling a congregation to worship	Initially you got involved through responding to a need and a request in church. You have a wonderful servant heart as well as loads of enthusiasm. This has become a journey of clarification and confirmation, as your leadership at St Peter's has visibly grown and been affirmed. The impact of your contribution on the singing group and the whole congregation should not be under-estimated.	Your growing leadership has been observed and appreciated by others. You have a big heart and relate well to all ages, especially those outside the church. Keep learning and serving. You have already been able to share personal testimony boldly in church and you received positive feedback. Listen to what others feed back to you. This will help to shape your ministry in the future. As you are faithful in the small things, so God will give you more.

Learning outcomes: Practical skills	Individual comments	Areas for future development
General musical or other skills Specific creative gifts Introducing and teaching new material to a congregation Running effective rehearsals	The singing workshop was a highlight for you, which led to an amazing encounter with God. This has opened you up to new vision and new possibilities. You have a strong voice, and your keyboard skills are gradually progressing. These skills are already being put to good use within the singing group. You relate well to all ages and want to model worship for others. Your enthusiasm and excitement are naturally infectious.	This encounter with God was both affirming and challenging. You embraced it with a straightforward honesty. How can you share this transparent approach and response with others to build their faith? Keep working at your keyboard skills, so that you will be able to fulfil your desire to cover when the regular organist is unavailable. As you have a strong voice, why not also explore the under-used and powerful art of unaccompanied singing.

Group work	Individual comments	Areas for future development
Participation Creativity Clarity of communication Confidence	You enjoyed working in your small group and learning from the various gifts and skills of others in the group. Together with the practical experience of working with other leaders, you have gone from strength to strength.	What have you learnt from this small group experience which you can take back to St Peter's and apply to the groups there? Continue to build up the team, inviting others to join you to share the load.

Review feedback	Individual comments	Areas for future development
Tutors Mentors Incumbent Parish 'link group'	You have had a tremendous year, which in turn has spilled over into the church. They are delighted to see how much you have grown and share your excitement. Growing up in the village, you know your context well. Consequently the Good Friday walk of witness was a big step for you. It was a significant public statement of your faith. You have a big heart for mission to your own community, and it will be a delight to see what happens next!	You value guidance from your incumbent. You work well with those in authority over you and do everything to the best of your ability. However, in your great enthusiasm you tend to want to do everything. The danger of burnout is a very real one, so do a few things and do them well. You have a passion for your own age group and can be a catalyst for mission into the locality. Together with your husband and family, you could be quite a powerhouse!

Recommendation			
We recommend that Sarah Jones should be authorised as a worship leader in the Diocese of Sheffield.			
Tutor signature	*Helen Bent & Liz Tipple*	Date	July/August

APPENDIX THREE

Other sample documents

Sample letters of recommendation
To be sent to each course participant and their incumbents

Working agreements
To be reviewed each year
A4 document to make an A5 folded leaflet

Sample *Worship4Today* certificates
To be given to each course participant at authorisation

To use this sample, you will need to reproduce the letters yourself,
inserting the details that are highlighted in brackets.

All these materials are available on the CD-Rom

(Date)

Dear (Insert name of course participant)

Worship4Today

Following the reviews and assessments at the end of the *Worship4Today* course, we are now able to make the following recommendation:

**We recommend that you should be authorised as a worship leader
in the Diocese of (Name)**

We hope that you found the training review helpful and that the recommendation we have made is in line with the discussions during the interview itself as well as with the discussions you have been having in the parish. In the event of any queries concerning the above recommendation, please contact us immediately.

We enclose your final course assessment and a *Ministry Agreement* form. A copy of this recommendation, together with a copy of your final course assessment and a ministry agreement form, have also been sent to your incumbent. The ministry agreement is a useful tool to help you clarify roles and responsibilities, fields of expertise and boundaries. We suggest that you meet up with your incumbent to fill this in as soon as possible. Hopefully it will undergird good working relationships in the future.

Those recommended will be authorised at a special service:

(Give local diocesan details here)

As lay ministers within the diocese, there is an expectation that those authorised will continue their study and development through a programme of Continuing Ministerial Education (CME).

(Give details of local CME sessions here)

You will also be invited to take part in worship teams for use around the diocese. These give us opportunities to continue friendships as well as opportunities to worship together.

You will be kept informed of what is going on by our *Warden of Worship Leaders*, who is there to offer encouragement, help and support:

(Give name and contact details)

It has been a great joy to spend a year with you on the *Worship4Today* course and we look forward to what God will do amongst us and our congregations in the future.

With all good wishes for your future ministry.

Yours sincerely,

(Your name)

(Date)

Dear (Insert name of incumbent)

Worship4Today

Following the reviews and assessments at the end of the *Worship4Today* course, we are now able to make the following recommendation:

We recommend that (Name) should be authorised as a worship leader in the Diocese of (Name)

We hope that you found the training review helpful and that the recommendation we have made is in line with the discussions during the interview itself as well as with the discussions you have been having in the parish. We enclose a copy of the participant's final assessment for your information. We hope that this is a confirmation of the process of discerning gifts and ministry which has been undertaken in your parish, and that your worship leader will continue with a renewed assurance of vocation to ministry. In the event of any queries concerning the above recommendation, please contact us immediately.

We also enclose a copy of the *Ministry Agreement* form. This is a useful tool to help you clarify roles and responsibilities, fields of expertise and boundaries. We suggest that you meet up with your worship leader to fill this in as soon as possible. Hopefully it will undergird good working relationships in the future.

Those recommended will be authorised at a special service:

(Give local diocesan details here)

We look forward to seeing you there.

Yours sincerely,

(Your name)

WORSHIP LEADER
MINISTRY AGREEMENT

Year 1 2 3 4 5

Valid: 20(??)-20(??)

The ministry agreement sets down helpful parameters at the beginning of each year of ministry, so that all those involved reach an agreed understanding of the work to be done and the level of commitment expected. These may be re-negotiated at each annual review.

The ministry agreement specifies lines of authority and encourages ongoing support. Worship ministry does not exist in isolation, but relates to the ministry and mission of the parish as a whole. Undertaking this exercise is intended to facilitate the development of effective lay ministry within the life of the parish.

Worship leaders are expected to attend **two** CME events and participate in **at least one** diocesan worship team in each twelve month period.

On completion, copies of the ministry agreement should be retained by the authorised worship leader and their incumbent, and a further copy returned to the *Warden of Worship Leaders* prior to the service of authorisation. Every **five** years there will be an 'in-service' review prior to re-authorisation.

311

Name	
Address	
Parish	
Ministry (as stated on the certificate of authorisation)	

Duties	

Hours per week	
Time off	
Accountable to	

Support group

Membership of committees or groups

Continuing Ministerial Education (CME)

Diocesan training events attended in the last 12 months

Any CME requests for the next 12 months

Participation in diocesan worship teams in the last 12 months

Any other comments

(Specific work undertaken this year: what has been effective? What has not gone well? How has the work complemented the mission and ministry of the parish? Any new developments? Any areas of difficulty?)

Signature of incumbent	
Date	
Signature of worship leader	
Date	

(Diocesan Logo)

Worship Leader Certificate

(Bishop's name) by Divine Permission, Bishop of (Diocese), to our well beloved and approved in Christ

(Name)

is hereby authorised to exercise the ministry of worship leader in the parish of

(Parish name)

And so we commend you to Almighty God, humbly praying, in the Name of our Lord Jesus Christ that His blessing may yet rest upon you and your work.

Given under our hand this (date) day of (month) in the year of our Lord two thousand and (year).

(Bishop's signature)

(Parish Logo)

Worship Leader Certificate

We hereby certify that

(Name)

has successfully completed the **Worship4Today** course

in the parish of

(Parish name)

May God's blessing rest upon you and your work.

(Date)

Signed:

Signed:

Incumbent

Course leader

(Diocesan Logo)

Worship Leader Certificate

We hereby certify that

(Name)

in the parish of (Parish Name)

has successfully completed the **Worship4Today** course

in Diocese of **(Name)**

May God's blessing rest upon you and your work.

Date:

Course Director

(Name)